To my Family

and

in Loving memory

of

Robin Gard

Cornishman,

Northumberland County

and Diocesan Archivist,

Christian Gentleman,

and Dear Friend.

GODS, SAINTS, AND A SCHOLAR

The Early Northumbrian Experience

Seven Essays

G.B. Thornton

CONTENTS

MAPS

INTRODUCTION

Since I retired twenty years ago I have been busy giving as many as thirty talks a season to local groups. In that time I have been much impressed by the number and diversity of these groups and by their eagerness to learn more about their region.

As the years advance all too rapidly so the attraction of turning out on a cold dark winter's night to speak in a village hall in the country fades. I decided therefore to record in writing the topics which appealed to me most: this has given me the opportunity to update and refine my material and, in some instances, to change my conclusions. If, at times, the essays sound more like talks to live audiences this is because that is how they began life. I have given only selected references lest I weary the reader but list all the authors and books consulted; there is, indeed, a wealth of literature available for those interested in the history of Northumbria. The free-hand maps shown in the books were used as hand-outs in the lectures: I trust they add a personal touch to this presentation.

I was a student at King's College Newcastle upon Tyne, then affiliated to Durham University, when, in May 1950, in a speech at his installation as Chancellor, G.M. Trevelyan spoke lyrically of the landscape of his beloved Northumberland: 'Ours is still the finest county of them all with its wide, distant views of heaven and earth, the sense of ancient freedom in its strong west wind that is written below in tribal mounds and Roman camps and border towns on the breast of Northumberland.' He had expressed similar sentiments in an essay on 'The Middle Marches' written half a century earlier where he described Northumberland as the 'land of far horizons where both heaven and earth are seen ….we walk all day on long ridges, high enough to give far views of moor and valley, and a sense of solitude above the world below'; such places evoked not a melancholic but a meditative mood.

I cannot match Trevelyan's eloquence but I do share his love of the northern countryside.

I have in the past been fortunate enough to travel quite widely in Europe, Africa and North America but nowhere has so thrilled the spirits or stirred the historical imagination as a stroll around the shores of Lindisfarne, a climb in the Simonside or Cheviot Hills, or a hike alongside Hadrian's Wall from Housesteads to Steel Rigg above Crag Lough. My choice of topics for these essays was determined by the close association of early Christianity in Northumbria with its wild and rugged landscape. Historians do, I feel, sometimes focus too much on time and too little on place: the men and women who populate these pages are the consequence of the interplay of their geographical environment and of the times they lived in.

Monks figure prominently in the glimpses of the early development of Christianity revealed in these pages from pre-Roman to Tudor times. It is a coincidence that the most eminent recent monastic historian, the Benedictine monk, Dom David Knowles, was Trevelyan's successor as Regius Professor of Modern History at Cambridge University. Trevelyan and Knowles are two of the main sources of inspiration for these essays. Lest my audiences felt too far removed from the monks of Jarrow/Monkwearmouth in the seventh century or of Rievaulx or Fountains in the twelfth, I did at times point out that they share two characteristics: monks, unless they are hermits, live in community dedicating their lives to a search for God in a spirit of fraternal charity drawing strength from each other; the members of the societies and clubs I meet gather to enrich their lives by discovering more about their region and to enjoy each other's company, meeting old friends and making new ones.

The late and much loved Cardinal Basil Hume was a monk and a lover of his native Northumberland who wrote that he lived his life in the shadow of the northern saints. He was in his element sailing among the Farne islands or on pilgrimage to Lindisfarne where I once had the great pleasure of meeting him. Wherever possible, I have included people in the photographs I have selected, for ours is a living history. There is no finer way of celebrating our rich heritage than by visiting at first hand the many places in our region hallowed by their association with the men and women who made this once an island of saints and Northumbria the cultural power-house of Western Europe; the enjoyment to be found in such visits is plain to see in the photographs from Iona (Chapter 2) and Newminster Abbey (Chapter 7). Readers who, for whatever reason, are unable to travel widely will still be able to make these journeys of discovery in spirit and therein, I trust, find much pleasure.

Bede writes at the beginning of Book 11 of his Ecclesiastical History of the English People: *'lege feliciter',* literally, 'read happily': to my readers I simply say, enjoy this book.

The lot marked out for me is my delight:
Welcome indeed is the heritage that falls to me!

Psalm 15

FOREWORD

In these seven essays we join the author on a pilgrimage of discovery of the earliest beginnings and golden ages of Christianity in the North of England. It is so well rooted in the history, geography and archaeology of the area that it will be of great interest to both residents and visitors for it will illuminate their visits to museums and historical sites of interest by helping them to make connections and understand the relevance and importance of what they see. You have only to look at the fine illustrations distributed throughout the book to realise what attractive places there are to visit.

The story begins in the period of Roman occupation and the boundary provided by Hadrian's Wall. We thread our way through the complex world of Celtic and Roman polytheistic beliefs and cults and their later mystery religions to discover, mainly through archaeological evidence, the earliest traces of Christianity and how some of the pagan feasts and customs were adapted to become Christian celebrations.

A more substantial Christian presence takes its origin from Columba's missionary foundation on the island of Iona in the mid sixth century. For this period we can draw much information from literary sources and the author carefully assesses their relative value and reliability. The main missionary work of the monks of Iona was in Scotland, but it happened that Oswald, a future king of Northumbria, sought refuge there for some fifteen years and became a Christian. When he eventually won his throne in battle he at once sent to Iona for a monk to come and win his people for Christ. The first to come was very severe and soon returned home complaining that the people were so barbarous as to be unteachable, but he was succeeded by the gentle and discerning Aidan who made great progress and established a community on Lindisfarne.

Not many years after Aidan's death Cuthbert who had been a monk and then prior at Melrose was made prior of Lindisfarne. His holiness and other fine qualities became famous in his lifetime and he was chosen to be a bishop which he very reluctantly accepted though he felt much more drawn to life as a hermit. We have some detailed knowledge of his life, achievements and miraculous events because within a few years of his death four different lives of Cuthbert were written which our author carefully compares to give us an accurate and balanced account. Many places in the Northeast are associated with Cuthbert.

Cuthbert died in 687 and the latter part of his life coincides with a remarkable spiritual, cultural and intellectual renaissance in Northumbria which continued until the middle of the eighth century. This owes much to Benedict Biscop, the founder of the twin monasteries of Wearmouth and Jarrow, who travelled frequently to Rome and brought back not only a large collection of books and the arch-cantor of St Peters to teach his monks the chant, but also a number of craftsmen in glass and stone work. They built the first stone churches organised by Wilfrid and Benedict Biscop following the Synod of Whitby and the adoption of Roman customs. They also adorned the churches with some fine stone carving which was an entirely new skill in the Anglo-Saxon world. This is also seen in the ornamentation of a number of beautiful carved stone crosses which date from this period and have survived all the ravages of time and wars. It is an interesting example of how much we can learn from monuments as well as from manuscripts.

The most inspired creator of this golden age of Northumbria was Bede, a monk of the monastery at Jarrow. He was a really great scholar and a very humble man and is rightly known as the Father of English History. He was very well read and possessed a wide range of knowledge. He wrote many books including some twenty five commentaries on Scripture and his famous Ecclesiastical History of the English People, but also covering geography, natural sciences, astronomy, chronology and even tide tables! His achievement is especially remarkable because he lived in such a remote, bleak and still barbaric part of the world. It was only possible because of the extensive library collected by Benedict Biscop but also owed much to Bede's extensive correspondence with many friends who supplied him with information.

The second golden age of Northumbria was brought about by the rapid growth of Cistercian abbeys in the twelfth century, and the towering saint of the time was Aelred, the Abbot of Rievaulx. He successfully combined his contemplative life with much activity because among other things he was a good diplomat and was called upon to help other abbeys and religious houses to settle disputes. He was a mild disciplinarian and was both courteous with friends and compassionate with those in need. He had great love and care for each of the monks in his charge so it is little wonder that he wrote a beautiful treatise on 'Spiritual Friendship' which has become a minor spiritual classic. Our author places it carefully in the context of the time and of Aelred's life and spiritual growth. He wrote other spiritual works and also quite extensive historical works pointing the way to spiritual advancement in which his sincere and candid Christian humanism aids the soul's progress from human to divine love.

In the final essay our pilgrimage takes us to the only Cistercian abbey founded between the Tees and the Tweed which is now in a wholly ruinous condition and overgrown with vegetation. We naturally wonder when and how it ever came to be there and why so many men should have dedicated their lives to God at this particular spot. We would also like to know what effect it had on the local people and the whole area. Our author unfolds the fascinating story and answers our questions from the general history of the area and available documents greatly supported by the fact that all Cistercian abbeys were built on the same plan and followed the same rule. The abbey of Newminster and the Blessed Virgin Mary, for such is its name, lies about a mile to the West of Morpeth. It was blessed with a remarkable and holy founding abbot, Robert of Newminster, who died in 1159 and therefore celebrates his 850th anniversary in 2009. That makes the publication of this book particularly opportune at this time. Thirty abbots followed him in succession and the abbey continued to flourish through four centuries although it did not escape the devastating impact of plague. It received many grants of land over the years and did much to develop agriculture and husbandry which led to its increasing wealth. This did not corrupt the individual monks but rather the purity of their original spirit of a life of prayerful contemplation in poverty and austerity. And it attracted the envious eyes of Henry VIII as soon as he had broken with the Pope. In five years between 1535 and 1540 no less than 800 monasteries and convents were closed and their wealth confiscated by the royal treasury. So the story and our pilgrimage ends on a sad but most interesting note with a clear explanation of the tragedy of the dissolution which so disrupted the social and religious lives of the common people.

This book is a joy to read.

Right Rev Ambrose Griffiths OSB
Bishop Emeritus of Hexham and Newcastle.

ACKNOWLEDGEMENTS

This book would never have seen the light of day without the cheerful and willing help of many people.

For their typing and computing skills I thank Betty Simpson, Alex Reis, Joe Murray, Des McGrahan, Fr. Paul Douthwaite and Peter Dias: their expertise more than compensated for my own deficiencies in this field.

For their constructive comments on the text, I am indebted to Professors Emeriti Richard Bailey, John Derry and Jack Watt, and to Lindsay Allason-Jones, Nick Hodgson, Bob Murphy, Bernard Robinson and John White.

Requests for permission to reproduce maps or photographs invariably met with a courteous and positive response which I gratefully acknowledge as follows: Durham Cathedral (p.109, 152); English Heritage (p.247); Museum of Antiquities and Society of Antiquaries of Newcastle upon Tyne (p.9, 12, 26, 247); National Trust (Back cover and p.99); Natural England (p.1, 34); Sancta Maria Abbey, Nunraw (p.220, 225, 264); The Post Office (Front cover, p.36, 48).

The following individuals also kindly supplied photographs: Howard Baker (p.116, lower); George Cairns (p.43, 52, 71,72); Derek Cutts (p.158); T.H.D. Horne Esq. (p.289); Maura Illingworth (p. 234); Kevin Milburn (p. 286-288); Luke Murray (p. 116 upper); Peter Stevenson (p. 72); Marie Temperley (p.286). Maureen Owens also provided valuable information on Newminster Abbey.

The Catholic Writers' Guild has been most supportive; I am especially grateful to the secretary, Mary Swales, whose talents as a calligrapher are evident in the uncial script of the Front Cover and the Dedications page.

I am also grateful to the parishes of St. Robert of Newminster at Fenham and at Morpeth for their generous grants towards the cost of printing this publication, my small contribution towards the joint celebration of the 850th Anniversary of St. Robert in 2009.

Much appreciated has been the practical advice on design and marketing given by Julia Grint of Ergo Press, Hexham, who will shortly be publishing my other book; 'The Percys and the Rising in the North, 1569'

My sincere thanks go to Averill Robson who cheerfully and efficiently undertook the complex task of compiling the Index.

Ambrose Griffiths was Bishop of Hexham and Newcastle from 1992 to 2004; his deep love of the region and of the northern saints is evident in the Foreword he has so kindly written. Thank you, Bishop Ambrose.

This book is dedicated to my family, in the widest sense of the meaning of that word, but it would indeed be remiss of me to conclude without thanking my wife most warmly for her patience, support and encouragement at all times.

1

OF GODS AND GODDESSES

INTRODUCING THE GODS

Hadrian's Wall, marking the extreme north west frontier of the Roman Empire, attracts some 12 million visitors a year. The popularity of the region has recently been given a considerable boost by the opening of a National Trail along its 74 mile length from Wallsend on Tyne to Bowness on Solway. In its first year, 2003, as many as 3,500 walkers completed the Trail, drawn to the region by the natural beauty of the landscape with its rich historical associations. However, the focus of this essay is on the beliefs of the native Celts, of the occupying Roman soldiers and the Roman-British inhabitants, and on the gods and goddesses they worshipped. Of particular interest are the first scant and, at times, tenuous vestiges of Christianity in Britain generally and more especially in Britannia Inferior, later called Lower Britain by the Romans; this region roughly comprises the five present northern counties of England north of a line from the Humber to the Mersey estuary.

Walker on the Wall above Crag Lough

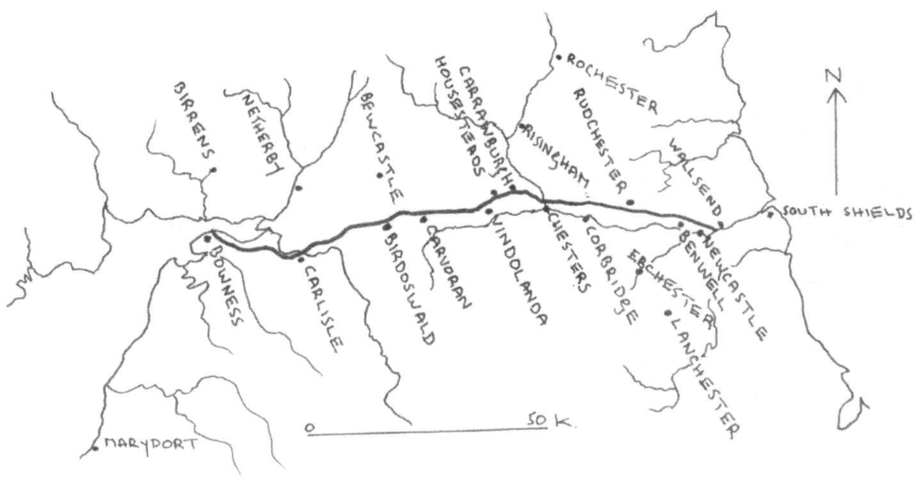

Hadrian's Wall Country

As befits a region so rich in Roman history there are many museums along the Wall at sites such as Carvoran, Vindolanda, Housesteads and Chesters. However, the best place to begin an exploration is in the Museum of Antiquities in the University of Newcastle, the chief archaeological museum of North East England, where the displays range from Stone Age to Tudors and Stuarts, though the emphasis is on the exhibits from the outpost wall and hinterland forts, and civilian settlements (vici) and places of worship before and during the four centuries of the occupation. The museum holds over a hundred Roman altars, not all on display. Admission is free. Expert advice is readily available and although the Museum has over 10,000 visitors a year it deserves to be better known[1].

A close look at inscriptions on altars, tombstones and jewellery displayed in the Museum reveals that there are four broad categories of gods, goddesses and lesser deities. The purely Roman gods, notably the Triad of deities were Jupiter (I.O.M. Jupiter Greatest and Best), Juno and Minerva; whose cults were celebrated in the Roman Capitol. Jupiter was sometimes identified with Zeus and Minerva with Athena revealing mixed Greek / Roman parentage. Native British / Celtic gods adopted by the Romans and Romano-British are shown in Roman guise and given Latinised names such as Antenociticus of Benwell, of whom more later. The exotic mystery religions from the East brought their own gods, Jupiter Dolichenus from Syria, Isis from Egypt, Mithras from Persia, and finally Jesus Christ from Palestine. In addition, dedications to deities personifying benefits like Fortuna, Victoria and Disciplina appear on altars along with spirits peculiar to particular places of districts such as Genius Loci, the lesser gods of the household Lares and Penates who presided over the household, Vesta of the hearth and a host of others.

Educated Roman and illiterate Celt alike were only too aware of their own human frailty, of the capricious nature of the elements and the brevity of life on earth, and therefore felt a real need to propitiate, petition and honour the gods whom, they believed, ruled every facet of life. Lives must be lived in harmony with the gods and in obedience to their will. Prayers and sacrifices were offered to the deities for the many and varied intentions that people pray for today: for the health, welfare and safety of family and friends, for bountiful harvests, for plentiful flocks and herds, for the regiment, and in thanksgiving for vows kept and favours received

In sacred groves and temples and beside springs Celts and Romans marked the changing seasons of the year into religious festivals and feasting just as Christians today have their own calendars of celebrations. The ways in which Christians adopted and adapted the old pagan festivals is a striking example of the new growing out of the old. The Romans saw themselves as the chosen people of the gods and strove to maintain the *pax deorum* so that the days of the *Feriale Duranum*, the Calendar of Feasts, as found in the fort at Maryport, were propitious occasions to approach the gods with prayers and sacrifices and to discern the signs and wonders the gods showed. Midwinter was celebrated with the Saturnalia, a time of merry-making and gifts, in honour of the god of agriculture Saturn and symbolising a mythical ideal world where gods and men lived in perfect peace. A mid-winter day, 25th December, was chosen as the birthday of both the Persian sun god Mithras and the Christian god Jesus. Imbola on 1st February was one of the four great Celtic festivals of the year and associated with the birth of new life, later it became the festival day of the Irish goddess Brigid and in Christian times the feast day of St. Brigid, legendary midwife to the Virgin Mary and now patron saint of healers and poets. The Jewish feast of Passover celebrating the end of bondage in Egypt and the renewal of God's Covenant with Israel became the most important event in the Christian calendar, Easter. Judaism was indeed the parent of Christianity. Easter follows the forty days of the penitential season of Lent, so called after the lengthening days of spring. Bede tells us that the name Easter derives from the Anglo-Saxon goddess of spring, Eostre, though the custom of associating Easter with the giving of eggs is an ancient one. Celts marked the beginning of summer with Beltaine on 1st May when household fires were extinguished, and druids lit bonfires to symbolise regeneration and regrowth after the ravages of winter. 1st August was the feast of the god Lugh and an occasion for celebrating the harvest. Later, in the Christian calendar, it became Lammas – 'loaf mass'. Samhain on the last day of October marked the beginning of the New Year in the Celtic calendar and became Halloween, All Hallows Eve, when witches and warlocks roam free and the natural and supernatural worlds meet. Christians keep the feasts of All Saints and All Souls at this time.

There was however a fundamental difference in belief between Romans and Celts. Rome produced outstanding leaders in many fields of human endeavour, Julius Caesar and Agricola as army generals, Virgil and Horace in poetry, Seneca and Cicero as orators and philosophers but few produced a sense of purpose for the universe nor proposed a promise of life after death for the Romans were essentially a pragmatic people whose beliefs were based on the observed world around them. A common inscription on tombstones is '*Dis Manibus*', 'To The Shades', implying a form of ancestor worship and a wish to placate the spirits of the departed though it is doubtful if it involved any notion of an afterlife. In Hexham Abbey there is a tombstone to Flavinius, standard bearer of the crack cavalry regiment, '*ala Petriana*', in full dress uniform. He is shown riding down a villainous looking barbarian, alongside the D.M. inscription decorating the top of the pillar are Tritons, the Greek sea-gods, perhaps an allusion to a voyage to the Isles of the Blessed in the afterlife. More typical is an inscription in the museum at Caerleon originally from a forum in Algeria; '*Venari, Lavari,Ludere, Ridere, occ est*' - 'To hunt, to bathe, to gamble, to laugh, these make life worth living.' Another inscription really sums up what was probably the attitude of the majority: 'I was not, I am, I am not, I care not.' The poet Lucretius (96-55 BC) believed that, after death, came the deep sleep of oblivion.

The Celts were never a nation like the Greeks or Romans but rather a scattering of tribes united in their common language as the Roman conquerors found. In the north as far as the Firth of Forth were the Votadini, in the south west of what is now Scotland were the Novantae and the Selgovae, in the rest of the region were the Brigantes and the Parisii, originally from France. Evidence of their beliefs and way of life is sparse for they built, not in dressed stone but in wood or rubble. Nor are there any Celtic written records for they had no written language. Their wisdom, folklore and oral traditions lay with the priests and therefore our knowledge is gleaned mainly from the subjective descriptions of literate but biased Greeks and Romans.

Chiefly stock-raisers, much given to cattle and horse raiding, they are described as vain, restless, quarrelsome, self-assertive and much given to self adornment, wearing 'ornaments of gold, torc on their necks, bracelets on arms and wrists, people of high rank wear dyed garments sprinkled with gold.... unbearable in victory, downcast in defeat they possess a trait of barbarian savagery'. Caesar writing on the druids states that 'they are chiefly anxious to have men believe that souls do not suffer death but that after death pass from one body to another, they regard this as the strongest incentive to valour since the fear of death is discarded'. Their values were heroic so that death in battle ensured a swift passage to the other world where feasting was on meat, especially pork, with plentiful ale and wine. One authority on the Celts, Ross[2], is quite definite 'one of their dogmas is that souls are eternal and that there is another life in the infernal regions'. Their gods were many and varied and often quite localised, as we shall see. As animists they saw the supernatural in all aspects of nature and invested the streams, rocks, forest glades and trees, most especially the sacred oak, with spirits.

Deities were thought to be able to assume the form of humans with all the strengths and weaknesses of men. Gods, it was believed, could also transform themselves into animals and birds so all living creatures were treated with respect: some were especially venerated, the speedy and fierce wild boar as a symbol of hunting and battle and a source of the favourite food, pork; the stag with its tree-like antlers as a symbol of the forest and majestic stature; the bull for its virility and strength with magico-divine attributes; birds, especially swans and cranes, for their ability to fly free from the earth into the skies symbolising the flight of the spirit from the body at death; ravens were messengers of doom and foretold defeat in battle.

THE OFFICIAL GODS

With the exception of the Legion based at York the garrisons in the Northern Frontier Zone were almost entirely composed of soldiers recruited from all parts of the vast Roman Empire, including Britain, so their own gods tended to dominate; however local gods were sometimes adopted, though in Roman guise and, at times, conflated with official gods. Thus dedications to the Capitol Triad who presided over the destinies of Rome are surprisingly uncommon except at the main forts where altars to Jupiter Optimus Maximus were the foci of religious festivals in the official Roman military calendar; these are best seen at Maryport, Birdoswald and Housesteads along with dedications to Victory, Virtue and Discipline. Jupiter dominated the parade ground and symbolised the finest Roman tradition.

At the western extension of the wall at Maryport as many as 22 altars to Jupiter were found, 13 by the parade ground used in the annual dedication by the fort garrison on January 3rd, a day when all the soldiers gathered in every fort throughout the Roman Empire to re-affirm their oath of allegiance to Jupiter, to the Emperor and to the army. In Jupiter they worshipped the sacred personification of the Empire: the army and the ceremonies were intended to demonstrate loyalty and promote *esprit de corps*. Many of the soldiers, while recognising that Jupiter was owed due worship as the senior god to the Roman pantheon, would see their own native gods as chief deities.

Jupiter Dolichenus, the ancient Hittite sky-god, was a soldier god from Syria always dressed as a Roman officer whose unofficial cult was popular in the army and who was often associated with other deities. At Corbridge part of a frieze from a Dolichenum depicts the sun god with Apollo and Dioscuri and has the inscription *Iussu dei*, for the cult fostered loyalty and prayed for the health and safety of the emperor. Minerva has her own temple at High Rochester but Juno only features doubtfully once as a statue at Corbridge.

Gods had their own specialist areas; Mercury was associated with commerce and travel, Neptune with rivers and seas, Silvanus with hunting, the Greek god Asclepius with medicine as attested at South Shields, the smith god Vulcan appears at Vindolanda. Venus appears only once in several pipe-clay figurines from high Rochester while the god of wine and giver of ecstacy, Bacchus, features on a silver patera handle from Capheaton. Apollo and Diana are known from Whitley Chapel and Housesteads respectively.

ROMANO-CELTIC GODS

One of the most interesting exhibits in the Museum of Antiquities is the bust of Antenociticus from the temple at Benwell. His name is variously spelt, though always Latinised, and its origin remains an enigma.

The fort of Condercum occupied a hill-top site, 415 feet above sea level, two miles west of the first crossing point of the Tyne, '*Pons Aelius'*. Its native name was *Condoncet,* 'the place with a fine outlook', for it commanded wide views to the north and guarded the valley of the Denton Burn. Built between 122 and 124 A.D. it covered 5½ acres and was home to a garrison of 500 men, first cavalry, then a cohort of Vangiones from the Rhineland. In the third century the First Ala of Asturians from North West Spain was stationed here, a crack cavalry regiment of some 500 men, the cream of the auxiliaries. They hunted down attackers in the open undulating land to the north. Water was brought from Denton Hill Head in a pipeline 3½ miles long[3].

The temple was built and destroyed within the late 2nd century A.D. Apart from the statue of the deity and the altars, few artefacts have been found, only two brooches and some bronze and silver coins and fragmented pottery.

The reservoir begun in 1848, later extended, obliterated the northern third of the fort, the busy West Road cuts through the Headquarters building and a housing estate covers the rest of the site. Fortunately the site was thoroughly excavated in the decade before the Second

World War to reveal three buildings of importance; a *mansio* or rest house for official travellers, an extensive bath-house comparable with that at Chester, and a splendidly preserved temple, the shrine of Antenociticus, first discovered in 1862 and now to be found in Broomridge Avenue. In style and form it is considered typical of temples as places of worship to unofficial gods for it is built outside the walls of the fort, only official gods of Rome were allowed in the fort housed in a shrine, *aedes*, in the *principia*, the headquarters building. The temple measures only 16' x 10', is rectangular in shape, with an apse at the southern end for the statue of the cult god, Antenociticus. The statue was broken in the barbarian raid of 197 when the altars were overthrown but the head remains and intact. Antenociticus is described as 'youthful god, the workmanship much influenced by Graeco-Roman models but the native elements clearly discernible, hair profuse, elaborately arranged, frontal locks bent back to suggest antlers of a stag'. Around his neck a torque, an ornament with magico-religious connotations in Celtic belief. Votive offerings found include two brooches and two silver coins.

The head of neighbouring Lemington Man is rougher, his features coarse, lips thick, nose flat and wide and incised eyes sightless symbolising death. The heads are a reminder that for the Celts the human head had a profound significance for it was the centre of emotions and place of the soul possessing both dignity and divinity. Honouring the head honoured the Gods. Antenociticus is a good example of a Celtic god, probably of native origin, adopted and Latinised by the Romans keen to find favour with local deities. He is unusual in that Celtic gods are rarely cast in human form but was clearly of some importance as inscriptions show: one inscription gracefully carved on the left of the altar is dedicated to Antenociticus and the Deities of the Emperor by Aelius Vibinius, centurion of the Twentieth Legion, on the right the inscription gives thanks for the promotion of the dedicator: "To the god Anociticus (sic) Tineius Longus, given senatorial rank and chosen as *quaestor* designate while cavalry prefect by decree of our best and greatest emperors, under Ulpius Marcellus A.D.180". One wonders why Tineius should have chosen an obscure and remotely situated Celtic deity to help him in furthering his career for quaestor was a rung on the ladder to senatorial rank. Had the other gods failed him or was this strong evidence of the status of Antenociticus?

The Bust of Antenociticus from the Temple at Benwell

Other dedications occur at Chesters, where he is called Antociticus, and as far afield as Germania and North West Spain. We cannot be sure that his cult centre was the temple at Benwell for he was widely known.

The small size of the temple allows room for no more than twenty or so worshippers who would be members of a *schola* or guild such as the popular burial clubs where soldiers contributed a portion of their wages to cover the expenses of an honourable funeral. Such unofficial societies were the only ones permitted under Roman law. Temples were not meant for public worship. The ceremony honouring the god involved the singing of hymns, the pouring of libations, prayers and the offering of a ram or pig by the priest or official clad in toga with his head covered as a sign of humility and to exclude distracting sights and signs of ill-omen. Music would be provided by a variety of instruments, flutes, pipes, rattles, cymbals and tambourines; the scent of garlands of flowers would mingle with the sweet smell of the incense from the thurible so that all the senses of the deity and of the worshippers would be satisfied. Such ceremonies bonded individual and group friendships for men stationed far from home and family and promoted loyalty to the regiment.

COVENTINA[4]

Some 25 miles due west of Newcastle on the old Stanegate, the Military Road, is the site of the fort at Carrawburgh, otherwise known as B(P)rocolita where there are two places of immense interest; a Mithraic temple, of which more later, and the other a shrine to the goddess Coventina. As early as 1732 the antiquarian John Horsley reported 'a year ago was discovered a well.... And a good spring almost filled up with rubbish.' As recently as 1954 Richmond was writing: 'At Brocolita the sacred spring of Coventina which still bubbles up limpid in its stone tanks, was covered by a temple of Celtic type in which the well or open basin took the place of a central shrine.' The altar was the focus of worship in this consecrated area open to the skies around the sacred water, a fine example of a Romano-Celtic temple.

Sculpture shows Coventina, whose name again is baffling, as a gracious nymph on her own or in a group of three reclining in a water-borne leaf. Whether of local origin or more probably imported from the Rhineland, she was highly regarded for three military commanders set up altars in her honour: Mausius of the Frisians 'for his own welfare as a vow gladly given; Aelius, prefect of the First Cohort of Batavians; Aurelius, prefect of the Cubernians joyously set up his votive offerings'. Coventina was chiefly a goddess of healing addressed as Deae Nimfae Coventinae and Nimphae Coventinae.

Sadly Coventina's well is no more for the site is now just a swampy hollow; the well may indeed have originally been dug as a sump to drain the hollow to allow the vallum to be built in a direct line. What a tourist attraction it would have been now, especially for those who know about Horseley's 'rubbish' for this proved to be a treasure trove revealing much about the history of the shrine and the nature of worship there!

The cult of Coventina was at its peak in the Flavian period from the late 2nd and 3rd centuries; most of the 14,000 coins found in the well date to this period. The last coins are dated 377 to 388 when the campaign against pagan worship was intensifying culminating in a decree closing pagan temples and declaring sacrifice illegal in 391. Animal bones from oxen, sheep and pigs, deer horns and boar tusks remained from sacrifices at the altar and feasting at the ritual meals. We know incense was burned during worship for a thurible bears the inscription 'For Coventina Saturnius Gabinius made this.' Many personal items were found, gold and silver signet rings, one inscribed 'Matre'; leather shoe soles with hob nails to help the deceased on the long journey to the other world, five bracelets, female offerings for safe childbirth, bronze masks of mirth and melancholy, a crude bronze horse, a statuette of a terrier dog with ears alert, pricked up ready for hunting, 'a little masterpiece of 2nd century naturalistic art.' Some offerings like the thurible were deposited carefully in the well for they were sacred objects, others were tossed in carelessly either as votive offerings rather as modern tourists throw three coins in a fountain or because they had to be hidden suddenly due to a barbarian raid as in 197 or Christian militancy in the late 4th century.

CELTIC GODS

The nearest equivalent in the Celtic world which stretched from Ireland in the west to Asia Minor in the east to a Father God like Jupiter to the Romans or Zeus to the Greeks was Lugus, known as Llew in Wales and in Ireland as Lugh. His strengths were in the arts and crafts and the subtler arts of war. His name is seen in the old name of Carlisle, Luguvalium – 'Strong in God'.

War gods were popular in an unsettled region much given to fighting. Cocidius (the red one?) was a god of some social status for he was honoured by commanding officers at eleven forts including Vindolanda and Housesteads where he is associated with Silvanus. He is afforded a rare honour at Bewcastle. Even though he is an unofficial god his shrine, Fanum Cocidi, is in the *principia* where the dedications are on silver plaques and he is shown as an armed warrior. He is found more in the west and in the Castlesteads – Stanwix area is invoked with Mars as is the grimly martial Belatucadrus who has inscriptions at Carrawburgh and Carvoran but has lesser status.

From South Shields a fine gem of red jasper with intaglio showing either Sylvanus the Hunter or Cocidius; the dog is sniffing a rabbit

Cernunnos was a horned stag god of ancient ancestry, well known in Gaul and Ireland and among the pastoral tribes of the northern hills. Horns were second only to heads in cult importance and stags and bulls, symbols of virility, were very much cult animals. The tribal people of Caithness in Northern Scotland were the Cornavii. 'People of the Horn'. Horns were symbols of courage in battle and of fertility in Celt tradition. Horned gods appear in various places; Antenociticus seems to bear vestigial horns, at Lanchester a little owl-like figurine has a large horned head, three horned heads come from Bremenium, at Aesica is a phallic figure conflated with Mercury protector of flocks and herds with long horns.

It is interesting to note that in Christian imagery horns take on a different meaning for Satan is often shown with horns, a powerful symbol of anti-Christ.

Mogons, 'The Great One', may also be seen as Maponus, a nature god associated with music and poetry. In the slype of Hexham Abbey an altar by an officer of the Sixth Legion is dedicated to Maponus with Apollo Citharoedus, Apollo The Harper; elsewhere at Corbridge, Ribchester and as far north as Lochmaben there are dedications by high-ranking officers to this god, usually associated with Apollo. At Netherby on a red sandstone altar he appears as Mogons Vitus, at Risingham as Deo Mogonti and Matunus and at High Rochester in plural form as Dis Mountibus.

Vitiris also appears in various forms as Vetus, Hueteres, Vitris, Deo Viteri, and Deo Sancti Veteris, all translating roughly as 'to the old Gods'. The invocations are numerous and as many as forty altars are known, a quarter from Carvoran alone, one with a serpent, another with a boar and a serpent. In the third century these gods were popular with the rank and file of the army but most inscriptions are crudely carved by barely literate sculptors, almost certainly native Britons. The Veteres are never in association with classical gods and are therefore indigenous.

Another nature god whose dedicants are of the humbler type is Condatis, 'God of the Watersmeet' with altars at the confluence of streams between the Tyne and the Tees at Chester le Street, Piercebridge and Bowes. Associated with Mars he is a warrior and a healing god.

Other gods appear only rarely: Mars Alator is known from a *patera* found in the sands at South Shields; seven altars to Vinotonus, 'God of the Vines', who equates with Silvanus, were found on the wild Scargill Moor above Bowes; at Binchester we find Belenus, one of the oldest Celtic gods out of Gaul and Italy; from the Antonine Wall comes the Belgic god Camulus and from Carlisle Ocelus with Mars, tribal god of Silurian tribe of South Wales. Taranis, a thunder god with votive wheels is found at Corstopitum along with the divine smith god Vulcan wearing a conical hat and with the tools of his trade, hammer, tongs, and anvil for smiths had a high place in Celtic society.

GODDESSES

Images of Mother Goddesses have long been dominant in world religions. Their roles were varied and crucial to the life of the community as sources of healing and fertility, as symbols of identity and mothers of their peoples and as mediators and intercessionaries between humans and male gods. For the Greeks Athena and Aphrodite fulfilled this role, as did Isis for the Egyptians and the Morrigan and Brigit for the pagan Irish. Christians see Mary as the virgin mother of God to be deeply venerated but she is not a goddess to be worshipped.

Brigantia, who reigned as the mother goddess of the north, lower Britain, was almost certainly a Roman import from the Rhineland whose cult flowered in the third century: she was the equivalent of Britannia who ruled in Upper Britain based on London. Brigantia, "High One", was a Roman creation owing nothing to Celtic beliefs who represented the personified spirit of the north region yet the cult of Dea Brigantia is little attested. From outside the fort at Birrens, perhaps from a temple, comes a fine stone relief where she is figured as Minerva winged as Victory with a mural crown as deity of a *civitas*; in one hand she holds a spear and in the other a navel stone symbolising her imperial character. At South Shields there is an altar to Dea Brigantia by Congennicus, unusual in that the dedicator has a Celtic name. A stately goddess at Corstopitum holds a sceptre and is invoked as Caelistic Brigantia.

The location of the shrine at Birrens, along with Bewcastle and Netherby, one of three outpost forts in the north west, is significant in that Brigantia is meant to keep watch on the warlike Brigantes tribe who lived throughout the Northern Frontier Zone and into Eskdale and Annandale north west of the wall. Brigantia may well have inspired the warrior queen of the Iceni, Boudicca. The other famous British queen Cartimandua invoked not a god but Brigantia. She is sometimes identified with Brigit, daughter of Dagda, the Irish Celtic Father God who has cultural and fertility attributes, and who in turn is seen as Brigid of Kildare, an early Irish Christian saint.

Mother Goddesses evoke images of home and fertility in childbirth and at harvest time, and were frequently invoked as the Matres or Matrones, the mothers. Originally Celtic in origin and from the Rhineland they are usually shown as Triads often with infants, baskets of fruit or cornucopia, and re-interpreted by Roman officials or officers as regional or household deities. At the cavalry fort of Condercum at Benwell the Matres presided over the parade ground: Housesteads has an altar to the Matres and at Castlesheads the commander Caius rebuilt a temple in their honour. Civilians too paid homage as at Bowness on Solway where the merchant Antonianus built a shrine in honour of the Matres. Votive treasure bore similar dedications for in the Backworth hoard was a gold ring inscribed to the Matres and a fine gold patera by Fabius.

Epona was an equine goddess, protectress of horses adopted by Roman cavalry, who was brought in from Gaul and has dedications at Carvoran. Horses were prized by Celtic warriors and Roman cavalry as essential in war and peace and as symbols of prestige. It is significant that the only Celtic deity honoured in Rome is Epona.

Nymphs figure prominently; apart from Coventina at Carrawburgh, sacred springs with water cults were common to both Celtic and Roman culture and usually associated with nymphs or water deities. At the outpost fort of Risingham on Dere Street an altar by a spring is inscribed: "Forewarned by a dream a soldier bade her who is married to Fabius to set up this altar to the nymphs who are to be worshipped. At Carrowburgh there is an open air shrine to the Nymphs and Genius Loci. Corstopitum features goddesses by a tub and is therefore associated with healing; at the same site we find Fortuna, a goddess regal with sceptre with bird attributes. At Maryport there are three naked goddesses, an unusual feature.

Celtic goddesses are sometimes closely associated with rivers; the Severn has Sabrina, the Dee Deva and by the Wharfe from Ilkley was an altar to Verbeia, "She of the cattle", wearing a pleated dress and holding a serpent in either hand. Other goddesses feature only rarely: at Birdoswald is Rata, 'goddess of the fortress' and Latis, 'goddess of the pool'; at Maryport is a 'goddess of long life', Setlocenia; and at Beltingham in the South Tyne valley is an inscription to Sattada who is associated with death and sombre funerary rites; in the Museum of Antiquities is an inscription to the Lamiae, the three witches, who are also vampire-like spirits fond of human blood.

The plethora of Celtic gods, goddesses and local deities reflects the diverse and scattered nature of Celtic society. Most deities dwell locally and lack the more specialist attributes of Roman gods. Where attributes are shared Celtic and Roman gods are conflated to give us Mars-Alator at South Shields and Mars Ocelos at Carlisle. The best known example is Sulis-Minerva who presided over the Roman baths at Bath.

EXOTIC MYSTERY RELIGIONS FROM THE EAST

As we have seen, gods imported by soldiers from their homeland to Britain were worshipped by military and civilians alike. Gods from the east were especially popular in the towns where traders and travellers gathered; at the busy town of Corstopitum on the key crossing point of the Tyne by Dere Street the temple to Jupiter Dolichenus from Syria has already been mentioned and inscriptions bear testimony to Astarte and Heracles of Tyre in Palestine. Up on the Wall at Carvoran the Hamian archers from Syria introduced the worship of Dea Syria and Jupiter Heliopolitanus. At the fort of Arbeia at South Shields, port of entry for supplies for the Wall garrisons, a tombstone dedicated by Barates of Palmyra to his wife Regina from Hertford bears an inscription in Aramaic, Christ's native language.

The second and third centuries were times of anxiety when enquiring minds began looking beyond the pragmatic world of Rome and searching for a deeper knowledge of the gods in the hope of gaining immortality; the strong moral code of the Stoics with its emphasis on personal asceticism and humility gained many supporters. This questing prepared the way for the so-called exotic mystery religions from the East.

Most enduring of all Egyptian deities throughout Hellenistic and Roman times was Isis, the great enchantress, the Mother Goddess whose cult spread west and reached Britain. Isis was the deity of all funerals, invoked on behalf of the sick and dying and patroness of all sea-farers. Her cult was centred in the temples of Alexandria. The legend surrounding Isis has echoes of the Christian belief in death and resurrection for she restored to life Osiris (Seraphis to the Greeks and Romans) who had been killed by the evil god Seth and now ruled the world as the supreme power of creation. The image of a mother suckling her infant son was powerful in the iconography and hymns of the cult of Isis and in Christian veneration of the Virgin Mary. Isis and Mary both bore the title "Star of the Sea".

Egyptians had a keen interest in the afterlife and preserved the bodies of the dead through mummification so that they might enjoy the idealised earthly life based on agriculture, with no famine or flood, in a better Egypt; first the deceased must appear before the husband of Isis, Osiris, and forty two judges to plead their causes and be weighed in the scales of justice. There was a temple to Isis in London but there is no evidence of the worship of Isis in the north of England as yet which is not surprising as her devotees, mainly women, needed to be rich to afford membership.

MITHRAS[5]

Though few in number the worshippers of Mithras held an importance unrelated to their numbers for they were men of influence, usually officers in the Roman Army.

I vividly recall the thrill of an outing with a classics group in 1949 to the temple of Mithras at Carrawburgh which had only recently emerged from the shrinking peat after a long dry spell;'one of the most interesting religious buildings the northern frontier of the Roman Empire has produce'. Our area scores well with Mithraea for they are found on the wall also at Housesteads and Rudchester, and probably at High Rochester, Carlisle, Castlesteads, Whitley Castle and possibly at Wallsend; elsewhere in Britain Mithraea were only at York, London and Caernarvon.

The temples on the wall are so few in number they have a special interest. The three temples to Mithras vary in size but are all small and the finds there are for ritual purposes rather than votive offerings. Perhaps the scarcity of temples is explained by the uncertainty of officers as to the length of time they would be stationed at that fort before being posted elsewhere. All the altars in the Mithraic temples on the Wall are dedicated by high ranking officers in the Roman army, five prefects, two centurions and a consular beneficiarus, an official. All dedicants made clear their names and their rank, no altars were dedicated to the regiment as Mithraism was a secret elite cult, nor is there any evidence of civilian worshippers of Mithras even though each major fort had an extensive *vicus* outside its walls. The suggestion is that Mithraism appealed to ambitious soldiers eager for promotion and to be noticed by their superior officers. Parallels with freemasonry have long been recognised.

While it is unwise and indeed impossible to ascribe motives to individual worshippers in any religion, nevertheless the fact that small shrines such as Coventina's at Carrawburgh had many personal offerings of coins and jewellery in the well whereas Mithraic temples have revealed only ritual objects such as lamps and cockerel bones may indicate that the worshippers of the Sun God see their membership as a shrewd career move as well as a source of spiritual fulfillment.

A visit to the reconstructed Mithraeum in the Museum of Antiquities offers a rare insight into the worship of this exotic religion. The building is rectangular with an ante-chapel, narthex, a nave with side benches and a sanctuary with altar. Centrepiece is a Tauroctony, a bull slaying relief, where Mithras in Persian costume plunges a sword into the neck of the primeval bull, the first living creature, caught after much struggle; thus the creative powers are released. Ravens feed on the bull's flesh, a dog and a serpent drink the blood where a vine shoots, ears of wheat sprout from the tail. Like the cave where the original drama is set, the temple is dark, being lit only by a few oil lamps, Mithras, with his two torchbearers Cautes and Cautopates, is backlit. Sacrifices are made, prayers offered and incense burned as initiates are welcomed. One can readily sense the atmosphere of drama and mystery.

Mithras was a Sun God originating in India c.1400 B.C. whose cult spread through Persia and Asia Minor to Rome in the first century and so to Britain, often as Sol Invictus, the unconquered Sun God. As a truth-seeking god of strict ethical conduct he had a special appeal for soldiers, traders and merchants and as he promoted loyalty and discipline he posed no threat to Rome. The cult was exclusive, male only, with elaborate initiation rites through seven stages from Raven through Lion to Father and involved payment of money and ordeal of heat and cold as evidenced by a pit on site at Carrawburgh. The status of devotees is well attested by the dedicants of three altars at Carrawburgh for Lucius Antonius, Aulus Cluentius and Marcus Simplicius are all prefects and all address Mithras as 'the Invincible God'. The dedicants of the four large inscribed altars found at Rudchester are also prefects or centurions, but apart from a stone laver, three lamps and an iron cleaner little has been recovered from this site. The temple at Housesteads was abandoned in the 3rd century. None of the three temples on the Wall were in continuous use and at times during the occupation there may have been no worshippers of Mithras in the region. As at Carrawburgh a spring rose within the shrine at Housesteads, water clearly played an important role in the rites and ceremonies of Mithraic worship. One piece of sculpture from this site ,shows Mithras emerging from the Cosmic Egg brandishing the Sword of Truth and the Torch of Light and showing the Signs of the Zodiac, their earliest depiction in Britain. Two large altars are inscribed 'To the Invincible Sun-god Mithras, Lord of Ages' and are dedicated by Publius Proculinus, centurion, and by Litorius Pacatianus, *beneficiarus*, staff officer of the governor for himself and his family….'. There were few small finds here and the fragmented tauroctony indicates deliberate destruction.

When in A.D. 377 the Christian prefect of Rome, Jerome, ordered the destruction of the metropolitan Mithraeum in Rome it seems a similar fate befell the Mithraea in Britain. Barbarians invading in the 3rd century had badly damaged the three temples on the Wall, Housesteads was abandoned but those at Rudchester and Carrawburgh were rebuilt and used intermittently. Desecration in the late 4th century was selective so that it is unlikely that it was caused by local vandalism or Pictish invaders but more probably by militant Christian commanders acting either on their own initiative or on orders from above. Perhaps they were fired by the zeal of recent conversion. Religious statuary was smashed and the bull-slaying relief attacked but, for some reason, the altars were left untouched. At Carrawburgh the lion guardian was destroyed and the two torchbearers of Mithras beheaded. At Rudchester the building was levelled and nothing is now visible but excavations in 1953 recovered four altars from the sanctuary.

It is ironic that iconoclasm is the first evidence, albeit of a negative nature, of Christianity in the Northern Frontier Zone; however it was not only local commanders who were bitterly opposed to Mithraism. Tertullian (c. A.D. 160-220), the Carthaginian theologian and the first notable Christian poet, called the sacred meal central to Mithraic worship 'a devilish parody of the Eucharist.' Justin Martyr wrote of the 'Satanic parodies of Christian rituals'; both blithely ignored the fact that the cult of Mithras had been in existence some one and a half millennia before Christ was born.

The two religions appeared to have some features in common; both demanded high standards of moral and political behaviour and sought the care of individual souls; both had baptism as the initiation rite, the one by honey on the hand, the other by water on the head; December 25 was the birthday of Mithras and of Jesus, both believed in a miracle birth, Mithras from a Cosmic Egg, Jesus from a Jewish maiden, Mary, by the power of the Holy Spirit; most importantly, for both new life flowed from a sacrifice, the slaughter of the primeval bull and the death of Christ on the Cross. A text found at Rudchester could apply to both religions, 'and you saved us by shedding the eternal blood'.

Yet the view that Mithraism contributed much to the development of Christian doctrine must be contested. Mithraism was an elitist and secretive religion whereas Christianity was universal and open to all. The choice of the winter solstice by the early church as the birthday of Christ was purely arbitrary; precise dates mattered less than the meaning of Christ's life, death and resurrection. The only significant source of Christian theology is Judaism of which it claims to be the fulfillment.

The death-knell of the cult of Mithras was sounded when Christianity was declared the official religion of the Roman Empire and pagan worship declared illegal.

The building of the Mithraeum in London after its destruction in 377 and its rededication not to Mithras but to Bacchus for use by worshippers of the wine-God shows that paganism was still very much alive, but marks the end of the fascinating and colourful cult of the Sun God.

CHRISTIANITY COMES TO BRITAIN

Politics in Rome dictated conditions in Britain. At first Christianity was tolerated as just another minority mystery religion from the East, though seen by Jews as disruptive for they denounced the followers of the Nazarene, according to St. Paul. As Christians grew in number they were at times perceived as a threat and persecuted by Emperors Nero, Severus, Decius and Valerian who interpreted the preaching on death, damnation and the Day of Judgement as prophesying the fall of Rome, the more so as many were ardent proselytisers. The steadfast courage of the martyrs was much admired: Tertullian described the blood they shed as 'the seed of the church'.

There was a strong political element in the arrival of Christianity in Britain, especially associated with York for it was here that Constantine had been proclaimed Emperor in 306 and evidence of coins suggest he returned twice in 312 and 314 before and after his conversion. The new Caesar had strong associations with the province and probably a personal following there. Constantine saw Christianity as a refinement of the cult of the Sun God, Deus Sol Invictus, the chief deity of the State, and many of his earlier coins describe him as Soli Invicti Comiti. There was a natural link between a single, unchanging, glorious Sun God and Jesus Christ, the single divine saviour of mankind. Indeed, a third century vault mosaic from a tomb under St. Peter's, Rome, depicts Christ as Christus-Sol; this was exceptional as both Judaism and Christianity opposed the idea of a sun god. Genesis 1 classes the sun as a creation of Yahweh.

The earliest recorded reference to Christianity in Britain is by Tertullian who wrote c. A.D. 200 'Parts of Britain inaccessible to the Romans were indeed conquered by Christ', almost certainly a reference to Ireland. Five centuries later Bede recorded that in the reign of Marcus Antonius (A.D. 154 – 180) Lusius, a British King, was baptised and "the British received the faith". Both claims are unsubstantiated and seem exaggerated.

The first British martyrs were Alban of Verulamium, St. Alban's, who was killed on 22 June A.D.301 and Julius and Aaron, the latter a Jewish name so probably a convert from Judaism, who died at the City of the Legions, Caerleon in South Wales, c.304 along 'with many others of both sexes in various other places', according to Bede. Perhaps the place name Merthyr (Martyr) Tydfil dates from this time. Caesar-worship was the test of loyalty and from the official standpoint these martyrs, and many others in Rome and the east, died not because they were Christians but because they refused to burn incense before the altar of Jupiter.

Attendance by British bishops at the early Church Councils to thrash out often controversial interpretations of Scripture and formulate an agreed dogma attests to a well-developed diocesan structure. At the Council of Arles in 314 four British dioceses were represented, London, York and Lincoln by Bishops Restitutus, Eborius and Adelfius respectively and a fourth, probably Cirencester, by a priest and deacon. No British bishop was at Nicaea but we were represented at both Sardica in 347 and Rimini 359, where the Emperor offered free transport for all who attended, a clear indication of state support.

Though the early Christian church was tolerant of lingering pagan practices heretics were fiercely attacked even though Augustine said an exact definition of heresy was impossible. It is ironic that one of the first names to gain prominence in the first centuries of the history of Christianity in Britain was that of an alleged heretic, Pelagius, a monk and theologian and probably a Briton. The charge was that Pelagius taught that man could gain eternal salvation by achieving high standards of morality by the efforts of his own human will without the saving help of God's grace: this was a deeply divisive doctrinal matter for it made Christ's death on the Cross and Resurrection pointless. The matter was deemed so serious that it occasioned the visit of two high-powered churchmen, bishops Faustus of south Gaul and Germanus of Auxerre. A well-attended conference at Verulamium roundly condemned the Pelagian teaching in 429 and Pelagius was finally excommunicated by Pope Innocent I. The choice of Verulamium for the meeting reveals that already the rites of burial of the holy dead, in this case the proto-martyr St. Alban, were becoming shrines, places of pilgrimage and foci of spiritual power where relics were venerated. It has recently been suggested that Pelagius was really concerned with drawing attention to the lax moral standards among churchmen, a worry echoed later by the monk-historian Gildas and by Bede in his last letter before he died to Bishop Egbert of York.

Henig[6] concludes that as early as the first visit of Germanus in 429 'a large proportion of British society, however materially impoverished, was Christian'. The Mediterranean lands produced high-powered church leaders in Jerome, Augustine and Gregory, ‘the Fathers of the Church’ and skilled biblical commentators of the calibre of John Chrysosthom, Origen of Alexandria and Eusebius of Caesarea, but in Britain on the north west fringe of burgeoning Christian culture no-one of intellectual stature appeared on the scene until Bede, A.D. 673-735.

EARLY EVIDENCE OF CHRISTIANITY IN NORTHERN BRITAIN.

Searching for evidence of Christianity in Roman Britain is a fascinating yet frustrating exercise where earlier researchers have been accused of showing more zeal than judgement. The evidence itself is scarce and often highly debatable. The latest study[7] of ‘small finds’ in Roman Britain examined 260 possible items and concluded that only 70 were definitely Christian with a further 60 to be confirmed or denied. Of the 70 definite only a handful, five, were from the Northern Frontier Zone (roughly the four present northern counties), the focus of this study, though as many as 43 had been claimed. What then are the signs we look for?

Epitaphs on gravestones or inscriptions on artefacts may be in a form recognised as Christian, or may bear Christian symbols such as a fish (the Greek ‘*ichthus*’ gives the acronym ‘Jesus Christ, Son of God, Saviour’), a dove, (*columba*), a peacock (also Juno’s symbol), a pomegranate, an olive branch or a tree of life. Best known, however, and most instantly recognisable are the *chi-rho* monogram (*Christos*) and the *iota-chi* (*Iesous Christos*). The illustrations show the various forms of these monograms, which first appeared as graffiti in the catacombs. It must be said that many Christians would recognise the symbols without necessarily understanding their deeper meaning and that in our region only a very few have been found, at York, Maryport and perhaps Catterick for example. The Cross as we know it today as the universal symbol of Christianity came much later, some time after AD600. Legend has it that its origins lie in Constantine’s vision of a cross in the heavens with the words ‘*In hoc signo vincas*’ in his famous victory over his rival Maxentius in the battle of Milvian Bridge in AD312; henceforth the cross was declared the official symbol of the Roman army.

Early Christian Signs

Chi-rho	Typed *XP* Combination of Greek letters *X (chi)* and *P (rho)*. Abbreviation of ***Christos* / *Christus***. Frequently combined with alpha and omega as *A XP W.*
Chi-R	Claimed to be combination of Greek letters *X (chi)* and Latin letter R, possibly abbreviation of **Chr**istus. **R**ex; perhaps more likely a variant of the hooked-loop chi-rho type. Also called 'Latinized chi-rho'.
Iota chi	Combination of Greek letters *I (iota)*, and *X (chi)*. Abbreviation of ***Iesous Christos*** / **I**esus **Chr**istus. Also (incorrectly) called 'chi-iota'.
Cross	Also called 'Greek cross'.
Saltire	Derived from Latin numeral ten, X (DECUSSIS) – hence also called 'crux decussata', and 'St Andrew's Cross'.
Swastika	Ancient symbol, probably a representation of the sun, found in catacombs, so possibly Christian.

Revelation to St John: 1.8. 'I am the Alpha and the Omega', and 21.6.

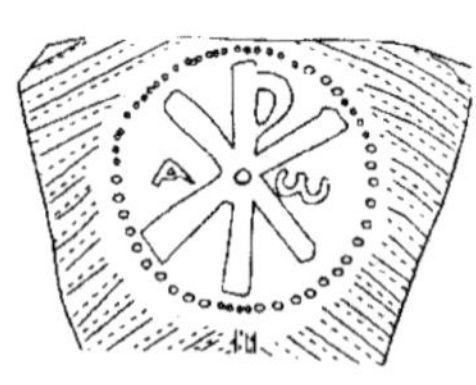

Several 'small finds' have come to light bearing Christian symbols but they only indicate a Christian presence, not necessarily ownership, for they may have been lost in transit, a collector's item, or part of a buried hoard as at Traprain Law in Lothian. From Beadlam in North Yorkshire come buckles and strap-ends showing peacocks and griffins, symbolic of immortality and doom and another strap-end bearing a fish. Chesters, Corbridge and

Coventina's Well have all yielded rim-fragments of amber-toned glass with fish engravings. It seems possible that these fragments are from glass vessels used then, as now, for wine and water central to the celebration of the Eucharist. A bone shaped like a fish, perhaps a pendant, has also been found at South Shields. The valley of the Tyne is quite a rich area for finds for the Romans made much use of river transport, especially here for supplying the Wall, and major crossing points like Dere Street at Corbridge were busy towns with much traffic and trade. In AD1760 a fisherman at Bywell had a lucky catch, a 4" tall silver beaker inscribed '*DESIDERI VIVAS*'; a fragmentary spoon with a similar conjectural 'Long life to…' inscription was recovered from the River Wear in 1869. Such inscriptions ending in '*vivas*' (or the Latinised Greek '*zeses*') may be Christian as they may be an abbreviation of '*vivas in deo*'; alternatively they may simply mean 'long life to…' which is purely secular. In 1736 erosion by the Tyne of the south bank below Corbridge revealed the magnificent silver plate known as the Corbridge Lanx as well as three silver vessels, one with a *chi-rho* and vine decoration; again, these vessels may have been used in the liturgy for wine and water. A 4th century silver bowl, part of the Corbridge hoard, found in 1736 on the south bank of the Tyne just below the bridge: in the centre a rose within a double circle; on beaded rim 6 engraved *chi-rho* symbols between light flourishes of vine scroll; function almost certainly liturgical, either for mixing water and wine or as an *agape* 'common cup' with a broad rim of 44cms. and a depth 10cms., so that it could easily be raised to the communicant's lips.

Agape, 'common cup' from the Corbridge hoard, 4th cent.

Two gold rings, both love tokens or betrothal rings, are of special interest. In the early 3rd century level of the *vicus* of the Roman fort at Vindolanda archaeologists found a polygonal gold ring with a cornelian centre showing a device variously interpreted as a cross, an anchor or a palm branch; round the edges in cameo is '*AN/IM/A/ME/A*', 'My soul' or 'My darling'. Again scholars disagree on the Christian significance, one argues that the dedication is secular and cannot be claimed as evidence for Christianity, another quotes the use of 'anima' in catacomb inscriptions as implying a Christian soul, though here admittedly the context is different. The second ring was found by a turnip picker in a field near Corbridge in 1840 and was the first openwork ring found in Roman Britain. The inscription reads '*AEMILIA ZESES*' and it may be that this beautiful love token, now on display in the Museum of Antiquities, was a gift to a Christian lady. In the British Museum is a ring similarly dedicated to Aemilia but showing also a fish, a dove and a tree of life, a convincing Christian juxtaposition. Chesters Museum has a jet ring with a possible *chi-rho* motif, again probably a love token.

Aemilia Ring, pure gold

The use of '*zeses*', the Latinised Greek form of '*vivas*', is interesting for, along with several epitaphs to Greeks as in Carlisle and South Shields, it indicates a strong Greek element in early Christianity even in this far corner of the empire. After all, the Gospels were written in Greek and the liturgy for the first centuries was celebrated in Greek. There is a similar connection between early Christian and Jewish communities.

Epitaphs deserve close study for they are the only means by which the people of the time can communicate with us and reveal their feelings. There can be no doubting the depth of emotion felt by this father grieving for his dead daughter: "To Corellia, 13, ye mysterious spirits who live in Pluto's realms whom these meagre ashes seek; sire of an innocent daughter, a pitiable victim of unfair hope, bewail her final end". The sad despair of Corellia's father contrasts with hope expressed in the epithet '*AVE SOROR VIVAS IN DEO*' found engraved on a strip of bone, possibly a casket-fitting, from a grave at York; significantly the greeting is 'ave' ('hail') rather than 'vale' (farewell). Two northern tombstones bear an intriguing phrase recognised as Christian. From Stainmore we have, 'Sacred to the memory of Titus who lived 32 years.... *PLUS MINUS*'. It is not that the age of the deceased is uncertain but rather that for a Christian the exact age in this short earthly life is of no consequence compared with eternal life.

Another form of words usually associated with Christian burials is seen on a tombstone from Vindolanda dated c.500. It reads simply '*BRIGOMAGLOS (HIC) IACIT*', 'Brigomaglos lies here'. Brigomaglos is obviously a British name but the earlier idea that he might be a priest sent from Gaul to join Germanus and a friend of St. Patrick has been dismissed in favour of the view that he was a leading British chief, not a cleric, whose name could translate as 'high lord'. The name seems to have Welsh connections so it is possible that Brigomaglos was a mercenary chief sent north to fight invading Picts.

Local scholars disagree on whether the 3rd century Carvoran tombstone of Aurelia Aia indicates that she was Christian; the inscription reads: "To the deified souls of the dead and to the soul of Aurelia Aia by Marcus to his most virtuous wife who lived most purely (*SINE ULLA MACULA*) for 33 years." One argues that this epitaph could apply to any good wife, another that the epithet 'who lived most purely' is most probably Christian and that Aurelia's home town was Salonas, in present-day Croatia, one of the earliest Christian centres. On the other hand, *D.M. (DIS MANIBUS)* on the gravestone is characteristically pagan.

Until recently the only churches recognised as Roman are at Lullingstone in Kent, at Silchester in Hampshire and at Caerwent in South Wales but local archaelogists are now positing probable Christian churches at South Shields, Housesteads and Vindolanda. At Housesteads by the west wall are the foundations of an apse and a building 20' wide and 33' long, some of the earliest churches, unlike later ones, faced west, alongside is a stone cist aligned east to west in the usual Christian style. The dating is late 4th century[8].

At Vindolanda a structure built above the courtyard of the former *principia* again has an apse at the west end, is 45' long and 15' wide and therefore capable of holding a small congregation of two dozen worshippers. On top of four of the stones a single course of regular masonry has been added to make a uniform flat surface probably for the base beams of a timber structure definitely post 370. The apsidal west and the small size of the building are similar to late Roman Christian churches elsewhere. Two leading authorities, Professors Cramp and Thomas, are confident that here we have one of the earliest Christian churches.

Mill Hill Father Bernard Phelan views the site of what is probably one of our earliest Christian churches. Vindolanda. 4th century.

At South Shields the base of a similar building in the forecourt of the praetorium has also been posited as a church, again the dimensions of 10m. by 13m. point to a small congregation.

In the on-site museum is a weathered table-altar of sandstone of the type found in cellars in Germany in the 6th century used by house-groups celebrating the Eucharist. An archaelogist in 1878 wrote 'In the forum towards the east end a most perfect table altar was found composed of two stones, one long and narrow and set upright as a pillar, the other broad and flat, poised on a pedestal', with a recess on the surface for a libation or to hold a relic. It is quite unlike Roman altars which are supported on columns and usually bear inscriptions and are sculptured. Again it is late 4th or early 5th century and of a type called *monopodia* in Gaul and Germany, found in house cellars where they would be used as altars by small groups celebrating the Eucharist.

These three Christian churches, if that is what they are, present the few traces of Christianity so far found in the archaeology of the many Roman forts in the Northern Frontier Zone. It is likely that the churches would serve the spiritual needs of the garrisons and their families and then, after the departure of the Legions c.410 of the dwindling local population, some undoubtedly Romano-Celtic, who lived in the fort and neighbouring *vici* along the only effective east-west route in the region, the Stanegate. Use of stone from old Roman forts is evident still in many of our Anglo-Saxon churches, often built on the actual site of the fort as at Chester-le-Street, Lanchester and Bewcastle. Stones from Corstopitum; some with mason's marks, form the walls of the crypt of Hexham Abbey. Wilfred saw a rich symbolism here, the new churches of Christendom arising from the ruins of the old pagan Roman Empire.

Some eighteen lead tanks from Roman times, often with *chi-rho* symbols, have been found throughout Britain. Most are quite large and may well have been used as fonts. Baptism in such vessels would have been by allusion (pouring water over the head) rather than immersion; it was carried out normally by the bishop. The only Roman lead tank in our area was found at Ireby in Cumbria and has only an 18" internal diameter so may have had a different function. The existence of these tanks is a fair indication of a Christian presence in the locality.

Both place names and ecclesiastical loan words from Greek indicate an early and continuing Christian presence. The word 'ecclesia' was adopted by Christians to mean 'a gathering' rather than 'a church building' and is still seen in various place names such as Eaglescliff on Teesside, Eccles near Duns with Eccles Cairn at nearby Kirk Yetholm, Eaglesfield near Cockermouth and Ecclerigg by Lake Windermere where there is also a White Cross. Except for wooden tablets as found at Vindolanda, the Romans wrote on papyrus which rotted all too quickly in our damp climate so no documentary evidence is extant but Latinised forms of Greek words like *Christus, presbyter, baptiso* must have figured in literature available to educate Roman Christians and are still in everyday use today in their anglicised forms.

AND AFTER THE LEGIONS LEFT

The traditional view is that with the legions gone there was a power vacuum and Britain was virtually defenceless and fell prey to plundering invaders; Irish from the west, Picts from the north and waves of Angles, Saxons and Jutes from across the North Sea. The Welsh monk-historian Gildas wrote 'the land is ablaze from sea to sea.' Thus were ushered in the so-called Dark Ages, the least documented in our history of the fifth and sixth centuries; significantly the Irish prefer the term 'the Early Christian Ages'. It was believed that Christianity was driven by these barbarian invaders into the remote fortresses of western Britain and kept alive by evangelising monks such as Patrick of Ireland, David of Wales and Ninian of Whithorn, 'Apostle of the North'. Bede pays fulsome tribute to the work of James the Deacon in the north.

Space precludes other than a passing mention of the 'Apostle of the Irish', the Romano-British Patrick (died c.AD492). From his surviving *Confessio* we learn that his grandfather, Potitus, was a priest and that his father, Calpurnius, was a deacon with a civil office. If Thomas' argument is correct that the family *villula* at '*vicus bannavem taburniae*' was in the area north of the river Irthing between Lanercost, Birdoswald and Bewcastle, then Christianity must have been established there for at least a century. It seems likely that Patterdale and Aspatria (Patrick's ash) mark locations where he began his preaching journeys as a missionary after his escape from Ireland as a youth and return from Gaul.

There is no doubt Christianity in Roman Britain was established much more firmly in the south than in the north. We have nothing to compare with the house-church of the Roman villa at Lullingstone in Kent with its wall plasters of *chi-rho* symbols and *orantes* (figures with arms outstretched in prayer), nor with the mosaic tiled floor of the villa at Hinton St. Mary in Dorset where a tiled representation of Christ is one of the earliest in Europe. Most finds identified as Christian come from the south-east, the present Kent, Essex and Suffolk, those areas most Romanised and with the largest towns, and nearest Gaul. Christianity was strongest among the landed gentry and a small but influential group in Romano-British aristocracy, classes largely absent in the north. Native Britons and garrisons along the Wall from as far away as Dacia, Dalmatia, Syria, even the Euphrates, worshipped the gods of their ancestors whereas the birth of Christianity was only a very recent event.

However, the most recent scholarship, notably by K.R. Dark[9], challenges the long-held view that Christianity all but died out in the north in the two centuries after the departure of the Legions. Dark argues that while paganism remained endemic not only in rural areas but also among the rich, there is increasing evidence that in the late Roman and sub-Roman period of the late fourth and fifth centuries, Romano-British culture was more deeply embedded and Christianity practised more widely than previously thought. Even in the lands of the Novantae and Selgovae in south-west Scotland and of the Votadini between the old walls of Hadrian and Antonine there is scattered yet impressive evidence; at Whithorn the monastery was a base for missionary work; at Kirkmadrine inscriptions on tombstones name local bishops of this time, 'Here lie the holy bishops Ides, Vincentius and Mavorius', and the stones show *chi-rho* symbols; at Selkirk a stone has the inscription '*Neitano Sacerdos*', Nathan the Priest, and a pillar stone displays '*orantes*' figures in the late antique style; there are many long cist cemeteries and east-west burials in the Christian manner.

South of the wall the Carvetti and Brigantes tribes used Carlisle and York as power-bases under the Dux Britanniarum and local chiefs and the west especially remained predominantly British and free from Anglo-Saxon influence until c.550. In the present Lancashire 'eccles' place names proliferate and attention has already been drawn to probably Christian churches on old Roman fort sites along the Wall; there is also increasing evidence for similar sites in remote rural areas then centres for dispersed communities or on drove roads. Cow Green, the site of the present reservoir in Upper Teesdale, is one such example.

Tradition has it that the site of the old Roman fort at South Shields was the birthplace of Oswiu, future king of the Anglo-Saxon kingdom of Deira, who was murdered in 651; this may indicate continuous use of Arbeia well into Christian times.

Dark readily admits that archaeological evidence is thin as most people in the north were too poor to build fine stone churches or leave inscribed tombstones, yet argues that as new knowledge comes to light it becomes increasingly harder to sustain the old view that Christianity only just hung on by its fingertips until the arrival of the Augustinian mission of 597 and the Irish mission from Iona to Northumbria in 635.

CONCLUSION

Though pagan worship persisted, Christianity eventually prevailed because of its inherent strengths and attractions: in the crucial early centuries it had a powerful central authority based on Rome and was closely identified with 'Pax Romana' and Imperial Rome even though many Christian communities were local in nature; it preached a belief in only one true God and therefore promoted unity as opposed to the conflicting loyalties of polytheistic religions; it provided new foci for worship and embraced a theology of mysteries on central dogmas such as the Trinity, the Incarnation, Death and Resurrection to engage enquiring minds seeking inspiration and ideals higher than the business-like relationship that traditionally existed between worshipper and god where the deity was only dimly visualised and the cult was everything.

Christianity was eagerly embraced by the late Roman emperors, with the exception of Julian 360 – 363, and by local chiefs for its strict moral code demanded obedience to lawful authority and was therefore conducive to political stability, peace and order. In their turn influential churchmen served the church well defending their dioceses and preserving Romanitas: in Britain the visiting Germanus encouraged active opposition to the invading heathen Saxon invaders.

Most importantly its appeal was universal for this new Covenant between God and men promised eternal bliss in heaven in the afterlife for all true believers in Jesus Christ who followed the Gospel precepts, whether they free man or slave, emperor or prisoner in the dungeon, rich or poor. In his letter to the Galatians 3.28 Paul was very explicit on this point: furthermore 'pagans now share the same inheritance.... That same promise has been made to them', Ephesians 3.6.

We have already seen how some Christian feast days grew out of the old pagan festivals throughout the calendar year: there were some similarities between the externals of the new and old forms of worship.

Pagan rituals usually involved the killing of a sacrificial ram, pig or cockerel and feasting on the flesh: Christians re-enact the sacrifice of Jesus Christ on Calvary in the Mass and partake of what they believe is His Body and Blood in the Eucharistic meal of Holy Communion. Libations are still poured as the gifts of bread and wine are offered, just as coins and personal ornaments were given to Coventina in her shrine at the sacred well. Prayers of praise and thanksgiving are offered now as then; hymns are still sung, incense burned, candles lit to help create an atmosphere of reverence, aura, mystery and drama. Scholas worshipping Antenociticus in the temple at Benwell were drawn into closer union with the god they were venerating and with each other no less than a community of Christians gathered in a church today to praise God.

Visitors to Roman temples or places of Celtic worship, often in lonely places, may well experience feelings of awe, even reverence, for the ancient deities who once inhabited Northern Britain: they may well have a sense of empathy with those who worshipped there on reflecting that had they been alive then they would have been their gods too.

It was the promise and the expectation that Christianity held that was so very different. It is not surprising that lore of the ancient religions persisted as they had already been in existence for 5,000 years and more when Christianity was born. Christianity is a late arrival on the human scene. A Roman citizen wrote a letter in the early 5th century in praise of *Dea Roma* and the *prisca religio*; 'Let me continue to practice my ancient ceremonies for I do not regret them. Let me live my old ways for I am free'.
Within two decades of Emperor Theodosius declaring Christianity the official religion of the Roman Empire the legions were leaving

and had probably all gone by 410. The strength of Christianity at this point in history and its persistence through the 5th and 6th centuries is a matter of debate awaiting new archaeological discoveries. We may be sure that fresh knowledge will come to light as some 90% of remains from the four centuries of Roman occupation still lie buried beneath the earth. We have barely scratched the surface.

'They built a strong wall of stone from sea to sea.... it is eight feet wide and twelve feet high'.
Bede. Ecclesiastical History 1.12

Along by Cuddy's (Cuthbert's) Crags.

REFERENCES

1. The Museum has closed on its present site in the University of Newcastle in April 2008 and will reopen as part of the Great North Museum in January 2009.

2. ROSS Ann. Pagan Celtic Britain, 1967.

3. SIMPSON F. G. and RICHMOND I. A., The Roman Fort on Hadrian's Wall at Benwell. Archaeologia Aeliana (AA),

4th Series, 1-42, 1941.

4. ALLASON-JONES L. and McKAY B. Coventina's Well, 1985.

5. ALLASON-JONES L. Mithras on Hadrian's Wall, 2002.

6. HENIG Martin. Religion in Roman Britain, 1984.

7. MAWER C. F. Evidence for Christianity in Roman Britain: The Small Finds, B.A.R., British Series 243, 1995.

8. CROW J., Housesteads, 1995.

9. DARK K. R., From Civitas to Kingdom, 1991 and Britain and the End of the Roman Empire, 2000.

OTHER MAIN SOURCES

CHADWICK Nora, The Celts, 1997. Chapter 6, Religion and Mythology, pages 145-189. Chapter 7, Christianity, pages 190-223.

GREEN M. J., The Gods of the Celts, 1986.

JACKSON K. J. ed., A Celtic Miscellany, 1971.

RICHMOND Ian, Roman Britain, 1955. Chapter 5, Religious Cults, pages 186-214.

SALWAY P., A History of Roman Britain, 1997.

THOMAS Charles. Britain and Ireland in Early Christian Times AD 400-800, 1971.
Christianity in Roman Britain to AD 500, 1985
Christianity in Celtic Britain, 1986.

WALL J., Christian Evidences in the Roman Period: the Northern Counties. Part 1 Archaelogia Aeliana (AA), 4th Series XLIII, pages 201-225, 1965 and Part 2 AA XLIV, pages 147-164, 1966.

2

HOLY MEN AND A STUBBORN PEOPLE OF A BARBAROUS TEMPERAMENT [1]

St Columba in boat.
1400th Anniversary, 1997

A WISH FULFILLED

My long cherished wish to visit Iona became a firm resolution when I read Kenneth Clark's impressions of the island in his excellent book *Civilisation* based on his television series:- "I never come to Iona without the feeling that some God is in this place. It isn't as awe-inspiring as some other holy places – Delphi or Assisi. But Iona gives one more than anywhere else I know a sense of peace and inner freedom. What does it? The light which floods in on every side? The lie of the land which, coming after the solemn hills of Mull, seems strangely like Greece, like Delos, even? The combination of wine-dark sea, white sand and pink granite? Or is it the memory of these holy men who for two centuries kept western civilisation alive?[2]

My wish was eventually fulfilled twice within a year; a short visit with a diocesan group, more of a reconnaissance for a longer stay with a parish pilgrimage some months later to celebrate the millennium.

And so it was that on the evening of our final day, midsummer day, I scrambled up Dun 1, 'Hill of Iona', at 100 metres the highest point of Iona, to enjoy the panoramic view. The cliché "The magic of the Western Isles" became a reality. Having visited the Hebridean islands several times in past years I readily recognised Skye and the Cuillins to the north with the 'Isle of Pillars', Staffa, only a few miles distant; southwards stood Jura with the Paps prominent and Islay; to the west silhouetted against the setting sun were the low outlines of Coll and Tiree and, on the far horizon across the Minch, the Outer Hebrides; eastwards were the 'solemn hills' of Mull and the coast of Argyll. As I savoured these moments I recalled reading in Adamnan's *Life of Columba (Vita)*[3] that the saint was sitting on the hill of Dun 1 when he saw 'a storm cloud to the north rising from the sea on a clear day' and foresaw that it was bringing a plague[4]. This incident happened over 1,400 years ago but when I considered that the gneiss rocks forming Dun 1 were formed some 2,000 million years before that, then the time perspective changed so that Columba became almost my companion.

My reflections soon changed when it dawned on me that I knew very little about the origins and nature of the Irish mission from Iona to my native Northumbria in the 7th century. I saw the darkness now rapidly descending over the mountains in the east as a symbol of my ignorance. I resolved then and there to seek enlightenment by focusing on the lives of two key figures in the story, Columba and Aidan, with Oswald in an intermediary role.

Columba has been variously described: for Adamnan he was a *peregrinus*, a wanderer, 'who sailed away from Ireland to Britain wishing to be a pilgrim for Christ'; for Bede he was the missionary who turned the pagan Picts to the faith of Christ by his words and example; for the medieval monks of Inchcolm (Columba's Isle) Abbey in the Firth of Forth he was Scotland's patron saint and protector in the struggle for independence for they sang, 'Save the choir which sings your praise / from the assaults of Englishmen / and from the taunts of foes'; others see him as a proto-Presbyterian as he was never a bishop, even as a 'Sabbatarian and Keeper of the Stone of Destiny'; most recently the leaflets celebrating the 1,400th anniversary of his death in 597 echo the view of Bede for 'he brought the Faith from Ireland to Scotland'[5].

SOURCES

There is such a wealth of literature on the life and times of this historical figure who continues to fascinate and provoke diverse views that here we will draw mainly on a selection of four primary sources, each typical of the genre of the time. Later writings, like the 10th century Vernacular Lives, see Columba as an ascetic and wonder worker but they obscure rather than reveal historical detail.

Accounts written by those who knew the saint or lived shortly afterwards may reveal how he was seen at the time.

Christianity brought literacy, and the power of the written word excited scholars for the past could now be recorded, the present chronicled and passed on to posterity. The popular view has long been of melancholic people brooding over a mighty and mystical past in a Celtic Twilight (as Yeats puts it) but recent scholars refute this view totally and point to the astonishing power of imagination of early literature[6]. The few examples selected here amply illustrate the point as will a reading, for example, of the monastic odyssey of seven years sailing in the *Voyage of Brendan* where he encounters Jaconius the whale, smoking mountains (volcanoes), the jaws of hell and an island paradise. *The Voyage* is a classic example of an adventurous sea voyage told in an allegorical Christian form out of an amalgam of truth, legend and literary borrowings[7].

The *Amra Choluimbh* or *Elegy of Colum Cille*[8] composed by Dallan Forgaill – his second name implies that he was blind – is rated as one of the earliest and finest literary works to emerge from the early Gaelic world. The *Amra* is dated c. 597 around the time of Columba's death and is both a lament and a praise poem in the traditional sense. Dallan was esteemed a saint and 'chief poet of Ireland' whose patron was Aed, a sub-king of the Ui Neill dynasty and a cousin of Columba. Bards or poet-laureates had long been supported by chiefs and kings: after long training in a bardic school they were employed by a chief or king to sing his praises, memorise his genealogy, celebrate his victories and lament his death. In the *Amra* Dallan blends eulogy, lament and Christian commitment not to his patron but to his hero-saint. The poem gives few firm details of Columba's life but, in an age of scant records, it casts a unique spotlight on the royal prince who became an example of Christian life; its composition exemplifies the integration of Christianity into Irish life at the close of the sixth century and points to the rapprochement between the secular aristocracy and Christian leadership.

Dallan may not have been a cleric but the quality of his Elegy, his familiarity with church matters and with Latin bear eloquent testimony to the high standard of education on offer in the first generation of monastic schools in places like Clonard, Moville and Bangor.

Colman Edo (d.611) was the founder of the monastery of Lann Elo in County Offaly in mid-Ireland, a contemporary and disciple of Columba, and a bishop. His *Alphabet of Devotion* is one of the earliest Irish spiritual writings where Gaelic is used to express Christian ethics. Its emphasis is on the pursuit of justice and truth and, as in the Rule of Benedict, on moderation. Colman urges monks to learn 'constancy at holiness, brevity at talks, tender brotherliness, rising at first summons, fasting with serenity, destruction of desire, lowering of pride, patience in suffering…' Colman clearly knew the *Bible*, the *Books of Wisdom*, Basil and Cassian and presents us with real insights into the thought world of Columba and early Irish monks in the progress of the human soul 'towards a tryst with resurrection on Judgement Day'. The *Alphabet of Devotion* could be called "A Primer in the Monastic Life" and is all the more valuable as no Columban Rule Book survives.

Beccan (d. c.677) was a poet-monk of the Columban *familia* who, some fifty years after Dallan, wrote two fine prose-poems, again in the old bardic style. In *Fo Reir Choluimb 'Bound to Colum'* and in *Tiugraind Beccain, 'The Last Verses of Beccan'* he combines deep affection with idolising praise of his hero-saint in his rejection of kingly power and wordly wealth in favour of a life of self-denial and asceticism.

Beccan spoke from the heart and practised what he preached. From community life on Iona he seems to have progressed to membership of a colony of hermits resident on the mysterious island of Hinba before finding his 'place of resurrection' and 'desert in the ocean' in the isolation and solitude of Rhum as an anchorite, the most highly esteemed level of religious life.

By far the richest source of knowledge is *The Life of St. Columba* written by Adamnan (Little Man), the ninth abbot and of Ui Neil stock, 'in response to the entreaties of the brethren' rather than at the behest of a royal patron. Dated to c.697 *The Life* is clearly meant to commemorate the centenary of the saint's death. The author draws on an earlier *'Book on the Virtues of St. Columba*' compiled by Cummene, who was abbot of Iona from 657 to 669 and on oral sources recounting 'what I have heard without any trace of doubt from informed and reliable old men'.

Divided into three parts, Prophecies, Miracles and Angelic Visitations, the *Vita* describes the life of monks at work and prayer and their dealings with the constant stream of visitors to the island. The focus is mainly domestic and shows above all the devotion of Adamnan to his patron saint. Columba is a man of God, a saintly abbot at the heart of his community, a model for Adamnan and future abbots of Columban monasteries.

Hagiography usually has a hidden agenda and the *Vita* is no exception.

Though composed primarily for the monks of the *paruchia,* Adamnan aimed to show that Columba's prestige was still high and that he should still be reckoned among the mainstream of Western saints, despite the perceived slight done to him at the Synod of Whitby when the decision was made against the old Irish and Ionan dating of Easter. *The Anonymous Life of Cuthbert* was being written at the same time by a monk of Lindisfarne so there appears to be an element of rivalry as Columba's star waned while Cuthbert's rose.

As works of hagiography are, by definition, studies in holiness they make no mention of the faults or foibles of this subject but describe only Christ-like qualities so that an idealised rather than a well-defined person emerges with whom we could more readily relate.

Though Adamnan's *Vita* is an outstanding piece of hagiography it leaves many questions frustratingly unanswered: did Columba engage in missionary activities in Pictland? What was the author's view of the mission to Northumbria, only mentioned in Oswald's vision of Columba before the crucial battle of Heavenfield? Where was Hinba? Where were Columba's 'hundred churches' mentioned in the Amra?

What is in a name?

From the days of infancy he was given the name Columba by divine providence, according to Adamnan. Later Irish writers say that his boyhood name was Crimthann, meaning Fox, a not uncommon name in early Irish medieval history. Certainly the name Columba, Latin for dove with its allusions to the Holy Spirit, would be considered more appropriate than fox for a man of God.

'He was called dove for his simplicity', Adamnan states. Perhaps he became Columba when he took his first monastic vows. Columba is the Latin form of the Irish Colum(b) or Choluimb, often seen as Colum Cille, 'Dove of the Church'. It is also the root of such names as Colm, Colin, Malcolm and Colman, Latinised as Columbanus, all names occurring regularly in later history.

The name Iona probably arises from a late medieval misspelling of Iova. Adamnan refers to the island as Insula Iova while Bede calls it Hi(1), a name deriving from the use of yew trees. It is likely that the form Iona has become popularised by the coincidence that the Hebrew word for dove is Jona[10].

Lineage and Early Life

Dallan, Beccan and Adamnan all make much play of Columba's noble ancestry and underline the crucial role of kinship in early Irish history. It is no coincidence that of the first nine abbots of Iona only the fourth, Fergnae, who was probably British, was not of the Ui Neill blood-line.

In the Amra 'truly the boy is a son of Conn's offspring.' 'Not newsless is Niall's land' for 'By the grace of God Colum rose to exalted companionship': 'in place of splendour, in place of pomp he bestowed the pure descendant of Conall ruled in his monastery.' For Beccan too Columba was 'Niall's candle', 'Great treasure in ever place Colum Cille, of all Niall's folk': he was 'Royal Kin of triumphant kings, lord, full of grace'. Not only was he 'Connacht's candle' he was 'Britain's candle' too, 'a splendid ruler, barque of treasure, people's counsellor, Conal's offspring'. Adamnan prayed 'the name of Niall's famous descendant, not small it's protection and I pray on great prayers to Eithne's son'[11].

The founder of the dynasty was the legendary Niall of the Nine Hostages, the great-grandfather of Fedelmid, an aristocrat of the Cenel Conall branch, who was Columba's father. According to the Annals of Ulster in the battle of Cul Drebene in 561 the Northern Ui Neills prevailed against the Southern Ui Neills 'through the prayers of Columba'. Thereafter the fortunes of the royal prince who became an exemplar of Christian life were much favoured as his kin ruled as High Kings of Tara throughout his lifetime.

Much of Columba's early life is shrouded in mystery. Even his birthplace is doubtful. A 10th century Derry historian records that he was born beside Loch Gartan in Donegal but this is unlikely as the Cenel Conaill did not rule in this region at the time. We may be sure, however, that his parents Fedlimid and Eithne were either pagan or first-generation Christians. Pagan practices lingered long after the coming of Christianity: as late as 564 the Kings of Tara were being inaugurated with pagan rites.

Scholars in Columba's time took pride in their ancestry and in their pre-Christian mythology where there was much that could be embraced, blessed and incorporated into Christian beliefs. Loyalty to the chief, worship of past heroes, a spirit-filled world and a belief in an afterlife were just some characteristics which cause one modern scholar to eulogise over pagan Celtic religion over which hangs 'a beautiful dignity, an orderliness, a sense of fitness… in the land of promise there is no sin or punishment, no lasting strife but an idealized existence amid beauty, perpetual youth and good will. The heathen Irish erected a spirituality on spiritual lowliness which comes close to an ideal spiritual existence.'[12]

Adamnan paints a different picture of everyday life on the ground; of fierce battles, of a woman slain by a spear before the saint's eyes; of demons carrying off to hell a grasping local chieftain; of a murderous attack on Columba by Lam Dass (Right Hand) whom he had just excommunicated; of fields parched by drought and clouds bearing rain that raised awful sores full of pus on the backs of people who suffer a terrible sickness even to death.

Columba was born into a world where hardship and violence prevailed and where life was all too often short and brutal.

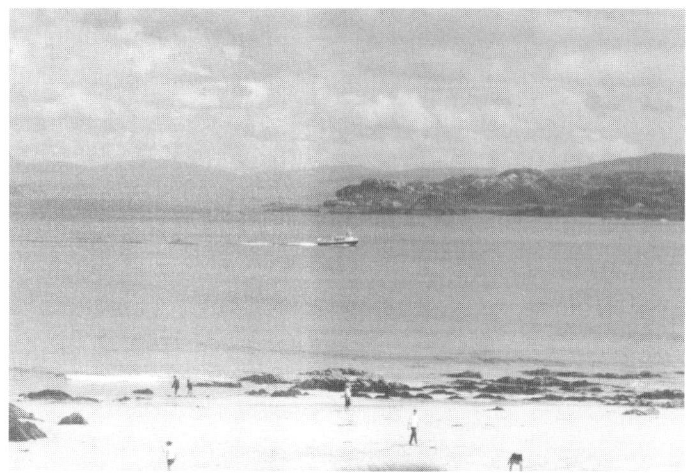

Bay of Martyrs, east coast Iona where Viking raiders slaughtered 68 Columban monks in 805, 'red martyrs'.

Columba, a 'white martyr?'

Alban of Verulamium, and Julius and Aaron of Caerleon, who had shed their blood for Christ in 4th century Roman Britain were deemed 'red martyrs': Ireland's first red martyrs were St. Donnan and 150 of his monks who were massacred on Eigg in 617, supposedly by Pictish warriors in a land dispute over sheep grazing rights. 'White martyrs' renounced home and family in an intensely kin-based society to practise an ascetic life in voluntary exile searching for Christ, either alone as an eremite or in a community; their journeying was then peregrination or pilgrimage. We hear of Irish monks settling on the island of Pappay off the east coast of Iceland, on the Faroe Islands, and as far east as Kiev in the Ukraine, at Bobbio and St. Gall in Switzerland and Brindisi in southern Italy.

Nearer home many offshore islands, some rocky pinnacles like Skellig Michael off the Kerry coast, others remote like Rona, forty miles north of the Outer Hebrides, became home to 'white martyrs' like St. Ronan.

By contrast Columba's choice of Iona, no more than a comfortable day's sail from the port of Derry and already part of the Irish kingdom of Dal Raita in Argyll, appears much less adventurous. Was his exile a penance, voluntary or imposed by the Synod of Teltown in 560 mentioned by Adamnan, for his part in the bloody battle of Cul Drebene? Or was it related to the well-known but unsubstantiated story of his illegal copying from a psalter or early vulgate bible in his time at Moville? He may well have been invited to found a monastery as a centre of learning by King Conall of Dal Riata: such an invitation would hold much appeal and could provide an escape from the political intrigue of the dynastic factions in Northern Ireland.

In the event, when Columba sailed for Alba (Britain) with the band of monks, chiefly kinsfolk, he stayed first at the royal palace before moving onto Iona to land granted him by the king, not by King Bridei of the Picts, as Bede tells us. Columba found himself in an Irish milieu where Irish was spoken and the people already Christian.

The Scottii tribe under their leader Erc had sailed across from the northern Ireland Coast to settle in the west of Alba, now Argyll, c.400. The Scottii, who gave Scotland its name, were Gaelic speaking and, by 563, already Christian so that Columba, far from sailing into distant and isolated exile, founded the monastery in a central situation of Dal Riata in what was in effect an Irish sub-kingdom. It is doubtful whether Columba would consider himself as a 'white martyr' as he made several return journeys to Ireland, nor did his secular activities cease.

Whatever the motives of Columba's sailing to Alba it was one that had profound implications for the history of Northumbria.

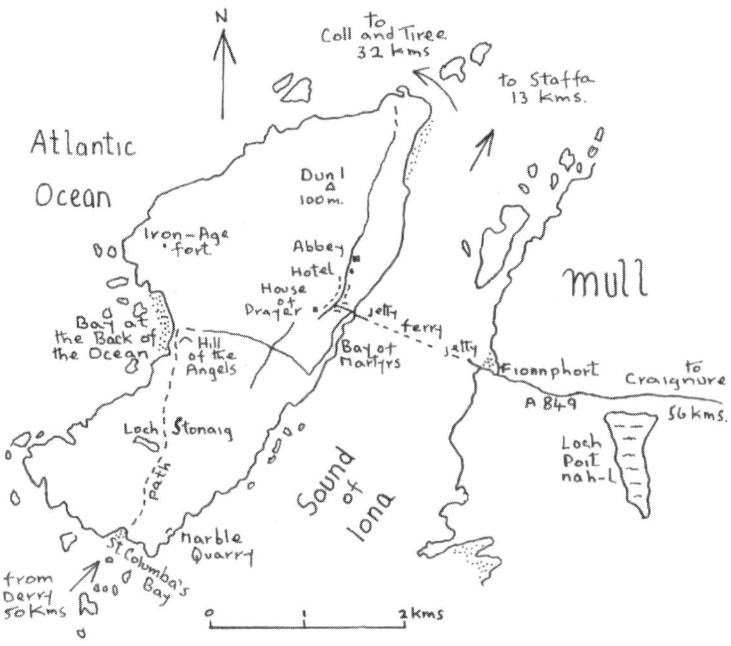

Columba, a diplomat.

Columba's royal blood, his growing status as a leading churchman and as abbot of an influential ecclesiastic centre almost invariably involved him in politics.

In a disputed kingship in Dal Riata he was invited to attend the coronation of Aedan, not his choice for king, whom he blessed while laying his hand on his head. This may well be the earliest recorded Christian ritual in a coronation ceremony. Thereafter he maintained close and friendly relations with the rulers of Dal Riata.

In 575 he was invited to a 'conference of kings' at Druim Cett to act as adviser and mediator in such secular matters as taxation and military service. Tradition tells how only Columba's casting vote saved the bards from being banned for making excessive charges for their services.

While at the conference he blessed King Aedan's son Domnall prophesying for him a long and happy reign: just as surely the saint's displeasure meant a short life and a violent death. Such was the fate of Feradach, a nobleman of Islay, who betrayed a trust Columba put in him to look after an exiled Pictish prince. Columba's success in bridging the divide between secular and ecclesiastical interests was assisted by ties of blood and religion with leaders on both sides of the Irish Sea. He was able to move easily in the company of kings, princes and nobles for he was one himself. His experience of secular overlordship in Ireland enabled him to organise the grouping of monastic churches into *paruchiae* ruled from Iona. Here were valuable lessons for future church leaders in Northumbria.

The Penitent

Beccan was the first Irish poet to give details of an exiled pilgrim: Columba was 'a bold man over the sea's ridge… a sage across the seas... he crucified his body on the grey waves… abandoned sleep… gave up bedding… embraced stone slabs – finest actions'. Dallan agrees; 'he fought a long and noble battle against flesh… his body's desire, he destroyed it.' There can be no doubting the life-style of Irishmen who found the most intelligible form of ascetic renunciation in exile; in the view of Beccan and Dallan this was all the more praiseworthy in Columba's case for he gave up wars, palaces and chariots as well as kith and kin and the prospect of becoming High King of Tara[13].

Iona became the destination of a constant stream of pilgrim penitents, many being misfits and outcasts of society, who came to confess their sins and seek forgiveness. Previously confession was in public and a one-off opportunity often deferred until the death-bed, as was the case with Constantine, the Roman Emperor..

Penance was a punishment for wrongdoing. In Columba's life the situation was transformed as Irish Penitentials envisaged a God of mercy, not of punishment. Penances were medicines for sick souls, dispensed by an *anamchara*, a father confessor, guided by the Penitentials. 'Let us bare our wounds to the healer, for he who binds up his wounds truly nurses them'. Finnian's Penitential states that 'there is no crime that cannot be forgiven through penance'.

Never despair of the mercy of God was the message. A poet lauds the beauty of 'a herd of thick-maned horses... the month of May with cuckoos and nightingales, summer days long and slow... the beauty of virtue in doing penance for glory, beautiful too when God saves me'[14].

Penitents did not stay long on Iona but were passed on to Tiree and Hinba where communities of penitents existed. Penances for serious sins were severe: for killing a man in his native Connaught one penitent had to spend seven years on Tiree as a hermit, eventually he became a monk; for sleeping with his mother Lugaid 'spent twelve years among the British with tears of remorse,' never to return to Ireland.

The Christian Celts had a strong sense of sin which was taken very seriously: there was a corresponding joy in experiencing the forgiveness and trust of a loving God. Columba's own life-style enabled him to become an exemplar of a soul friend, an *anamchara*, for he was 'a sound austere sage of Christ... a shelter to the naked... a teat to the poor... no slight refuge after penance'.

The Scholar

Dallan's Amra portrays Columba as a scholar's saint for he was 'learning's pillar in every stronghold... foremost at the books of complex law... he separated the elements according to figures among the books of the Law'. He knew the writings of Basil and 'the books Cassian loved'. He was skilled in computation and astronomy for 'he could number the stars of heaven' and 'set in motion seasons and calculations'. In his teaching role he distributed the Scriptures among the schools and as an exegete he commented on them. He studied Greek grammar. Dallan's picture of Columba as an active intelligent theologian of many interests complements that of Adamnan who stresses his love of books and talents as a scribe.

We read that Columba spent time copying books and preparing service books, but of the many prayers and hymns attributed to him only two carry a high degree of probability. *Altus Prosator*, 'Exalted Sower', is orthodox, powerful and rich in biblical imagery and succeeds in filling the heart with godly fear, yet says little on the mercy or love of God. *Adiutor Laborantium*, 'Helper of Workers' has a litany of titles for God and is a plea for help and protection:- 'I beg that I, a little man, trembling and wretched rowing through the infinite storms of this age… may be led into the joy of paradise… to the most beautiful haven of peace'.

Columba's love of learning, inspired by his first teacher Cruithnechan the priest, to whom he was fostered, and by Gemman and Finnian, was an integral element in Celtic spirituality in Ireland and Alba, most especially in Northumbria.

The Missionary?

Was Bede correct in writing that 'the priest and abbot named Columba came from Ireland to Britain, to preach the Word of God in the provinces of the northern Picts'?[15]

This has been the long held popular view restated in the 1997 centenary celebrations literature. Yet the evidence points rather to this 'pilgrim for Christ', who was never a bishop, seeing himself primarily as abbot of a monastic community teaching his monks to live a life of contemplative prayer in mutual and sincere charity.

Columba did make several journeys into Pictland and neighbouring islands, like Skye, Tiree and Hinba, but the only hint that he came as an evangeliser is found in the Amra where Dallan records that 'he preached to the tribes of the Tay', in Perthshire. In his best known visit to Pictland he met Bridei, King of the Picts, in the royal fort near Inverness. There is no suggestion that he succeeded or even tried to convert the pagan king to Christianity: the purpose of the visit was probably to secure the release of hostages and the safety of the hermit Cormac and other monks on Orkney, part of Bridei's kingdom.

Adamnan records baptisms of Picts but these are isolated events: on Skye by the water of Artbrannan an old man, chief of a war band became a Christian just before his death at the very place of his baptism; in Glen Urquahart by Loch Ness a Pictish household was baptised. There are also references to Columba preaching the gospel through interpreters to Pictish converts and of the saint 'staying for some days in the presence of the Picts' yet Adamnan does not depict Columba as a missionary to Pictland. It is interesting that Bede's informants a century later should remember Columba in that role.

We know that others were drawn to join monasteries of the Columban *familia* on Iona, Hinba, Tiree, and on the mainland at Loch Awe, for all four of the races living in the British Isles were represented in these communities; Irish, Picts, British and English (Anglo-Saxon). Pilu and Genereus the baker on Iona were both English. Yet the religious houses were there for a life of work and prayer not as bases for missionary work, though each would exercise a degree of pastoral care for needy locals and visitors.

Though Adamnan does not mention them we know from other records that there were Christian missionaries at work, as many as eighty, among the Picts: St. Donnan, the future martyr, was active on Eigg, Skye and northern Pictland; St. Kessog in the Trossachs; St. Serf in Fife; St. Tiernan in the Dee Valley; St. Mungo (Kentigern), the first Bishop of Glasgow, in Strathclyde. We hear too of Molvan on Lismore, Blane in Perthshire and Maelrubra from his base at Applecross evangelising in Banff.

In the light of the evidence available it would be misleading to count Columba in that number: that role was to fall to the next generation of Ionan monks, most notably Aidan.

A Thaumaturge

Columba, and in the following century Cuthbert, are exemplars of thaumaturges, early medieval wonder-workers. Adamnan's *Vita* contains as many miraculous events as the two later lives of Cuthbert; many of events recounted are strikingly similar. In an age of faith both the learned and simple country folk expected miracles and assessed the favours given to the thaumaturge by God by the extent and nature of the wonders he worked in his lifetime and after death. Thus an individual's sanctity was attested by popular acclaim, '*Vox populi*': there was no formal recognition of canonisation to sainthood until 1163, three years after the death of St. Thomas à Becket. The miracles are wide-ranging in their nature: some are clearly latter-day Gospel stories; some seem to arise from local folklore; others are meant to demonstrate the superiority of the Christian God over the heathen gods or may be down to what seem to us to be common sense, yet there remains 'an indissoluble core that cannot be explained by any natural means and are attributable safely to the supernatural power of God displayed and through His saints... God is not bound or restricted in the means by which he manifests his power or answers the prayer of faith'[16].

Adamnan asks that the reader of his book 'should contemplate how great and how special is the honour in which our glorious patron stands with God'. The miracles he recounts are because 'God deigned to hear his prayers' of our praiseworthy patron's life.
Let a few examples of the forty-six miracles cited by Adamnan illustrate the reputation Columba enjoyed as a wonder-worker in the early Irish church and, Adamnan hopes, even as far 'as Rome itself, the chief of all cities'.

Significantly, the first miracle recorded is by the deacon Columba under Bishop Uinnian (Finnio) when the wine for Mass runs out and he changes water from a nearby well into wine, 'the same first miracle Christ himself has worked at Cana of Galilee'.

Early in his life Columba is closely identified with Christ, later he draws water from a rock when none is available for the baptism of a child in Ardnamnchan and raises the dead son of a Pictish family who had just been baptised to life, commanding: 'in the name of the Lord Jesus Christ, wake up and stand upon thy feet'. Adamnan here places his patron in the company of the prophets Elijah and Elisha and with the apostles Peter, Paul and John who also raised the dead to life.

Several instances are given of Columba's power over the elements; by his prayers he calms stormy seas, he changes wind directions to give favourable voyages, he procures rain to end severe drought over the fields of Iona, he preserves a hymn book he wrote from rotting in the water in which it had lain, he overcomes the devastation of plague in Ireland by sending Silnan there to cure afflicted men and cattle with water and blessed bread. While attending the 'Conference of Kings' at Druim Cett he 'cured the ailments of various invalids who received full healing… some by merely touching his cloak'. On Iona he cured his servant who was desperately ill and prophesied that Diarmait would outlive him by many years. Wonders could be worked at a distance – given a vision of a 'poor girl tortured by the pains of a most difficult childbirth who was now in Ireland calling on his name' the saint got up from his reading and entering the church, prayed for a safe delivery. His prayers were heard so that he told the assembled community 'she has safely given birth'. A different cure was effected while he was staying as a guest in Rathlin Island where the wife of the steersman Luigne hated him for his ugliness and 'would not allow him to lie with her', even threatening to cross the seas and enter a woman's monastery. Fasting that day and praying at night, Columba reconciled the unhappy couple; 'for the husband I hated yesterday I love today' the wife declared. The abbot revealed himself as a successful marriage-counsellor.

Pictland is usually portrayed as hostile territory where Columba is seen jousting with wizards who mock him as he blesses a poisonous well so that the water now cures sickness, where previously it caused leprosy and crippled those who drank there.

By the shores of Loch Ness he drives off a terrible water-beast (the first recorded mention of Nessie) which had already seized a man; on Skye he encounters a wild boar 'of amazing size' which he commands 'Go no further, die where you are', whereupon the beast collapsed dead. The fate of the boar is in contrast to that of the crane, arriving exhausted on Iona blown across from friendly

Ireland. The bird was cared for in the guest house until it recovered and was able to fly home.

Some tales are bizarre, even ridiculous, to our modern ears yet are recorded as everyday events, perhaps with their origins in old pagan folk-lore: Columba expels a devil from Colman's pail as it was making the milk constantly spill out; milk is drawn from a bull; deer impale themselves on stakes set in the ground; a poor man's herd of five cows is increased to one hundred and five upon Columba's blessing.

These strange and enchanting tales offer glimpses of the early medieval world in and around Iona in which Columba and his monks lived and travelled.

Angels

Book III of the *Vita* includes twenty three 'visions of angels and manifestations of heavenly light', spanning his whole life. While the unborn child was still in the womb his mother had a vision of an angel telling her that she would bear 'a son of such flower that he shall be reckoned as one of the prophets for he is destined by God to lead innumerable souls to the heavenly kingdom': at the moment of his death just after the midnight office 'the whole church was filled with angelic light around the saint' and a monk on a neighbouring island saw Iona 'bathed in the bright light of angels'.

Stained Glass Window of St Columba, Abbey Church, Iona.

A blacksmith, St. Brendan and a monk, ‘a saintly Briton’, were just some of the souls seen being carried to heaven by angels by Columba in visions; occurrences not uncommon in the lives of saints.

On our visit to Iona we stood on the rocky *Cnoc nan Aingel*, ‘Angel’s Knoll’, on the machair beside the Bay at the Back of the Ocean. Adamnan recounts how a spy followed Columba to that place and witnessed ‘holy angels, citizens of the heavenly kingdom, flying down with amazing speed gathering around the holy man as he prayed’.

Adamnan advises us that ‘we know little of the extent and nature of the sweet visits by angels for they generally came as he remained awake on winter nights or as he prayed in isolated places’.

In prayers attributed to Columba the saint strikes a note of nostalgia for his homeland as well as a sense of the ever present angels as these excerpts show:-

‘Were all the tribute of Scotia mine
I would give all for one little cell
In my beautiful Derry
For the white angels that go
In crowds from one end to the other.
I love my beautiful Derry
For its quietness and purity.
For heaven’s angels that come and go
Wander every leaf of the oaks’[17].

In the ‘Protection of Columcille’ we read:
‘The path I walk, Christ walks it.
Bright angels walk with me – dear presence –
In every dealing’.

It may well be that the angels took the place of the wee folk of old pagan folklore; certainly an angelic presence was never far from saints in the tradition of Columba and Cuthbert.

LIFE ON IONA

What do we know about everyday life on Iona in Columba's time and in the following years when Aidan was a novice monk and the Bernician royal household was in exile there?

The only visible remains from this time are the outlines of a vallum or ditch marking the boundary of the monastic site enclosing some twenty acres. A rocky knoll in front of the main entrance of the abbey church is reputedly the site of Columba's writing hut. We can only surmise the original wooden buildings: the church, refectory, dormitory, guest house, forge, bakery, barns, stables and work-shops; for nothing remains[18].

Yet references in the *Vita* and archaeological research have revealed a variety of agricultural and craft activities occupying much of the monk's daily routine. The aim was self-sufficiency, the work highly organised and the workers well-equipped.

Dairy cows were milked and cattle slaughtered; crops were sown, tended, harvested and stored; horses were bred for draught and travel; herbs were grown by gardeners; millers ground corn; blacksmiths shoed horses; stonemasons built and repaired walls; carpenters built boats for fishing and transporting people and goods such as timber from the mainland.

The daily round was broken by the ringing of a hand-bell summoning the community to worship in church at the time of the Hours. Mass was celebrated only on Sundays and feast days when the brethren wore white, and special meals (later called pittances) were eaten. Monks fasted every Wednesday and Friday.

Adamnan portrays everyday life on Iona as busy and purposeful. As well as following the daily routine of prayers, study and work there was a steady stream of visitors ranging from kings and their envoys, ecclesiastical pilgrims including a bishop, who tried unsuccessfully to hide his true identity, and the sick and penitent. One of the busiest places on the island would be the harbour for all visitors arrived by boat: Adamnan records or infers as many as fifty-seven sailings. The place name Port na Muinntirr may indicate where the harbour was. Visitors arriving on the coast of Mull hailed the ferryman on Iona who then rowed them across the narrow strait.

Visitors brought eagerly sought news of the outside world: from Ireland of the killing of two Northern Ui Neill rulers, Baetan and Echord; of an Italian city overcome by sulphurous fumes, probably Naples below Vesuvius, a prophecy of Columba, later that year confirmed 'by Gallic sailors arriving here from Gaul'; of fascinating and eye-witness descriptions of the Holy Places in Palestine and Rome recounted by the Frankish Bishop Arculf after spending nine months there. Arculf's information was written up by Adamnan as a book, later circulated in Northumbria, to form the basis of Bede's *De Locis Sanctis*. Bede informs us that Arculf 'was brought by contrary winds to our island, after not a few dangers' on his return journey from the Mediterranean; this may well be only conjecture by Bede but the story shows the remarkable ways knowledge was disseminated in the early medieval world and then recorded for the enlightenment of scholars.

Though they were skilful and intrepid sailors, Irish monks were only too aware of the dangers of the deep. The vulnerability of a sailor in a frail boat on the open sea was an eloquent symbol of the Christian life and required a deep faith in the protection of God. St. Brendan prayed: 'Oh Christ, will you help me on the wild waves?' The poet Beccan sings of the *peregrinus* in his curragh as he crossed the 'wave-strewn wild region, foam-flecked, seal-filled, savage, bounding, seething, white-tipped, pleasing, doleful'. Columba is often invoked to exercise his God-given power in rescuing sailors in peril, calming storms, changing contrary winds. His view was that hazardous sea voyages help the pilgrim to grow in faith and trust in God's providence.

When Colman was in great danger in the surging tides of the whirlpool of Corryvreckan Columba urged him 'to pray more fervently that he may sail through the peril and reach us here'. Not all sailors made harbour safely; in the Annals of Ulster we read of many drownings in the 7th and 8th centuries, including monks of Iona.

The sea continues to exact a terrible toll.

On our millennium visit we sailed to Staffa, seven miles north of

Iona, where we landed to explore the wonders of Fingal's cave. We enjoyed the company and admired the seamanship of the young men in charge of the boats. Tragically, only a few months later, four of their number, the only unmarried young men on Iona, were drowned when their boat was overcome by waves as they were crossing the narrow strait from Mull where they had been attending a dance in Bunessan.

The monastic library

A recent study[19] has revealed the wealth of books held in the *scrinia*, the book-chests in the library on Iona. It is remarkable that such a fine collection could be assembled throughout the 7th century for we hear of no Irish Benedict Biscop, the bibliophile.

Most important was the *Bible*, both the old Latin version and the new Vulgate, St. Jerome's translation were there. Colman's *Alphabet of Devotion* at least gives us the spirit of the Rule Book no longer extant. In Augustine's *City of God* the reader shared a vision of a community of people, touched by the grace of God, who respond by living in Christian love – the ideal for any monastic community. The teachings, trials and ascetic practices of the Desert Fathers of Egypt, the founders of both western and eastern monasticism, could be studied in the two prototype hagiographies, *The Life of Anthony* by Athanasius and the *Life of St. Martin* by Sulpicius Severus, and in Cassian's Conferences.Local saints' lives were represented by *The Life of St. Brigid* by Cogitosus and the *Book of the Powers of St. Columba* by Cummene Find, Abbot of Iona 657 – 669, on which Adamnan drew in his *Vita.*

The writings of Isodore (d.636) bishop of Seville, were seized on eagerly by Irish scholars and were immensely influential for they displayed an encyclopaedic knowledge on a wide range of subjects, grammar, mathematics, medicine, cosmology and astronomy. Both his *Etymologies*, a collection of twenty books, and his *De Rerum Natura*, were available for study in the library.

Iona's deep involvement in the life of the church brought copies of texts of church councils and synods and letters on key matters like the Easter controversy. The Divine Office required hymn books, Psalters, texts of prayers to celebrate the changing seasons of the liturgical year and different feast days.

Even the small sample of books mentioned here indicate that Columba and his successors led a monastic community 'not out on a limb doing its own Celtic thing but one steeped in the culture of Latin Christianity, participating fully in the literary expression of the faith of the church, 'The People of the Book'[20].

Books were worth their weight in gold. Words were precious and novel after centuries of oral traditions and, where they were the words of Holy Scripture, they were sacred and enshrined in the sumptuous illustrated *Books of Kells* and of *Durrow*, both probably originating on Iona.

Perhaps it is not too fanciful to see the seeds of the future flowering of the Northumbrian Renaissance being sown in the minds of zealous young monks like Aidan, Finan and Colman as they acquired knowledge and wisdom from the books stored in the *scrinia* of the library on Iona.

Heavenfield

'No symbol of the Christian faith, no church, no altar had been erected in the whole of Bernicia before Oswald set up the standard of the holy cross before he fought his savage enemy. This place is held in great veneration'. Bede HE III 2.

The scene now shifts to Northumbria, still divided by Bernicia in the north and Deira in the south.

Some twenty miles west of Newcastle on the old Roman Stanegate, now the line of the B6318, stands the latest replica of 'the standard of the holy cross', the first in Bernicia according to Bede. If not in this precise place - some argue for Hallington to the north, others for Steel a few miles south - then certainly near here was fought one of the most significant battles in Northumbria's long and bloody history. The year was 634.

Bede describes how Oswald 'mustered an army small in numbers but strong in the faith of Christ' to do battle for the future of Northumbria with 'Cadwalla's vast forces'[21]. Later historians likened it to a David and Goliath contest. The background to the confrontation lay in the continuous political infighting for power between rival claimants, characteristic of 7th century Britain and Ireland. Exile was the usual fate of the losers and became an important factor in royal conversions. Oswald was born in 604 but was forced to flee while only a youth with other members of the royal Bernician household when his father Aethelfrith was killed in battle by Edwin in 617. Northumbria had long-standing ties with the Scottish Dal Riata; Aethelfrith exacted tribute from the province after defeating King Aedan in the battle in 603 at Degastan, thought to be in Dumfriesshire.

Irish exiles found refuge in Iona where Oswald spent the next fifteen years of his life, where he learned to speak fluent Gaelic and was baptised into Christianity.

The death of Edwin, Northumbria's first Christian king, in battle against the joint forces of Welsh chieftain Cadwalla, probably an apostate, and the Mercians, marked the end of another phase in our turbulent history. Bishop Paulinus, and Edwin's widowed queen Ethelberga, fled to Kent and the momentum of the Roman mission to Northumbria was spent. The church was left in the care of James the Deacon, based on Catterick.

Oswald's brother Eanfrith, who had married a Pictish princess while in exile, claimed Bernicia while Osris, Edward's cousin, took Deira. Both rulers reverted to paganism but when they were in succession killed by Cadwalla, a power vacuum again existed giving Oswald the opportunity to return from exile to stake his claim for the throne.

Bede and Adamnan, our two main sources, though agreeing on the outcome and profound consequences of the battle of Heavenfield, differ in their accounts of the preceding events. For Bede Oswald's army was already Christian for the King commands them: 'Let us kneel together and ask the true and living God Almighty of His mercy to protect us from the sorcery of our enemies'. The whole army obeyed and 'at the first light of dawn won the victory their faith deserved'[22].

Adamnan has only Oswald and twelve companions as Christians (returned exiles from Iona?) and describes how the rest of the army was baptised after the victory. It may well be that Adamnan's version is more correct for Christianity had long been established among the Welsh whereas it had only recently arrived in Northumbria with Paulinus, but Bede would not wish to portray this battle so crucial for the conversion of Northumbria as a victory of pagan English over Christian British; it would go right against the theme of his works.

Bede does not mention Columba in his account but to Adamnan the saint played a crucial role: while Oswald was asleep on his pillow on the eve of the battle he had a vision of Columba who 'shone with angelic beauty', and whose 'head touched the clouds'. 'Be strong and act manfully. Behold I will be with thee … the Lord has granted me that at this time your foes shall be put to flight … you shall return'[23].

For Adamnan the great victory was due to the prayers of Columba on behalf of Oswald and yet another example of the saint's prophetic powers and the special privileges he enjoyed in relation to kings.

THE NORTHUMBRIAN MISSION

Bede writes that as soon as he became king Oswald 'sent to the Scottish elders among whom he and his companions had received the sacrament of Baptism when in exile, asking them to send a bishop by whose teaching and ministry the English people over whom he ruled might receive the blessing of the Christian Faith and the sacraments'[24].

It is just as likely that Oswald delivered the request, even the command, in person when he revisited Iona 634-5 for in quoting his source for the story of the King's vision of Columba Adamnan states: 'this was confidently narrated to me by my predecessor, our abbot Failbe. He asserted that he had heard the vision from the mouth of King Oswald himself, relating it to abbot Segene'. Adamnan took great care to state his sources in recording the posthumous miracles of Columba.

Oswald's decision to send to Iona rather than to York or Canterbury was not surprising. The Roman mission was associated with Edwin who had killed his father, and with Paulinus who had fled, whereas in his fifteen years among the Dal Riata Irish he had been much impressed by the simple and holy life of the monks. He had been baptised as a Christian and experienced the advantages Christianity could bring to a king ruling his people justly. Furthermore he owed his success to Columba's prayers. Oswald's request, whether by envoy or in person, came at a propitious time in the affairs of Iona.

The abbot Segene was a strong leader of a confident community, now well established after thirty years. Fifth in succession to Columba, Segene was of Cenel Conaill stock maintaining the strong family ties of that dynasty; Columba was succeeded by his cousin Baithene, then came Baithene's cousins Laisren and Fernae (Virgna) who, though probably British, may well have had Conaill connections, according to some genealogists. Throughout Segene's long rule from 623 to 652 as abbot three powerful Cenel Conaill kings ruled in Ireland, providing some of the patronage which fuelled Iona's new ebullience[25].

Segene's abbacy had three notable characteristics: his staunch support for the Irish dating of Easter (Iona did not finally conform to the Roman method adopted at the Synod of Whitby in 664 until 719); his strenuous efforts to hear and record stories about Columba in written rather than oral form, Silnan 'gave testimony in the presence of Abbot Segene and other elders', all of which yielded material for Cummene's book; finally, and most importantly from our perspective, he gave immediate and continuing support to the mission requested by Oswald. It may well be that Segene's decision was to meet a particular request rather than to embark on a policy of wider missionary work for the only other monastery founded in this time was at Rochtu, either Lambay Island off the coast north of Dublin or Rathlin Island.

Segene may have reckoned that, as well as winning souls for Christ, a successful mission to the Kingdom of Northumbria would extend the influence of the Columban *familia,* would find new supporters in the Easter dating dispute, and would gain a powerful new ally in King Oswald. Indeed, Adamnan refers to Oswald as 'Emperor' with powers greater than the 'High King of Tara'. Bede says Oswald was given by God 'a more extensive kingdom than any of his ancestors', he had under his rule all the peoples and provinces of Britain where people 'spoke four languages, I mean the British, Picts, Irish and English'. The extent of Oswald's hegemony is disputed but the term '*bretwalda*', overlord, used in the Anglo-Saxon Chronicle, seems appropriate.

Only Bede tells us that the first mission from Iona was a failure. Segene's first choice was 'a man of a more austere disposition', at times referred to as Bishop Austerior, who returned frustrated to Iona reporting that the English refused to listen to him as they were 'an ungovernable people of an obstinate and barbarous temperament'[26]. A conference was convened when Aidan spoke up advising that 'ignorant heathens should first be given the milk of simpler teaching and gradually nourished with the Word of God to enable them to follow the loftier precepts of Christ.

In attributing these words to Aidan Bede clearly had in mind Paul's first letter to the Corinthians 3.2. "I fed you with milk, not solid food; for you were not ready for it".

Aidan was duly elected to lead a second mission to preach the faith of Christ to a province of the English for he was 'particularly endowed with the grace of discretion, the mother of all virtues'. He was at once consecrated Bishop so that he could ordain well-trained English men to the priesthood in his mission territory.

Oswald's gift of Lindisfarne to the Ionan monks as a base for their mission was as wise as Segene's choice of Aidan as leader of the mission. Formerly called Innis Med in Irish (Isle of Winds) and Medcaud by Nennius, it is in fact not an island but a tombolo for as Bede picturesquely puts it: 'as the tide ebbs and flows, this place is surrounded by sea twice a day like an island and twice a day the sand dries and joins it to the mainland'[27]. Twice a day there was easy access across the wet sands to the mainland and protection was given by the encircling sea. It is significant that in the later Middle Ages, when the island became known as *Insula Sacra* (Holy Island), the abbey here was the only one in Northumbria to escape pillaging by the Scots.

In a time when most communication was by sea Lindisfarne boasted a fine natural harbour overlooked by the commanding height of Beblow Crag (Bible Law) and was ideally situated for coastwise travel between Bernicia to the north and Deira to the south. Most importantly, the King's royal palace on Bamburgh Rock just seven miles to the south was well within signalling distance if help was needed[28].

The environment of Lindisfarne would help newly arriving monks to settle quickly for it closely resembled Iona in many respects: both are off-shore islands with rocky cliffs and foreshores, sandy bays and dunes and similar wild life in seals, fowl and flocks of sea birds. Life on both islands was very much at the mercy of the elements, the wind, the seas and the tides.

A recent study[29] explores the most likely route from Iona to Lindisfarne taken by Aidan and 'the many who arrived in Britain day by day from the country of the Scottii to proclaim the Word of God… in all the provinces under Oswald's rule'. Even today the journey from Northumberland to Iona takes a full day as it involves two roads and two ferry rides. In the 7th century the route traversed difficult mountainous and unmapped terrain across disputed borders where fighting and brigandage were prevalent.

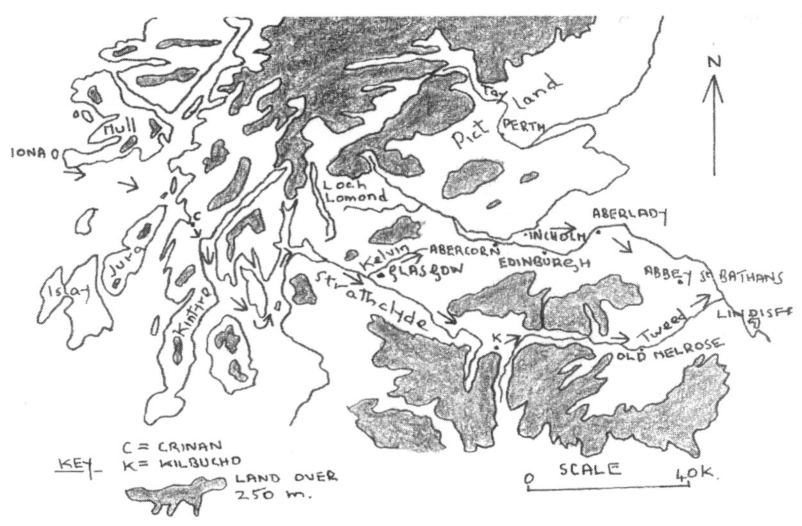

Routes from Iona to Lindisfarne
Based partly on Simon Taylor, Spes Scotorum. p.50.

The first leg of the monk's journey was by sea and land to the region of Strathclyde where Columba's earlier friendship with the Christian King Rhydderch would help to ensure safe passage east to the Firth of Forth, where the monks could rest at the monastery on the island of Inch Colm (Columba's Isle). The second leg involved a steep ascent of the Lammermuir Hills and then down the valley of the Whiteadder River (the line of the B6355 road) to Abbey St. Bathan's, named in honour of Iona's second abbot, Bathene, Columba's cousin. From here it is only a short journey to Tweedmouth from where the isle of Lindisfarne is clearly visible only eight miles to the south.

AIDAN'S ACHIEVEMENT

Left: Stained Glass Window of St Aidan, St Aidan's Chapel Lindisfarne.
Right: Sculpture of Bishop Aidan by local artist, Kathleen Parbury, unveiled by the Queen, 1958.

Aidan, spelt as Aedan or in its diminutive form Aed, was a popular name among early Irish nobility. In the text and notes of the 1995 edition of the Vita twelve different Aedans are named though Adamnan does not mention Aidan of Lindisfarne at all in the text. We rely almost entirely on Bede[30] for our knowledge of Aidan for no one wrote his life and he figures only briefly in Alcuin's *History*. We glean a few facts on his background from later sources. A 14th century book called the *Lebor Brece*, a collection of pieces from ancient Irish sources, gives the pedigree of Aidan: Aidan, son of Lugar, son of Ernin, son of Cael, son of Aed, son of Artcharp, son of Niacorp. The Kalendar of Scottish Saints, 1872 says Aidan sprang from the regal stock of Eochaidh Finn, of which St. Brigid was a descendant. Several old chronicles record his death; the *Lebor Brece*, Innis Medcuit Aidan lies here; the Martyrology of Oengus August 31 ' Aidan, the bright sun of Innis Medcoit', the Tigernach annals 651, August 31, 'the repose of Aidan, bishop of the Saxons'.

Such evidence as there is certainly points to an ancient and noble lineage.

Oswald's role as patron, protector and interpreter fluent in both Gaelic and English was as crucial to the success of the missions as was the example of Aidan's personal life. It is not unlikely that in his long years of exile on Iona Oswald had formed bonds of friendship with the young monk Aidan.

Bede is keen to hold up Aidan[30] as an example to the lax clergy of his own time, and illustrates his humility and that of Oswald's successor as King, his son Oswin, who had also been in exile with his father.

Aidan gave the king's gift of a fine horse to a beggar he met on his travels who asked for alms. Questioned at dinner about this by the king: "Why did you give a beggar the royal horse meant for you?", the bishop replied: "O King, what are you saying? Surely this son of a mare is not dearer to you than that son of God?" The King, filled with remorse, sought forgiveness, which was gladly given. Bede tells us how Bishop Aidan was dining with King Oswald when a servant entered to inform the king that 'a great crowd of needy folk' were outside begging for alms. The King at once ordered the dish of rich food set before him to be taken out to the poor and the silver dish to be broken up and distributed among them. The bishop was deeply moved and holding the King's right hand, exclaimed: "May this hand and arm never wither with age." At the same time he wept, for gifted with prophetic vision, he foresaw that the King would soon be killed in battle; indeed in 641 Oswald died fighting the Mercians near Oswestry (Oswald's tree?) in present day Shropshire. He is revered as Northumbria's first red martyr.

Dining at the royal table presented ascetic monks like Aidan, and later Cuthbert, with a dilemma. The king's patronage and approval was essential for it gave access to the royal courts and to influential thegns and aldermen; furthermore the king's country seats were bases for preaching expeditions. Yet at Anglo-Saxon banquets 'revels ran high and the troops became flushed with wine'. Bede tells us that Aidan solved the problem by 'attending the banquet with one or two clerks and taking a small repast before making haste to be gone, either to read or write'.

Nowhere is the divine favour shown to men of God more than in their power over the elements as seen in two miracles related by Bede.

Utta, the priest, was given holy oil to calm the waves which Aidan prophesied would beset his ship as he returned by sea from Kent bringing Eanfled as wife for King Oswald. As was foretold 'in a rising gale the roaring seas broke into the ship from every side and it began to fill. Everyone felt his last hour had come until Utta took out the flask of oil and poured some over the sea which immediately ceased its raging'. Though far distant the miraculous power of Aidan's prayers was evident.

Again when praying alone and undisturbed on Inner Farne Aidan saw 'a column of smoke and flame wafted by the winds above the city walls' as Penda and his Mercian army laid siege to the royal city of Bamburgh. In tears he raised his hands and eyes to heaven; 'Lord, see what evil Penda does'. At once the wind shifted and drove the flames back, so unnerving the besiegers that they abandoned the assault on a city so clearly under God's protection.

It is significant that Aidan was alone on Inner Farne praying and meditating when he saw the smoke and flames from the assault on Bamburgh. He was following the custom of Irish abbots and bishops who, especially in the seasons of Lent and Advent, sought solitude in order to balance private prayer with abbatical and episcopal duties in their lives. Columba on Hinba, and later Cuthbert on Inner Farne, followed this practice in fulfilling both the contemplative and active demands of their vocations.
We hear only scant details from Bede on Aidan's preaching journeys among the country folk in his role as '*episcopus vagans*', a wandering bishop in the Celtic style rather than a diocesan bishop in the Roman tradition.

We glean that he based his expeditions on the King's country seats; that his companions on the road were required to meditate, read the *Scriptures* or learn the *Psalms*; that many who became his disciples were instructed and ordained to the priesthood; that any gifts of money were distributed for the needs of the poor or paid as ransom for anyone who had been unjustly sold as a slave. Travel on foot enabled Aidan to meet villagers face to face rather than from on high from a horse which was very much a status symbol unbecoming for a monk vowed to poverty. It was preaching by example.

After sixteen years as bishop and founding abbot Aidan died in 651. Bede describes how he left this life leaning against a post that buttressed the outer wall of the church at Bamburgh. His body was buried in the monks' cemetery on Lindisfarne and later, when a larger church was built, at the right side of the altar. The troublesome Penda returned and, on this occasion, succeeded in burning down the village and church but the beam against which Aidan had been leaning when he died was miraculously preserved. The beam survived two more fires intact, and is now set inside the church where all who enter might kneel and ask for God's mercy. Chips of wood from the beam, like those from the cross at Heavenfield, dipped in water were held to cure disease.

Oswin, Oswald's son and successor, and probably a former exile on Iona, gave the same royal patronage as his father to Aidan so that the bishop was able to found as many as twelve daughter houses from Lindisfarne. Each was granted about ten hides of land. Following a custom found in Gaul, double houses, where religious men and women lived separately, were established at Gateshead, on St. Abb's Head north of Coldingham, at Hartlepool and Whitby. The abbesses were invariably ladies of royal blood who had taken the veil such as Ebba, Ethelreda, Audrey and the celebrated Hilda. Single houses for men were founded at Abercorn on the Firth of Forth, at Norham on Tweed, at Gilling in North Yorkshire, and at Old Melrose where the youth Cuthbert chose to enter the monastic life rather than Lindisfarne which he would know well enough.

BEDE'S ASSESSMENT

Though careful to disassociate himself from Aidan's dating of Easter, Bede is fulsome in his praise of the '*episcopus vagans*' who 'cultivated peace and love, purity and humility', who was 'above anger and greed, despised pride and conceit', and who 'tenderly comforted the sick, relieved and protected the poor and was diligent in study and prayer'. Aidan is held up as 'an inspiring example to the clergy of self discipline and continence', for 'he lived as he taught, never seeking or caring for worldly possessions', he always travelled on foot and stopped to speak to people, high or low, he met on his walks[31].

It is to Bede that Aidan owes his saintly status.

Bede saw the turning of 'an ungovernable people of an obstinate and barbarous temperament' from the darkness of paganism to the light of the Christian gospel as the providential unfolding of history under the guidance of the Holy Spirit. That many Northumbrians returned all too readily to pagan practices, a source of concern to Bede to his dying day, detracts but little from the immense success of the Irish mission when, for three decades, the church in Northumbria was ruled effectively from Iona and was in many respects part of the church in Ireland and Dal Riata. Lindisfarne rivalled York and Canterbury in importance as an ecclesiastical centre. The Synod of Whitby 664 was a watershed after which the influence of Iona waned, though it did not disappear.

After King Oswin's decision at Whitby some English churchmen regarded Christians of the Ionan tradition as schismatics or even heretics: Bede did not go this far but he is more than once critical of Aidan's adherence to what he regards as the mistaken dating of Easter. This adherence, which persuaded Colman and a party of monks to quit Lindisfarne to return to Iona and then back to Ireland, explains why no hagiographer has written a *Vita* of Aidan. He was honoured in his own time by men as distant as Honorius of Canterbury and Felix of East Anglia and is universally regarded as the founding father of Christianity in Bernicia yet is eclipsed by Cuthbert.

We may presume that the original monastery on Lindisfarne closely resembled that of the mother-house on Iona; an extensive area of land of up to twenty acres surrounded by a ditch and low earth rampant, a church of hewn oak and thatched with reeds in the centre and elsewhere a refectory, scriptorium, bee-hive shaped stone cells with numerous ancillary buildings for farming purposes, craft and storage.

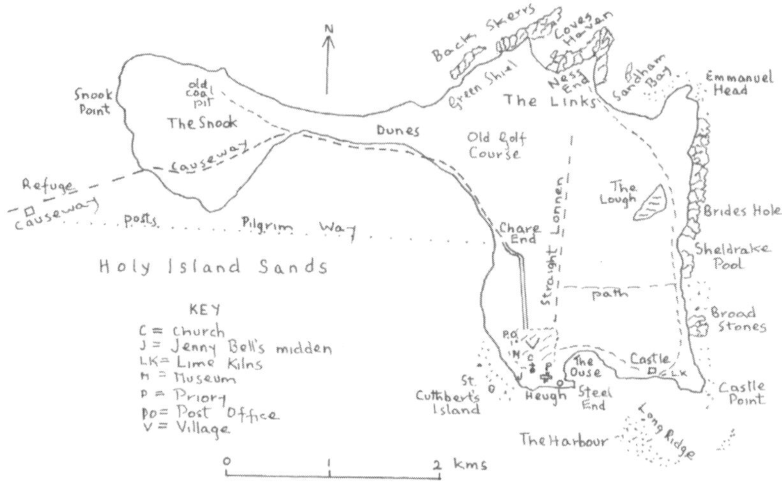

THE HOLY ISLE OF LINDISFARNE

Most importantly, Aidan and his monks established a flourishing school for Anglian boys, some of whom were destined to become renowned missionary priests and bishops. Of four priest brothers who were students Chad, a disciple of Aidan, became a bishop based in Lichfield to evangelise among the pagan Mercians; and Cedd, as bishop of the East Saxons, preached to the Mercians and Middle Angles, assisted by Adda, Betti and Diuma, all alumni of the Lindisfarne school. Bede records no discord between the Roman missionaries from Kent and the Irish-trained monks from Lindisfarne in the work of converting the pagan peoples of the English midlands. The work of conversion was zealously pursued by Aidan's successors Tuda, Finan and Colman who were all Irish-trained and appointed from Iona. Not all Lindisfarne students followed the Irish tradition, for Wilfrid became the chief spokesman for the Roman cause at the Synod of Whitby.

CONCLUSION

Well schooled as a young monk on Iona, Aidan introduced the essential elements of Celtic spirituality to the aspiring Christians of Northumbria. His model was his own monastic father Columba though whether they ever met we cannot know. Distinctive features of this way of life may be summarised as: a strong sense of the enveloping presence of God in their lives at all times and of angels; a deep personal relationship with Jesus Christ; a love of learning, especially of the scriptures and the writings of the Church Fathers; a belief in the value of renouncing earthly goods and values in order to follow a life of asceticism; a keen awareness of the reality of sin and of the joy of forgiveness; an affinity with the creatures of God's creation and an appreciation of the wonders of the natural world; a conviction that everyone had a unique role to play in the unfolding history of salvation; a faith that wherever they were, Providence and not chance had put them there; a love of their native Ireland and a pride in their heritage, pagan and Christian; a lively understanding of the concept of the communion of saints whereby they felt at one through baptism with Christians of other times and other places, be they in Palestine or Egypt in the time of Christ or in Ireland, Iceland, Iona or Lindisfarne in their own time[32].

Adamnan considered that Oswald's vision of Columba exhorting him to be brave in faith on the eve of the battle of Heavenfield was crucial to the success of the Irish mission to Northumbria, Iona's finest achievement. Bede would have us believe that Cuthbert's vision while minding sheep at night in the Lammermuir Hills beside the River Leader was Providence providing for the continuing success of the newly founded church led by a native Anglo-Saxon monk. In his vision Cuthbert saw 'choirs of a heavenly host returning to their home above, a human, marvellously bright… the gate of Heaven opened and a band of angels led in the spirit of some holy man'. The next day when Cuthbert was told Aidan, bishop of Lindisfarne had passed into the Kingdom of Heaven at the time of his vision, 'he at once delivered the sheep back to their owners and decided to enter a monastery'[33].

Though he conformed after the Synod of Whitby Cuthbert remained Celtic at heart, and throughout his monastic life cultivated the same ideals and ascetic practices Aidan had learned from his patron Columba 'on a little island on the edge of the ocean'[34].

Iona ferry.

Chaplain Father Michael (left) and author on board.

View of village and Abbey church

Top Left: St Martins Cross, c.750-800, sculpted from single slab of stone from Argyll, east face richly carved with bosses and serpents.

Top Right: St John's Cross, replica (original in Abbey museum) c.800.

Song of praise in Abbey church.

REFERENCES.

1. See BEDE: A History of the English Church and People (HE) trans.
   L. Sherley-Price. 1968. III 5 p.149 for full quotation.

2. CLARK K. Civilisation. 1969. p.10.

3. ADAMNAN OF IONA. Life of St. Columba. (Vita or V.C.). Trans. R. Sharpe. 1995. Almost all unattributed quotations are from V.C.

4. V.C. 114. p.156.

5. See G. MARKUS. Article in Spirituality: Columba, Missionary and Hijack victim.

6. JACKSON, K.H. A Celtic Miscellany. 1971. Preface.

7. See Lives of the Saints. Trans. J.F. Webb. 1965. The Voyage of Brendan, p. 35 – 68.

8. CLANCY T.O. and MARKUS G. Iona. The Earliest Poetry of a Celtic Monastery. 1995. The chief source for Dallan, Beccan, Colman and the library on Iona.

9 HERBERT M. Iona, Kells and Derry. 1998. Chapter 1 The Saints and his Times.

10. V.C. note 56, p. 257.

11. Ibid CLANCY and MARKUS. p.149.

12. CHADWICK N. The Celts. 1971. p.186.

13. Ibid n.10.

14. MARKUS G. The Joy of Penance, Article in Spirituality. 1996.

15. BEDE (HE). p.146.

16. BEDE (HE). Introduction. p.30.

17. Attributed to St. Columba in The Wisdom of Saint Columba of Iona compiled by Murray Watts. 1997.

18. See IONA, A Guide to the Monuments. HMSO. 1995.

19. Ibid, CLANCY AND MARKUS. Iona's Library, p.211-222.

20. Ibid. p.222.

21. BEDE (HE). p.142.

22 Ibid. p.144.

23. V.C. 1. p.111.

24. BEDE (HE). p.144.

25. V.C. Introduction.

26. BEDE (HE). p.149.

27. BEDE (HE). p.145.

28 King Ida built the first recorded royal castle here in 547.

29. Spes Scotorum Hope of Scots.
Saint Columba, Iona and Scotland.
Ed. BROUN D. and CLANCY T.O. 1999.
Chapter 2. Simon TAYLOR.

30. Bede in HE devotes chapters 5, 14, 15, 16, 17 to Aidan and the miracles described here.

31. Bede (HE). p.165.

32. T. O'LOUGHLIN. Journey on the Edges, The Celtic Tradition, 2000. The author incisively and eloquently explores the witness of early Christian Ireland, especially for what it reveals about spirituality today.
Richard Woods, O.P.

33. BEDE, Lives of the Saints. Life of Cuthbert. 1965. p.77.

34. V.C. p.233.

OTHER USEFUL BOOKS.

O. DAVIES (Trans)	Celtic Spirituality. 1999.
FINLAY I.	Columba. 1990.
HERBERT M.	Iona, Kells and Derry. 1988.
LYNCH M.	A New History of Scotland. 1991.
MACQUARRIE A.	The Saints of Scotland. Essays in Scottish Church History AD 450 – 1093. 1997.
MAYR-HARTING H.	The Coming of Christianity to Anglo-Saxon England. 1972.
SMYTH A.P.	Warlords and Holy Men. 1984.
THOMAS C.	Celtic Britain. 1997.

3

CUTHBERT REVISITED

IN CAVES

Walking in the Kyloe Hills in north Northumberland one sunny June morning I made a point of visiting St. Cuthbert's Cave for the first time: it is a deep and impressive cave etched by the forces of nature in the base of the sandstone cliffs which form the escarpment of the Kyloe Hills overlooking the Millfield Plain, a former glacial lake. The approach to the cave from Holborn Farm up a grassy path in a grove lined with tall fir trees has a Greek feel about it, as if one would soon be meeting with the oracle at Delphi. Before the cave came into view I heard the unexpected sound of singing and soon saw a group of people who were evidently venerating the saint with hymns. I held back until the group was departing, we exchanged friendly greetings, and I was left alone in this evocative place.

St Cuthbert's Cave, Kyloe Hills

Having admired the magnificent view between the fir trees across the plain to the Cheviot Hills I retired to the inner recesses of the cave where the silence and confined space induced a reflective mood as I recalled the close association of caves and holy men in the past: Elijah, the prophet, in his cave on Mount Sinai wishing he were dead as he despaired of the people of Israel and finding the Lord was not in the fierce wind, earthquake or fire, the usual manifestations of a divine presence, but in the silence[1]; Martin of Tours, soldier, monk and bishop seeking solitude away from his episcopal duties in his cave high up in a cliff face above a gentle bend of the River Loire[2]; Benedict of Nursia, last of the great Romans, author of the Rule, patron of Europe, forsaking his father's house and wealth, to be hid in a cave at Subiaco, forty miles south of Rome, for three years 'after the manner of the Hidden Life of Christ'[3].

Returning to the present I wondered why this cave, where a chance meeting between fellow pilgrims had just taken place, was associated with Cuthbert. Did the saint come here for a time of quiet reflection when he was a young monk or, like Martin in his cave, when he was a busy bishop? Or did his body rest here awhile in its wanderings following the retreat from Lindisfarne in 875 under the threat of further Viking raids? Perhaps the association has no basis in history but is part of local folklore for there are many place names scattered across the map of Northumberland which commemorate the name of Cuthbert: there is another, though less impressive, St. Cuthbert's Cave on Dod Law a few miles to the south; Cuddy's (Cuthbert's pet-name) Crags form a prominent stretch of the Whin Sill on which Hadrian's Wall is built; Cuddy's Well at Bellingham still spouts water used in baptisms in the local parish church; just off the south-west corner of Lindisfarne is St. Cuthbert's Island where fossil remains of sea-lilies found on the strand are known as St. Cuthbert's beads; the best-known and most trusting bird on Inner Farne is the eider or Cuddy duck.

Leaving the cave to continue my walk I resolved to discover as much as I could about Cuthbert by exploring some of the places he is recorded as visiting and assessing the significance of what happened there.

The difficulty of the task I had set myself soon became apparent.

SOURCES

Archaeological evidence on the ground is hard to find. A friend and I searched in vain for the vallum surrounding Cuthbert's monastery two miles below Melrose on the banks of the Tweed which I had been informed was still visible in places, as it is on Iona.

Scott's View, Eildon Hills in distance.
Old Melrose Monastery on flat land on inside bend of river Tweed.

As the invaluable relics of the saint held in the treasury of Durham Cathedral, of which more later, tell us more about Cuthbert in death than in life, we find ourselves almost entirely dependent on literary sources.

Here again, it is a surprise to find out that neither Cuthbert, nor indeed any of his illustrious contemporaries – Aidan, Wilfrid, Chad, Cedd, Hilda or Ebba – has left us any memorials of themselves in writing. Two revealing letters written by St. Patrick are still extant, as is an account of his early life by St. Augustine of Hippo. Bede includes brief autobiographical notes in his *History of the English Church and People* (HE), and indeed it is to Bede and an anonymous monk of Lindisfarne, that we turn for almost all our knowledge of Cuthbert.

Alcuin of York (d.804), scholar, theologian, friend and adviser to the Holy Roman Emperor Charlemagne wrote a poem c.800, later given the rather wordy title, *Bishops, Kings and Saints of York*[4], where he praises Cuthbert as an 'outstanding monk… a teacher of the Gospel… a shining light in that time' but, in effect, adds little to the knowledge we acquire from the *Life of St. Cuthbert* by an Anonymous Author (VA)[5] and Bede's metrical *Verse Life of St.*

Cuthbert (VM)[6] and his prose *Life of Cuthbert* (VP)[7]. Bede also features Cuthbert in six chapters of HE[8].

THE LINDISFARNE LIFE

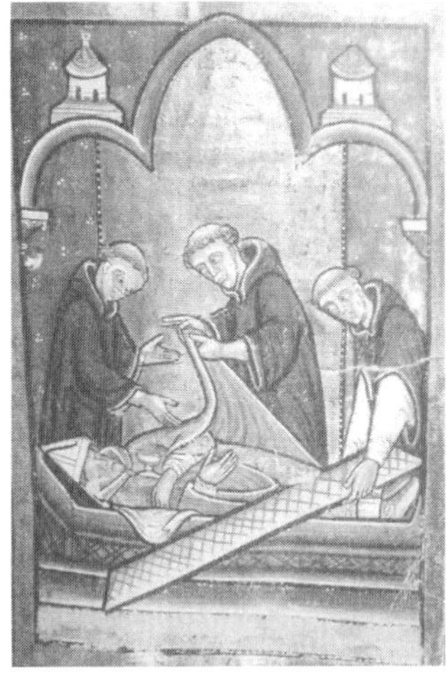

'They found the body intact and whole as if it were still alive and much more like a sleeping than a dead man'.
Bede. HE IV 30.

Perhaps it was the revelation that the body of Cuthbert was perfectly preserved when his tomb was opened at the elevation eleven years after his death that prompted Eadfrith to commission one of his monks to write a Life and to inspire the bishop himself to begin work as scribe and artist of the Lindisfarne Gospels. The Anonymous, as the unknown author is called, may well have known Cuthbert personally for he was writing only some eleven years after his death. Memories were still fresh and many miraculous events are described by eye-witnesses with the intention of demonstrating beyond any doubt the sanctity of the saint. Adamnan's *Life of St. Columba*[9] has much in common with the Anonymous *Life of St. Cuthbert*; both are tracts for their times, both present the lives of their subjects in a thematic and chronological way with such headings as prophetic early life, visions, miracles; incidents are set in a scriptural context in biblical language.

The two lives were being written simultaneously with the clear intention of promoting the cult of their respective saints and enhancing the prestige of their monastic houses; furthermore Cuthbert was portrayed as the powerful patron of Northumbria, newly united from the old Bernicia and Deira, just as Columba was patron of Iona and Ireland.

THE VERSE LIFE

Bede's *Verse Life of Cuthbert* is a substantial poem of forty six verses. Bede sees symbolism in number so it is probable that the number of verses represents the years it took to rebuild the temple in Jerusalem, for the saint was for Bede a living temple of God in his life. Surviving manuscripts indicate an earlier version of the poem and c.716 a later refined version dedicated to a priest-friend, John, for reading as he undertook the long journey to Rome.

The *Verse Life* is a re-working of the Life by the Anonymous, with the addition of ten new miracles. Only in this poem, and then only in the earlier version, do we hear the charming tale of the seals. 'What shall I say of the seals weighed down with the burden of pregnancy, who did not dare to drop the offspring of their womb unless the saint had blessed them beforehand with his holy right hand?' In Adamnan's *Columba* we read of another wondrous event concerning seals.

Bede's poem is a reflection on the *Life of Cuthbert*, it is not historical narrative; the real importance lies not in the factual details of the events but in their figural significance. When Bede describes how Cuthbert extinguished the flames of a burning house through prayer the flames are 'the fiery arrows of Satan's temptations... nor is it any wonder that a mere fire should give way to a saint who was accustomed to repel the arrows from Satan's fiery quiver with the heavenly shield of Christ'. Faith in the power of prayer is the lesson to be learned here. A similar story is told of Martin of Tours who 'placed himself before the flames advancing on a village'; as he prayed the flames bent back against the force of the wind 'till it looked like a battle between warring elements. Such were his powers that the fire destroyed only where it was bidden', a pagan shrine[10].

THE PROSE LIFE

Bede's Prose *Life of Cuthbert*, completed c.721, marks a high point in the evolving art of hagiographical writing. At first there were only lists of saints with the dates of their birth and death: then came martyrologies and sermons for major feast days; the first hagiographies as such were the *Life of Antony of Egypt* by

Athanasius translated by Evagrius of Antioch in the late 4th century, the *Life of Paul of Thebes* by Jerome and the *Life of Martin of Tours* by Sulpicius Severus. For several centuries these classic early lives became models for later lives of saints in Western Europe: they were widely copied but this was regarded as evidence of wide reading not of plagiarism.

One might wonder why Bishop Eadfrith, having already commissioned a *Life of Cuthbert* by a Monk of Lindisfarne, invited Bede of Jarrow/Monkwearmouth to write a second Life. There were probably two reasons: new edifying material kept coming to light as further proof of Cuthbert's sanctity; Eadfrith considered that the polished Latin of one of Western Europe's leading scholars would furnish a more fitting memorial to the saint than the plainer style of the Anonymous. Yet I agree with the view that while Bede is indisputably the finer scholar yet the direct simplicity of the *Lindisfarne Life*, with its many details of local interest omitted by Bede, seems nowadays to give a more faithful reflection of Cuthbert's age than the more elaborate prose of Bede[11].

Unusually, though Bede draws extensively on VA for his source material, he makes no acknowledgement of his debt to the Anonymous. Of the forty miracles described by Bede only eight are not in VA.

The special merit of VP is that for the first time a saint's spiritual progress is charted; from childhood to novice monk, from prior to hermit, from bishop to hermit again, and finally to death on Inner Farne where a moving and much debated eye-witness account is given by the priest Herefrith.

The Bible was the focus of Bede's life and all the wondrous events he describes should be seen through the lens of Holy Scripture for they are intended to show how the saintly Cuthbert enjoyed God's favour and shared in divine qualities, even in the power of miracles. The early church in Northumbria needed miracles 'in order that she might grow firm in the faith' no less than in Palestine in the time of Christ. The God of the Christians had to be shown as demonstrably superior to the pagan gods.

Bede omits many names of places and individuals as he places the miracles in a context undefined by location or time; as in the Verse Life it is the moral of the story that matters not the historical narrative. In the tale of the monks storm-bound on Inner Farne because they neglected to cook the goose as ordered by Cuthbert the significance is not where or how this happened, but a lesson in the importance of monastic obedience. The provision of a goose for a meal exemplifies the kindly hospitality offered to guests in the best traditions of the hermits of the Egyptian desert; 'a jar of wine for the visitor, brackish water for one's self'.

The medieval preference of VP over VA is seen in the number of surviving manuscripts; thirty eight of the former, only seven of the latter. However, for the purposes of this quest to identify some of the places and people associated with the *Life of Cuthbert*, VA is the more valuable source; for example it is only here that we learn that Cuthbert had a foster-mother called Kenswith (Coenswith) who lived in the village of Hruringaham.

THE BOY

We know nothing of Cuthbert's parents though we can safely guess they were of Anglo-Saxon stock and either first generation Christians or pagans, perhaps converting to Christianity after hearing Aidan preaching in the villages. The name they chose for their son, Guthbertus, means 'worthy of God'[12]. No credence should be given to the story of Cuthbert's royal Irish ancestry[13], nor was he the son of peasants for his parents could afford to have him educated by a foster-mother. It is most likely that he came from the middle ranking of a Northumbrian society strictly stratified into slaves, commoners, nobles and those claiming royal descent; country gentry sounds most apt.

A key figure in Cuthbert's early years was Kenswith 'a nun and a widow' who 'brought him up from his earliest years and was therefore called mother'. Monasticism was at the heart of early English Christianity and could take many forms from a royal foundation to a few churches gathered to serve local pastoral needs, or indeed an individual living at home under personal vows, like Kenswith. Fostering was popular in Scandinavia, Ireland and

England among nobles and gentry and lasted till the youth was 17 years old when he would decide to enter a monastery or lead a lay life.

The location of Kenswith's home village of Hruringaham where Cuthbert visited regularly in later life remains unknown. Various unlikely suggestions[14] include Risingham in the North Tyne valley on Dere Street, Roddam near Wooler; my own preference would be Wrangham, still a farm, to the east of the two St. Cuthbert's caves in the Kyloe hills. The elements in the place name, 'homestead of the people of Hrur?' indicate an early Anglian settlement on or near the east coast, like Coldingham or Tyninghame, rather than further inland where 'ton' and 'ington' suffixes point to later settlement. Wrangham could well be a simplified spelling of Hruringaham and is only some twelve miles inland and the same distance south of the Tweed valley.

Two revealing incidents are recorded from Cuthbert's early boyhood years.

As a boy of eight he surpassed all of his age in agility and high spirits as they played games and tricks in the fields, some were naked in the Germanic manner. A child scarcely three years old began weeping and wailing, beseeched Cuthbert to 'leave this foolish play', 'O holy Bishop and priest Cuthbert, these unnatural tricks are not befitting to you or your high office'. Young Cuthbert heeded the words of the precocious infant and 'kept in mind the prophetic words, just as St. Mary kept in her memory all the words prophesied about Jesus'.

Bede concludes: 'Out of the mouths of babes and sucklings thou hast perfected praise'. Prophesy of high office is not uncommon in the early life of holy men; it happened with Athanasius, Samson of Dol, Columba and again with Cuthbert as he approached the gates of the monastery at Melrose to seek entry. The authors of both VA and VP see Cuthbert from the outset as a chosen vessel destined by God to become a man of exceptional holiness.

While still a young boy Cuthbert's agility was brought to an abrupt halt for 'his knee swelled, his sinews contracted and he became so lame that one foot could not touch the ground'. He was carried outside the walls of the house into the sunshine by servants – another indication that the family were not peasants – when a horseman, clad in white and on a fine mount, approached seeking hospitality. The boy told the stranger about his problem and was advised: 'Cook wheat flour with milk and anoint your knee with it while it is still hot.' After a few days he was healed and restored to good health.

Both the problem and the cure sound straightforward to us; Cuthbert was suffering from synovitis, water on the knee, and the remedy was hot poulticing. However, in both VA and VP the horseman is perceived as an angel of God 'sent by One who once deigned to send the archangel Raphael to cure the eyes of Tobias.'

From that time, whenever Cuthbert 'prayed to the Lord in times of his greatest distress he was never denied the help of angels'.

THE YOUTH

The youth Cuthbert was standing with a crowd of onlookers as monks transported wood for use in a monastery 'not far from the mouth of the Tyne, on the south side'; this monastery at South Shields 'once full of monks now houses a noble company of women'. A sudden storm of wind from the west sprang up and the force of the river dragged the rafts 'far out to sea so that they looked like five tiny birds riding on the waves, for there were five rafts'. Death seemed imminent. Despairing of human help the monks from the monastery gathered on the rocks and 'fled to the divine'. The reaction of the crowd was very different for they jeered 'with boorish words': 'Let no man pray for them and may God have no mercy on them for they have robbed men of their old ways of worship.'

When Cuthbert heard this he knelt on the ground to pray. Immediately the violent wind turned round and bore the rafts safe and sound to land amid much rejoicing of those guiding them. When the countryfolk saw this they were deeply ashamed and ever after praised the faith of Cuthbert.

This dramatic incident, all the easier to visualise as the location of the headland at Tynemouth where the Spanish Battery was sited is so familiar, yields a rich harvest of incidental detail. The incident is recounted only by Bede who heard it 'from the lips of a worthy brother of our monastery' and may not have been known at the time of the writing of the *Lindisfarne Life*.

It is the first recorded reference to a monastery at South Shields; the site is unknown. The tale shows the importance of water for the transport of heavy building materials of wood and stone; we know the timber for the construction of the monastery on Iona was floated on rafts from Argyll. The attitude of the jeering spectators was probably typical for many countryfolk (*rustici*) were still loyal at heart to the old heathen Saxon gods: or were they new Christians disillusioned because they were left without a priest? The courage of the young Cuthbert in the midst of a hostile crowd was evident to all. A cynic might simply attribute the outcome to a sudden shift of wind from off-shore to on-shore, a frequent occurrence on the coast. But for Bede, 'from this time the boy was wholly given to the Lord... because he prayed with kindly piety for others who were in danger. He was heard by Him who hears the cry of the poor and delivers him out of all his troubles'.

Both Bede and the Anonymous tell the tale of the miraculous provision of foods for Cuthbert in his travels, the first of several such miracles. In VA we learn that the location was by the river Uuis (Wear) at Kuncacester (Chester le Street).

Cuthbert may well have been on the king's business returning from York north along the old Roman road when he sought shelter from the winter storm in a deserted shepherd's hut, known as a sheiling. Writing the *Life of St. Oswald* Symeon described the land between the Tees and the Tyne in the sixth century as one vast deserted region and the haunt of wild beasts, so the hazards of making long journeys in winter were real enough.

As Cuthbert knelt in prayer his unsaddled horse 'greedily seized part of the thatch and there fell out a warm loaf and meat carefully wrapped in a linen cloth, food provided by God through an angel'. He blessed the food, ate it and satisfied he set forth prosperously glorifying the Lord, according to V.A.

Bede's fuller account adds meaning to the story. Before reaching the sheiling Cuthbert had been offered a meal at the home of a devout married woman but declined as it was Friday so he must fast till the ninth hour. After his food in the hut he prays, 'O God, I was fasting for love of Thee and in return thou hast fed both me and my animal, blessed be Thy Name'. Bede stresses that when the bread was broken half was given to the horse. Cuthbert's unfailing courtesy towards animals is a recurring feature of events in his life. The incident is placed in a biblical context for did not the Lord send birds, day after day, with food for Elijah in the wilderness? Bede's source was the 'holy priest Ingwald from our monastery at Monkwearmouth who heard it from Cuthbert himself when he was bishop'.

A defining moment in Cuthbert's life came as he was minding the flocks of his master by the River Leader which flows out of the Lammermuir Hills into the Tweed a mile below Melrose. This tale is the origin of the popular myth that Cuthbert was a shepherd boy of peasant stock. It is probable that guarding the king's flocks was part of his military service for in VA we read he 'dwelt in camp with the army, in the face of the enemy, having only meagre rations'. He might well have fought against Penda as he besieged Bamburgh. Benedict Biscop, the Northumbrian noble and founding abbot of Monkwearmouth Monastery, also served in the army.

During his night vigils Cuthbert had a vision of 'angels ascending and descending and, in their hands, was borne to heaven a holy soul, as if in a globe of fire'. He knew it was the 'soul of a most holy bishop' and in the morning (VP), a few days later (VA) news came of the death of Aidan. Visions of souls being carried to heaven by angels occur regularly in the lives of saints: it happened on the deaths of Anthony of Egypt, Columba, Martin and later of Robert of Newminster to select a few examples.

The effect of the vision on Cuthbert, then aged about seventeen years, was dramatic: 'forthwith he delivered the sheep to their owner and decided to seek a monastery'. He knew that the monastery on Lindisfarne 'contained many holy men' but preferred the daughter house of Melrose because he had heard of Prior Boisil's 'reputation for sublime virtue'. By chance Boisil was standing at the gate when Cuthbert rode up. Handing his horse and spear to his servant, a sure indication of his social status, he sought entry. Boisil greeted him with prophetic words: 'Behold the servant of the Lord' thereby 'imitating him who, looking upon Nathaniel as he came towards him, said: "Behold an Israelite in whom there is no guile".'

NOVICE AND GUESTMASTER

When the abbot Eata, one of Aidan's original founding group of monks on Lindisfarne, returned to Melrose he gave permission for Cuthbert to be tonsured and thereby become one of the brethren. Interestingly, the Anonymous has Cuthbert tonsured later at Ripon in the Petrine style where the crown of the head is shaven symbolising Christ's crown of thorns; was the author rewriting history to suit the decision of the Whitby Synod in favour of the Roman tradition? It is more credible that Cuthbert did indeed receive the Irish tonsure at Melrose when the front part of his head would be shaved from ear to ear.

Cuthbert's confidence in Boisil as a teacher was well-founded. The prior, whose name lives on in the town of St. Boswell's, was as influential a figure in the spiritual formation of the young Cuthbert as was the novice-master Coelfrith on the boy Bede at Monkwearmouth.

Under Boisil's guidance 'the novice watched, prayed, worked and read harder than anyone else'. He took no alcohol even though some beer was allowed in Columban monasteries, but fasted only moderately so that his work did not suffer, an early hint, perhaps, of the moderating influence of the rule of Benedict on ascetic Irish practices.

He had an early experience of the value of fraternal charity in monastic life when he fell desperately ill, stricken with the plague which was raging throughout the land. In the morning, learning that the community had spent the whole night praying for him, he rose from his sick bed to resume his daily routine. Yet Bede tells us that the swelling on his thigh seemed to move inwards and for almost the whole of his life he was troubled with some internal pain, 'strength was made perfect in weakness.'

Cuthbert's first move was to the new monastery founded by Eata on land at Ripon granted by King Alhfrith of Deira. Though 'still a neophyte' Cuthbert was a 'pleasant and affable young man' and so he was elected by the community to the important position of guestmaster of Ripon monastery, the link-man between the brethren and the outside world. No brothers were chosen for this post unless they were men of tact and virtue, for guests who call are to be welcomed as if they were Christ, for he will one day say, 'I was a stranger and you took me in'. The spirit of Chapter 53 of the Rule of Benedict was followed in the Celtic monasteries and was in line with the traditions of the Desert Fathers of Egypt. Martin of Tours acted as guestmaster to all his visitors, bathing and drying their feet and bringing warm food.

One snowy December day a 'well built young man in the flower of his age' called at the Ripon monastery. Cuthbert washed and dried the stranger's hands and feet and rubbed them to warm them up and, eventually, persuaded him to stay for a meal after the office of Tierce at 3 p.m. Sitting the guest at a table Cuthbert left to bring some loaves which were still baking but, on his return, found the young man had disappeared, not even leaving footprints in the snow. He did, however, find three warm loaves 'white and fine' on the table and 'his nostrils were filled with the odour of choicest bread'. Cuthbert at once concluded that the visitor was an angel of the Lord come to test him; 'no wonder he refused human food when he can enjoy in heaven the food of eternal life', was his observation.

This was the second of several miracles involving the provision of food – the first was in the shepherd's hut at Kuncacester – and 'from that day on he was held worthy to see and talk with angels and the Lord fed him when he was hungry'.

As with other miracles there are scriptural precedents: ravens brought bread to Elijah in the desert; the feeding of the five thousand by Christ with the multiplying of loaves and fishes.

The stay at Ripon was short. In the run-up to the Synod of Whitby King Alhfrith, persuaded by Wilfrid, expelled the Columban monks as Abbot Eata refused to conform with Roman traditions. The community returned north to the mother-house of Melrose and Alhfrith gave the monastery at Ripon to Wilfrid. The expulsion from Ripon taught Cuthbert the lesson that division brings only hurt and conflict: for the rest of his life where division existed he strove for reconciliation.

VA and VP treat the Ripon episode very differently; the Anonymous omits it completely, Bede finds it rather embarrassing, simply referring to the Ripon community 'as those who follow the Irish' and observing 'all the ways of the world are fickle and unstable as a storm at sea… they were thrown out of Ripon and the monastery they had built given to other monks'.

Hagiographers typically give detailed accounts of the saint's death: the three saints central to this story, Boisil, Cuthbert and Bede, are no exceptions as their 'entry to eternal bliss' is highlighted as the fitting climax to their life on earth.

On returning to Melrose Cuthbert again submitted himself humbly to the direction of Boisil.

Soon, however, the prior fell ill and advised his pupil 'I warn you not to lose the chance of learning from me' as he had only seven days to live for 'by next week my body and voice shall have lost their strength'. 'Then tell me the best book to study, one that can be read in a week'. 'St. John the Evangelist', Boisil answered. 'I have a commentary in seven parts. With the help of God we can read one a day and discuss it'. They were able to finish quickly as they dealt not with profound arguments but with the simple things of 'the faith which worketh by love'. In those final days Boisil declared all Cuthbert's future to him 'prophesying that he would become a bishop and a hermit, where drawing on 'the faith that works by love', he would unite his vocation for solitude walking alone with Christ on Inner Farne with that of bishop serving the pastoral needs of his people.

This moving scene of a dying man studying St. John's Gospel with his pupil would be re-enacted nearly half a century later in 735 when, in his last days, Bede strove with his servant, another Cuthbert, to complete his translation of the same Gospel into Anglo-Saxon.

The choice of this particular gospel in both instances is significant for the 'eagle Gospel', by the disciple Jesus loved, deals essentially with 'the divinity of Christ… the rest of contemplation… the mysteries of God', all of which lay at the heart of Cuthbert's and Bede's spiritual life. The seven days of prayerful study represent the seven days of creation; on the eighth day, the saints entered into a life of eternal re-creation[15].

PRIOR

Cuthbert was elected prior of Melrose in place of Boisil; having received from his tutor 'knowledge of the Scriptures and the example of a life of good works, the new prior, filled with holy zeal, counselled the monks in the religious life and set a high example himself'.

Following Boisil's example he began his preaching journeys. Travelling either on foot or, at times, unlike Aidan, on horseback and sleeping in a tent he was 'often away from home for up to a month, living with rough hill-folk in villages in steep and rugged mountains'. He preached 'so gloriously that they would confess every sin openly, and when they had been absolved, he would celebrate Mass which he could never finish without shedding tears'. 'No-one left unconsoled, no-one had to carry back the burdens he came with'. This work was for Cuthbert a labour of love made all the more difficult as the raging plagues caused many 'to flee to idols, amulets, incantations or any other diabolical rubbish'. The common view, shared by Bede, was that such afflictions were punishments sent by God on evil-doers.

From surviving pieces we can gain a remarkably clear picture of the liturgical vessels Cuthbert would carry with him on his missionary journeys. All were exceptionally small so that they could easily be carried in a pocket or haversack and all were, and still are, of high quality, pointing to leading monastic centres like Lindisfarne, Whitby and Hexham where artists, scribes, book-binders, goldsmiths and metalworkers produced material of fine quality for the glory of God and the practice of the liturgy.

In the treasury of Durham Cathedral is a portable altar of a slab of oak, only five inches square, encased in silver plate and inscribed + IN HONOREM S. PETRV, five crosses decorate this tiny altar, one in the centre and one in each corner. Displayed in the wall of the choir of Hexham Abbey is a beautiful 7th century bronze chalice, only five inches high; the British Museum commented; 'the chalice seems to be precisely the sort that would have been used with a portable altar on those numerous journeys St. Cuthbert made to the outlying villages of Northumberland to preach and administer the Sacraments'.[16]

Two missals from the time have miraculously survived: the so-called Stowe Missal is an 8th century Irish Mass Book measuring only 5" by 4" containing St. John's Gospel and prayers for Mass; a 7th century copy of St. John's Gospel in its original binding resides in the library of Stonyhurst, again it is a real miniature, only 5" by 3 ½", eloquent testament to the skill of the calligraphers and binders. Some have suggested that this is indeed the Gospel studied by Boisil in his last days with Cuthbert but this is improbable as it was not associated with Cuthbert until 1104.

THAUMATURGE

In the three periods of missionary life, as prior of Melrose and later Lindisfarne and, finally as bishop, Cuthbert's reputation as a thaumaturge, that peculiarly medieval term for a wonder-worker, grew steadily. Folk came increasingly to believe that here indeed was a man of God gifted with divine qualities, most dramatically shown in his powers of healing. In selecting only a sample of the forty miracles attributed to Cuthbert in VA and VP I follow in the best traditions of hagiographical writing where authors, having expressed their unworthiness, explain the brevity of their accounts: 'I have omitted much lest the reader be wearied by the mass of material' is the final sentence of Sulpicius' *Life of St. Martin*; Adamnan makes the same point in VC; the Anonymous notes 'The rest of his abundant works I pass over in silence lest I engender a distaste in the reader'. All writers could point to John 21.25 as a scriptural precedent.

Bede names the pious priest Aethilwold 'abbot of Melrose, as a witness to the story of how Cuthbert, on one of his teaching journeys, came to a village where a nun, a kinswoman of Aethilwold, 'was afflicted by a severe illness and intolerable pain and had been given up by the physicians'. 'The man of God had pity on the wretched woman and anointed her with holy oil'; after a few days she was restored to full health. The Anonymous names the village as Bedesfield, possibly Bedrule in Roxburghshire. It is likely that the nuns had taken refuge here after fleeing from their monastery at Abercorn on the Firth of Forth following King Ecgfrith's death at the disastrous battle of Nechtansmere in Forfarshire in 685.

Aethilwold later became bishop of Lindisfarne and had an elaborate case made for the carrying of the Lindisfarne Gospels and a stone cross erected in Durham churchyard in memory of Cuthbert.

The tale of the wife of a 'certain religious man specifically dear to the man of God' called Hildmer shows Cuthbert in the role of exorcist and the prevailing attitude to mental illness. Hildmer's wife 'was much vexed by a devil, grinding her teeth and uttering fearful groans, greatly ravaged to the point of death'. Cuthbert rode on horseback with his friend, who was weeping and mourning because his wife was dying and, more especially, because of 'her disgraceful insane condition so horribly degraded and polluted with spittle'. Cuthbert reassured his friend and it was as he prophesied. As they approached the house the wife, as if rising from her sleep, came to meet them, held the horse's reins and, with the demon driven away, ministered to them, having been restored to full health.

The same reeve Hildmer later became ill to the point of death when his friends realised that they had some bread with them recently blessed by Cuthbert. Having all professed that Hildmer would be cured by partaking of this blessed bread they put a little portion in a cup of water and, as soon as it reached his stomach, the inward pain and the wasting of limbs disappeared. 'His health returned at once and all praised the holiness of the man of God 'who had the power to work wonders even when not present'. This was in fact the first of several miracles of association which continued even after Cuthbert's death, and only one of many effected by drinking a draught of water in which a holy relic had been placed.

Cuthbert as prior and bishop responded equally to calls for help from common folk or those of rank.

Called by the thegn Sibba, one of the king's nobles, to his vill at Examford on the Tweed just about Wark where a servant was in great pain, 'tortured by an evil disease… the saint blessed some water and poured it three times down the sick man's throat. In the morning, after a quiet sleep, the servant was found to be cured'. The witness to this story is 'Baldhelm, a priest at Lindisfarne is still alive, we are told'.

At Medilwang (Middlefield), probably Middleton near Wooler, the priest Tydi told Bede that before Cuthbert left the plague-stricken village he asked if there was anyone still suffering from the pestilence: a woman was pointed out to him who was weeping for her dead son and holding another 'half dead and breathing his last'. At once Cuthbert blessed and kissed the infant, saying: "Woman do not weep, your son will live and none of your household who are alive will perish by the plague." Typically, Bede concludes this touching tale by informing us that 'mother and son are still alive and are witnesses to the truth of this'.

The story of the two fires, one real and the other illusory, illustrates the power given to Cuthbert to change the natural elements.

He was visiting the village of Hruringaham when a house at the east end of the village caught fire; with a strong east wind blowing there was a real danger the whole village would be destroyed by the flames. Kenswith, who had 'brought him up from his eighth year until manhood' ran to Cuthbert, begging him to ask God for help. 'Falling prone upon the earth he prayed in silence and there arose a mighty wind from the west which drove the flames harmlessly from the houses. The villagers gave thanks and blessed the Lord, seeing that a miracle was plainly wrought about them by his protection'.

This tale, as recounted in V.A. and V.P., reveals the differing styles of the two authors. The incident is described by the Anonymous in a matter-of-fact straightforward way and loses nothing thereby, whereas Bede elaborates and dramatises the situation as 'the great wind tore away the blazing thatch… the fierce flames kept off those who were throwing water; "do not be afraid mother, be calm for this fire, however fierce, will not harm you or yours",' Cuthbert reassures Kenswith.

Nowhere is the language of Bede more colourful than in his account of the illusory fire, a story omitted in V.A., sent by the devil to prevent the villagers hearing the Word of God preached by Cuthbert on the hills. ‘That most evil foe produced a phantom fire and set alight houses nearby… firebrands seemed to be flying all through the village, fanned by the wind, their crackling rent the air’. All the villagers threw water on the fire to no avail until ‘at the prayers of Cuthbert the man of God, the author of lies was put to flight carrying with him the phantom fire into the empty air’.

Bede concludes his account with a strong moral point; ‘the devil never ceased, even for an hour, from hindering the work of man’s salvation.’ The crowd on bended knees begged forgiveness for their fickleness and ‘he continued his interrupted discourse’.

Instances of fires, real and illusory, extinguished by the prayers of saints are not uncommon: St. Martin drove back the flames from a village ‘where it looked like a battle between warring elements’; Gregory in his *Life of St. Benedict* describes how the whole kitchen seems to be ablaze when a bronze idol is thrown on the fire; once when St. Fintan and his brethren were eating in the refectory the whole room was filled with illusory flames; the house in which St. Wilfrid was being born appeared to be on fire.[17]

The illusory fires were interpreted either as the work of the devil and extinguished by prayer or as a sign of the divine presence as when the Lord spoke to Moses out of the midst of the burning bush as he tended his flocks in the wilderness of Horeb, the mountain of God.[18]

Two further examples of miracles involving the miraculous provision of food, earlier seen in the shepherd’s hut at Kuncacester and in the guest house at Ripon, are worth recording for they yield incidental insights.

Cuthbert, accompanied by a boy, was travelling south along the river Tesega (Teviot), teaching and baptising the country folk among the mountains (Cheviot Hills). Sensing that the boy was becoming anxious for a mid-day meal, as they had no provisions with them, he pointed to an eagle flying in the sky and said: ‘This is the eagle the Lord has instructed to provide us with food today’. The eagle settled on the bank with a large salmon at its feet which was divided equally between the bird and the travellers, who cooked their share and, giving thanks, ate it before resuming their journey.

The most extensive missionary journey recorded was to the region of Niduari in Pictland, wrongly identified as Nithsdale in Galloway, but more probably on the north east coast of Scotland. Cuthbert, with two brothers, set out to sail there just after Christmas, intending to spend Epiphany with the Nids. Unsurprisingly, at this time of the year, they encountered storms and became stranded on a deserted beach, where a great hunger assailed them. A night spent in prayer revealed in the morning three portions of dolphin's flesh on the sand, 'as though cut by human kind with a knife'. Giving thanks, they cooked the pieces and 'enjoyed the wonderful sweetness of the flesh'. After three days the storm died down, as Cuthbert had foretold, and a calm voyage brought them safely to their destination. The story reveals the extent and dangers of their evangelistic endeavours, the characteristic Anglo-Saxon confidence in boats, even for mid winter journeys, and the depth of their faith that the Lord would provide for them on the way. The visit also shows Cuthbert on friendly terms with the Christian Picts after he had adapted the Roman tradition of the dating of Easter but well before the Picts conformed finally in 716.

Two islands, Lindisfarne and Inner Farne, figure prominently in Cuthbert's life for he had two spells on each, a total of nine years on the latter. When Cuthbert was first sent to Lindisfarne as prior by Eata, who was both abbot and bishop, he would see a scatter of buildings lying now somewhere beneath St. Mary's parish church, the Norman priory and on the Heugh headland, but not even the latest archaeological research can say where precisely. Centrally situated would be the church 'built of hewn oak and thatched with reed' by Aidan's successor Finan, and later roofed with lead and re-dedicated by Archbishop Theodore after the Synod of Whitby, significantly to St. Peter. Around would be scattered cells of bee-hive type huts and, outside the vallum or cashel, now possibly identified, he would see cow byres, barns, stables, a kiln and bee hives – all very much like Iona, the mother-house, from where the founder Aidan had come in 635.

St. Cuthbert's City of God, Inner Farne

Initially, Cuthbert's tact and patience as prior were fully tested. Abbot Colman, with a group of twenty four monks of the Lindisfarne community, unable to accept the decision of the Whitby Synod, departed for Iona, then Inishboffin, before finally settling at Mayo where the monastery became known as *Magheo nos Saxon*, Mayo of the Saxons. Cuthbert quickly discovered 'the community found it difficult to adopt to new ways'. Assailed by bitter insults in the daily chapter meetings, he would calmly rise and leave, only to return the next morning with cheerful countenance after a night of prayer, so he gradually won them over 'to a rule of life which we composed for the first time which we observe along with the rule of Benedict' – a triumph of sensible compromise. Bede tells us that Cuthbert relieved the tedium of prayer and psalm-singing by walking about the island: any reader feeling jaded would do well to emulate Cuthbert and enjoy, as he did, the invigorating air and sights and sounds of an amazingly rich natural environment. In these respects little has changed and our present day visitor will find it possible to walk again in spirit with Cuthbert and then return to everyday life refreshed and recreated.[19]

St. Cuthbert's island lies off the south west shore of Lindisfarne and is only a short walk over slippery rocks and seaweed at low tide; here Cuthbert, one suspects, first felt strongly the pull of a solitary life, for he spent the penitential days of Lent and Advent in watching and praying alone. In this he was following the example of Aidan. All the visible remains today are post-Saxon; most marked are those of the medieval chapel of St. Cuthbert in the Sea which may well lie above the original oratory. Only a dig will reveal if the mound to the north of the chapel is the site of a cell.[20] The modern visitor searching the shore may find the fossil remains of sea-lilies, crinoids, popularly known as St. Cuthbert's beads, and will hear the same sounds as Cuthbert did, most evocative of all the plaintive, melancholy cry of the curlew. It is an atmospheric place.

St Cuthbert's Island in winter storm.

From short spells of solitude to permanent isolation was a step on the path to spiritual perfection where the anchorite could experience and savour 'the stillness of divine contemplation'. At the age of forty years with the permission of his abbot and following the example of Aidan, Cuthbert sailed the seven miles south to Inner Farne, 'an island frequented by evil spirits, utterly lacking in corn, water and trees', where he built his 'city' so well described by Bede. His oratory and dwelling may lie beneath the present medieval chapel, his guesthouse was by the jetty where some 30,000 visitors sailing from Seahouses land every summer; 'the spring close by' is still there, though now only one metre deep and filled by run-off water; unchanged is the sea-filled gully, known as St. Cuthbert's Gut, where the storm threw up a piece of timber which the monks had neglected to provide, so that the gully could serve as a '*necessarium*'. Nature thus compensated for the shortcomings of men in serving the saint's basic needs.

At first the hermit had problems with his new neighbours. The ravens tore the thatch off of the guest-house with their beaks for their nest building; admonished twice by Cuthbert, they returned 'with feathers sadly ruffled and drooping heads', asking pardon and, duly forgiven, brought a piece of hog's lard as a gift which, for a year, visitors used to grease their boots. Like Columba in Iona, his first attempt to become self-supporting failed, for spring-sown wheat 'produced no fruit', yet the barley sown much later, out of season, yielded 'an abundant crop' which the birds began 'eagerly to consume'. Ordered to depart, the flock flew off and thenceforward refrained from attacking his crops, just as Antony' with one exhortation restrained the wild asses from injuring his little garden'. Cuthbert would read in Job: 'Even the birds and animals have much they could teach you, ask the creatures of earth and sea for their wisdom'.[21]

Visitors to the Farne Islands in early summer will immediately realise that creation is an ongoing saga, not a seven day wonder. They will see up to 100,000 birds engaged in a whirl of activity, laying, incubating, hatching their eggs and flying back to the nests to feed the chicks with sand-eels – here is surely one of the great sights of Nature. Cuthbert is recognised as one of the first conservationists for he ordered the protection of the birds. Most trusting of all are the Cuddy ducks; the females a drab brown, the males with striking black and white plumage.

Cuddy drake on nest

Cuthbert preferred to be alone, ‘satisfied with the converse and ministry of angels, full of hope in God’, but he soon discovered the paradox that visitors were attracted ‘even from the remoter parts of Britain’ by the wisdom and insights he found in his prayerful solitude; Antony in the Egyptian desert, Columba on Iona, and Guthlac in the Fens had the same experience.

BISHOP

King Egfrid landing on the Farne Islands to summon Cuthbert to become bishop.
William Bell Scott (1811 – 1890) Wallington, the Trevelyan Collection.

Unwelcome visitors arrived in the persons of King Ecgfrith, Bishop Trumwine and ‘chosen men of our community’ who, having met at a synod at Adtuinfyrd (‘at the double ford’ possibly Whittingham, more probably Alnmouth) unanimously decided to appoint Cuthbert as Bishop of Hexham. Earlier letters and messengers had met with no success and now, ‘on bended knee, the king adjured him by Our

Lord Jesus Christ'. Reluctantly Cuthbert agreed and was led away 'weeping and wailing'. It is a scene colourfully portrayed by the local pre-Raphael artist William Bell Scott and exhibited, along with a series of other paintings of important scenes from Northumbrian history, in the atrium of Wallington Hall. Many saints, including such illustrious men as Augustine, Ambrose, Martin, Chad and Wilfrid, shared a similar reluctance to accept a bishopric and only agreed after protest. Ammonius even cut off part of his ear and threatened to tear out his tongue in protest, so was left to live a life of quiet contemplation.[22]

The prophecies of the precocious boy in the playground and of Prior Boisil were fulfilled late in the winter of 685 when Cuthbert was consecrated Bishop in the church of St. Peter's, York, in the greatest gathering of ecclesiastics to date in this country. The remarkable Archbishop of Canterbury, Theodore of Tarsus, already 84 years old, presided and was assisted by six bishops. When Theodore died in 690 his contribution as an organiser and administrator of the early Church and as a patron of arts and letters was inestimable.

Cuthbert's virtues as a bishop as described by the Anonymous are identical with those chosen by Eddius in his *Life of Wilfrid* and by Isodore of Seville as befitting the ideal bishop: his 'special care was to take part in fastings, prayers, vigils and reading of Scriptures where his memory served him instead of books… he fed the hungry, took in strangers, protected the widows and orphans'. He prophesied that his 'time as bishop would be shortlived, in fact it was only two years, but in that period he continued his missionary journeys so that many signs and wonders were wrought among the people'.

However, there was one important change in the nature of his work. His ever-growing reputation as a man of wise counsel and his enhanced status as a bishop brought him increasingly into contact with nobles and royalty who sought his advice. One has the distinct feeling that Cuthbert was more at ease in royal company than Aidan who was more of an ascetic and perceived as a foreigner.

Coquet Island, off Amble, was the scene of a meeting between 'the hermit of God and a certain nun, a virgin and royal abbess, Aelfflaed,' the daughter of King Oswin and Hild's successor at

Whitby. Aelfflaed was a staunch supporter of Wilfrid and yet a close friend of Cuthbert: the wounds from the Whitby Synod were healing.

Aelfflaed was anxious about the future of her brother King Ecgfrith and wept bitterly when Cuthbert prophesied that he had but twelve months to live and, when pressed on the succession, replied that the next king presently lived 'on an island beyond the sea'. She at once realised that he meant Aldfrith, her half-brother, then on Iona.[23] Asked about his own future as bishop, he prophesied: 'after the brief space of two years I shall rest from my labours'. 'After many prophetic words, all of which came to pass, he sailed to his own place'. His counsel was sought here, not on spiritual but on dynastic matters concerning royal succession, a new dimension to his prophetic powers. 'It is salutary to note the political dynastic alignment of even this apparently eremitical figure, Cuthbert was far more than the recluse of hagiographical tradition'.[24]

Queen Iurminburg too was anxious about her husband who was campaigning against the Picts, against Cuthbert's strong advice. She invited the bishop to Luel to seek reassurance. Luel, (named after Lugubalia, a Celtic war god) now known as Carlisle, had a town reeve, Waga, who was showing Cuthbert the walls and the Roman fountains still playing. At one point Cuthbert, leaning on his staff, lifted his eyes heavenwards and with a sigh said: 'Oh! Oh! Oh! I think the war is over and that judgement has been given against our people'. The worst fears of the queen were realised for, at the hour of the vision, the King and his army had been destroyed in an ambush at Nechtansmere by the Picts under Ecgfrith's cousin, King Bruide.

Widowhood transformed Iurminburg for she took the veil, Cuthbert receiving her religious profession, and from 'being a she-wolf she was changed into a lamb of God, a perfect abbess, an excellent mother of the community'. Interestingly, the story reveals Carlisle as a town with an active administration and, with York, the only sizeable town in the north of Britain, for the Anglo-Saxons were essentially country dwellers and mostly shunned the old Roman cities calling them 'tombs surrounded by nets and built by giants'.

Best known of all the tales about Cuthbert is that about the saint and the otters.

Double monasteries where nuns and monks lived in corporate and liturgical unity were an importation from Gaul and formed a key element in early Northumbrian monasticism. Invariably these institutions, which were supported by both the Celtic and Roman parties, were ruled by those formidable Anglo-Saxon ladies, the royal abbesses who had taken the veil.

On the prominent windswept St. Abb's Head on the Berwickshire coast are the remains of an ancient fort with buildings inside it: here is the probable site of the monastery founded by Aidan. In 672 Queen Aethilthryth left her husband King Ecgfrith, at the instigation of Wilfrid, to become a novice nun at Coldingham; in later life she became St. Audrey, abbess of Ely. Another royal lady Aebba (hence St. Abb's Head and probably Ebchester), sister of Kings Oswin and Oswiu, was chosen as abbess of Coldingham, 'a widow and mother of them all in Christ'. Only at Coldingham was there any scandal; the visiting abbot of Iona, Adamnan, Columba's biographer, warned against the lax life led by monks and nuns; soon afterwards Bede relates that the monastery was consumed with fire as a punishment. Aebba invited Cuthbert to visit 'to open the community to the paths of righteousness'. Cuthbert spent the night in the sea up to his armpits, praying and singing psalms, before slipping back to church to sing the first office of the day. In the dawn a curious monk who had been spying on the saint from a cave saw '*animalia maritima*', as Bede describes them, otters more likely than seals, emerge from the waves to dry the holy man's feet with their fur and warm them with their breath, and then, having received his blessing, they returned to the sea. Overcome with guilt, the spy fell ill and only recovered after confessing to Cuthbert and receiving his absolution, on condition that he tell no one what he had seen until after Cuthbert's death, echoing Christ's message to the disciples at the Transfiguration.

Otters feature in the story of Irish saints; salmon were brought each day by otters from Lake Glendalough to supply the community under St. Coemgen (Kevin) and an otter retrieved his psalter from the waters of the lake.

Such tales illustrate perfectly that most attractive characteristic of Irish spirituality, a deep and close affinity with the natural word. It was a tradition in line with the Desert Fathers where we read of Jerome befriending a lion, of Pachome riding across the Nile on the backs of crocodiles, of a penitent wolf, a grateful hyena and helpful wild asses;[25] all a world away from the half-man, half-beast were-wolves, the fearful semi-human monster Grendel of Beowulf, and the Fenrir wolf and serpent of Norse mythology, for these creatures represented the powers of evil and darkness fighting against 'the light with which God penetrated the primordial darkness'.

The beach where the incident of Cuthbert's encounter with the otters took place can be identified fairly positively today: it lies immediately to the west of the headland where the monastery stood and where easy access to the sea is possible whereas to north and south are high and steep cliffs. The spy saw in Cuthbert in the first light of dawn a man transformed by prayer and penance into a Christ-like figure who was in total harmony with the creatures of the deep; Man and Creation were in union; here was Eden before the Fall. The idea that man's dominion over the lower orders of creation had been lost by sin is quite commonly seen in the lives of the saints.

St Abb's Head looking north; the bay at the foot of the cliffs is the only possible site for Cuthbert's encounter with the otters.

There is a close correlation between many of Cuthbert's journeys and the old Roman roads whose worn cobbles still provided routes through the difficult hill country of Northern Britain more than five centuries after they were built. Stanegate, along the lines of Hadrian's Wall, gave easy east-west access through the Tyne Gap.

Though neither Life mentions it, it is hard to believe that Cuthbert, journeying west, failed to visit his fellow bishop Eata and Wilfrid's 'finest stone church north of the Alps' at Hexham. However, he is recorded as preaching and confirming at Ahse (probably Aesicia, the old Roman fort of Great Chesters). Luel, otherwise written as Lugubalia ('wall of Lugus' – a Celtic war-god) now Carlisle (Caer – Welsh for fort), near the western end of Stanegate, where he had been granted lands by King Ecgfrith, features prominently in Cuthbert's travels. That he was a regular visitor is shown in Bede's account of his meeting with Herbert, the hermit from an isle in Lake Derwentwater who, 'constantly on previous occasions' met 'the holy bishop for spiritual converse' at Luel. Herbert's prayer that he would die on the same day as Cuthbert was granted, 20th March 687. It is encouraging to note that men of God do, at times, crave human friendship as much as lesser mortals: Herbert and Cuthbert's friendship is akin to that of Robert of Newminster and Godric of Finchal in the mid-twelfth century.

At Osingadun (probably Ovington) Cuthbert dedicated a new church in a daughter-house of Abbess Aelfflaed of Whitby. Whilst feasting with the abbess, Cuthbert's countenance suddenly changed and the knife fell from his hand. When asked the reason, he replied lightly 'Can I eat all day? I must rest sometime'. In truth, he had seen a vision of a shepherd dying in an accident. Next morning, during the canon of the dedication Mass, the abbess 'came breathless into church with woman-like astonishment, crying I pray you my lord bishop, remember at Mass my Hadwald who died yesterday falling from a tree'.

At the eastern end of the Wall Cuthbert visited the monastery of Abbess Verca at South Shields, where he was given a splendid reception and a fine linen cloth as a present. Invited to drink wine or beer, he asked for water, but when his cup was passed around, all who supped agreed that the water tasted like fine wine.

HERMIT

Both VA and VP point to Cuthbert's increasing asceticism and desire to be left alone.

One episode is particularly revealing.

On Christmas Day a party of monks sailed to Inner Farne to celebrate the feast with Cuthbert. ‘Let us be joyful today’, they said, ‘because it is the birthday of our Lord Jesus Christ’. Soon they were ‘indulging in feasting, rejoicing and storytelling’. Cuthbert, filled with foreboding, warned: ‘I beseech you brethren, let us be cautious and watchful less by recklessness we are led into temptation’. The monks replied: ‘You give us good, yea excellent instruction, but nevertheless because the days of fastings, prayer and vigils abound, today let us rejoice in the Lord’. The cause of Cuthbert’s foreboding was the plague which broke out on Lindisfarne the next day.

Bede uses the word *fabulae* for story-telling implying secular tales, the heroic sagas of old beloved by Anglo-Saxons. Alcuin in 797 shared Cuthbert’s worry: reflecting on why God should allow Vikings to pillage Lindisfarne, he concluded that it was because the monks had the custom of listening to heathen poems at dinner. ‘What has Ingeld to do with Christ?’ he asked. ‘Narrow is the house, it will not be able to hold them both’. In admonishing his partying monks Cuthbert was mindful of the tenth step in humility of the Rule of Benedict, ‘The fool lifts up his voice in laughter’. (Ecclus 21).

DEATH

There is a marked change in Cuthbert’s attitude to visitors to his hermitage on Inner Farne who came not only from the neighbourhood but also from the remoter parts of Britain attracted by reports of his miracles.

At first ‘he went forth from his cell and ministered to them, washing their feet in the customary way … having confessed their sins and been refreshed by his pious exhortations, no-one left unconsoled’.

Cuthbert’s episcopacy lasted barely two years. Foreseeing that death was not far distant he resigned and, having spent Christmas 686 with the brethren on Lindisfarne, he sailed off to Inner Farne where he awaited the end freed from outside anxieties. Yet his desire to prepare for entering into eternal life by continuous prayer and psalm-singing was still disturbed by visitors. He shut himself up in his hermitage and only conversed through the window;

eventually he shut even that except to give a blessing. He would remove his own boots only once a year for the washing of the feet on Maundy Thursday and a long and thick callous was revealed on his feet from so many genuflexions at prayer. Cuthbert, in his scorn of washing, was emulating Antony of Egypt 'who neither bathed his body nor ever washed his feet'.

The rather unattractive image of a man, most probably bearded, who rarely washed and changed his boots only once a year, is offset by his countenance as described by the Anonymous: 'at all hours he was happy and joyful, neither wearing a sad expression at the remembrance of a sin nor elated by the loud praises of those who marvelled at his manner of life.' Bede's description of Cuthbert's clothes is an echo of the advice given in Chapter 55 of the Rule of Benedict; 'he wore ordinary garments... noteworthy neither for their elegance nor for their slovenliness'.

The story of the last miracle wrought by Cuthbert in his lifetime was told many times by his servant Walhstod who had a 'grievous sickness which had long afflicted him'. As he came to minister to the dying saint in his cell he was cured of his chronic dysentery at Cuthbert's first touch.

Some scholars query the authenticity of the detailed and moving farewell oration of Cuthbert as recorded by Bede who names the priest Herefrith, an eyewitness, as his source: others are downright sceptical: 'it is highly unlikely that he said any such thing, Bede's whole account of Herefrith's testimony has every appearance of substantial elaboration'.[26]

Bede has Cuthbert issuing a solemn warning: 'Have no communion with those who depart from the unity of the Catholic faith, either by not celebrating Easter at the proper time or in evil living'.

However, there can be no doubting Cuthbert's suffering in the final few days. Alone, storm-bound, in his last agony, a near despair and sense of desolation oppressed him as no bird or beast came to minister to him. He had only the sea, the sky and the rocks for company, a Gethsemane on Inner Farne. 'My adversaries have never persecuted me so severely as during these past five days,' he told the monks from Lindisfarne who finally reached him after the storms had died down; ‘as my mouth was parched and burned through excess of dryness, I sought to refresh and cool myself by tasting these’, and he indicated seven onions, one half nibbled.

No longer alone, ‘he passed a quiet day in the expectation of future bliss’, and at the time of night prayers, ‘fortified by the communion of the Lord’s body and blood, raising his eyes to heaven, he sent forth his spirit in the very act of praising God to the joys of the heavenly kingdom’, where ‘God’s tribe are seated at the banquet and where there is eternal joy’.

The news of the saint’s death was at once signalled by two torches to the brother in the watch-tower on Lindisfarne. He quickly ran to inform the community who were gathered in church for the service of Lauds singing the 59th psalm: ‘Oh God, thou hast cast us off and broken us down; thou hast been angry and had compassion on us’.

Miracles attributed to the intercession of Cuthbert continued even after the saint’s death. A visiting bishop of the Frisians, Willibrord, fell grievously ill while visiting Lindisfarne and was cured by prayer ‘at the sepulchre of the most holy man receiving strength from the incorrupt body’; a paralytic youth, for whom ‘the physicians of Lindisfarne could do nothing’ recovered completely when Cuthbert’s shoes were taken from the tomb and ‘placed upon the nerveless feet of the sick man’; Felgild, who lived in the hermitage on Inner Farne after Cuthbert’s death, was cured of an inflamed and disfiguring swelling covering his whole face by bathing it in water in which had been dipped the calf skins the saint had nailed over the cracks in the oratory wall.

That some of the forty miracles recounted in VA and VP seem to us hardly extraordinary at all, and that others are plagiarisms of stories from the Gospels or other Lives, did not concern folk who lived in an age of faith and in a world shot through with divinity. That Cuthbert could use his powers of healing in life and posthumously only confirmed the popular view, *vox populi*, that he was indeed a man of God.

<u>THE FINAL RESTING PLACE</u>

Our journey of exploration ends where Cuthbert’s earthly journey finally ended, in the Cathedral at Durham, built, as the Lindisfarne Gospels were written, 'to honour God and St. Cuthbert'. When the tomb was opened at the translation in 1104, and again at the ransacking of the shrine at the Dissolution, 'the body was found lying whole and incorrupt'. Whether the true grave is beneath the slab of slate simply marked Cuthbertus' behind the high altar or elsewhere is a matter of debate, for there is a Catholic tradition dating from the 1620's that, just prior to the Dissolution, monks moved his body to a secret grave in the cathedral. The secret is still extant and is held by the Abbot President of the English Benedictine Congregation.[27] In 1891 Abbot President Augustine Walker declined a request to remove the body to the English Benedictine monastery of Lambspring in Belgium on the grounds that 'it would be cruel to deprive the faithful of their protector'.[28]

Many local people believe Cuthbert still serves as their protector.

The night of May 1st 1942 was clear and moonlit as German planes crossed the English coast with the aim of bombing Durham in retaliation for RAF attacks on the historic cities of Lubeck and Rostov. A member of the Royal Observer Corps noted that as the bombers approached a thick mist arose from the River Wear shrouding the city and cathedral. Unable to locate their target the planes turned for home. Cuthbert was still interceding on behalf of his people.

The cult of relics in medieval minds meant that the saint was not only in heaven with God but was also present in his or her earthly remains and could therefore respond to prayers made at the shrine by interceding for the supplicant. This firm belief is expressed clearly in the epitaph of the tomb of St. Martin of Tours: 'Here lies Martin the Bishop, of holy memory, whose soul is in the hands of God: but he is fully here, present, and made plain in miracles of every kind'. When the body in the shrine was incorrupt his intercessionary prayers were even more efficacious.

The historian Lingard drew attention to Anglo-Saxon burial customs: 'the distinctions of office were preserved on the bier and in the grave: and the bodies of Kings and Ealdormen, of Bishops, Priests and Deacons were interred in the ornaments of their respective ranks. St. Cuthbert was laid in his coffin in his Episcopal vestments with a paten, chalice, portable altar, offletes and all that was necessary for the celebration of Mass'.[29] It is therefore no small wonder then that the tomb yielded up such a rich haul of objects when it was opened in 1827, despite the destruction of the shrine in 1537.

The collection of antiquities in the Cathedral Treasury is of inestimable interest and value and some may feel closer to Cuthbert here than on Inner Farne.

Among the objects displayed are his coffin of small fragments of oak boards incised with the figures of Christ, Virgin and Child, the apostles and archangels rather crudely portrayed compared with the fine figures on the Ruthwell Cross and on the pages of the Lindisfarne Gospels; the portable altar previously described; an ivory comb, for either personal or liturgical use, found in the saint's robes; a burse or small linen bag for holding hosts; fragments of silks from Persia and Byzantium brought by pilgrims to the shrine as gifts as well as a stole and maniple, ornamented with figures of prophets and saints, exquisitely embroidered in gold threads by ladies of the West Saxon court and presented by King Aethelstan at the shrine when the body was still at Chester le Street, c.934.

St. Cuthbert's pectoral cross

Of supreme interest, however, is the pectoral cross found in the 1827 opening 'deeply buried among the remains of the robes nearest to the breast of the saint'. Only 6 cm. tall, the cross is made of gold with a decoration of garnets in gold cloisonné, at the centre is a garnet set in gold on a bed of shell. Each arm of the cross is in twelve segments representing the tribes of Israel or the apostles. As in the Dream of the Rood the association of the red of jewels and gold symbolizes the blood and the glory of the Crucifixion and of martyrdom. One scholar believes the style of the cross is unique and that the cross is the solitary example remaining to us of the goldsmith's work of the Britons of the fifth-century Strathclyde who were Christians working with some surviving knowledge of the Roman crafts and some acquaintance with the continental 'Gothic' fashion in jewellery.[30] I think it more likely that the cross was made in the workshops of Lindisfarne monastery by the same craftsmen who adorned the Gospels with jewels. All agree that the cross and Cuthbert have been together since the 7th century. It may have been manufactured especially for the occasion of his consecration as Bishop in York in 685, or as an ornament to be placed in his tomb. Whatever the date or provenance, this exquisite jewel evokes the same feelings of awe and reverence at first sight as the Lindisfarne Gospels.

The Lindisfarne Gospels: 'to honour God and St Cuthbert'.
St Mark seated writing his Gospel: his symbol an angelic lion, king of the beasts, representing the majesty of God, with horn heralding the Good News.

Though our emotions are stirred by these precious relics it must be conceded that they tell us more about the dedication and skill of the craftsmen and the wealth of art of medieval times than about the man Cuthbert. It is evident that a holy monk, who lived a simple life vowed to poverty, was buried and honoured in later centuries like an emperor.

If indeed, so little is known about Cuthbert why is it that he is northern England's best known and most loved saint, patron of Northumberland, with some eighty-three churches dedicated to him in England and Wales, forty-nine in the six northern counties? His fame is all the more remarkable when one realizes he was not a scholar like Bede, not the first preacher of the Christian Gospel in Northumbria like Paulinus or Aidan, not a builder of magnificent churches like Wilfrid, not a traveller and collector of books and relics like Benedict Biscop, not a martyr like Alban before him or Beckett after him. His episcopy was exceptionally short, less than two years (Christ's public ministry lasted only three years) and was undistinguished by any event of signal importance. What is the secret of Cuthbert? What was it that won for him a reputation that no churchman of Northern England has surpassed or even rivalled since?[31]

Certainly politics played a part for Cuthbert had always maintained close links with the Bernician royal house. After his death his cult received the full backing of the now powerful and wealthy church of Lindisfarne and of the Northumbrian kings. Cuthbert was portrayed as the patron and protector of the newly united Northumbrian, hence the prominence given to him by Alcuin in his poem *Bishops, Kings and Saints of York.* He was the Northumbrian equivalent of Martin of Tours, also a soldier and bishop, the patron of the Frankish kings who ruled France, the Low Countries and much of Germany.[32]

A greater part of the saint's reputation lies not so much in the troubled politics of a region constantly at war in his lifetime but rather in certain personal qualities evident in The Lives.

An Anglo-Saxon by birth, Cuthbert had the gift of friendship whether as guestmaster at Ripon, prior of a troubled Lindisfarne, diligent bishop anxious for the needs of his flock or counsellor to the stream of diverse visitors to his hermitage on Inner Farne. He moved easily in the company of princes and peasants alike for his was a personality that attracted by its peaceful and gentle nature.

Despite a life of ascetism he was not always in control of his emotions for 'when celebrating Mass he could never finish the service without shedding tears; he shared the gift of tears' with St. Dunstan and the desert fathers. Only towards the end when illness and old age were taking their toll did Cuthbert appear to become rather curmudgeonly.

The popular view that the scandals he witnessed at Coldingham left him with a fear of women – Walter Scott in Marmion calls him 'that well-known woman hater' – is not borne out by the evidence. His love for his mother, Kenswith, the warmth with which he was received by royal abbesses Aebba, Aelfflaed, Iurminburg and Verca, shows that his affection for them was reciprocated. Verca's gift of white linen in which his body was first wrapped symbolises Cuthbert's relationships with high-born women who often held prominent places in Saxon society, and gives the lie to the Norman propaganda .

Reconciliation was a key feature of Cuthbert's life, where his affable nature would be of much assistance. Just as in his spiritual life he successfully melded the active and the contemplative in his roles as missionary prior and bishop and eremite, so he strove to heal the wounds caused by the Synod of Whitby. His expulsion from Ripon early in his monastic life led him to see, as did Bede, that unity was essential; this insight enabled him to carry forward the vibrant Celtic spirit into the new emerging Anglian tradition. It was this deep desire for unity that persuaded him to conform after the Synod rather than join the exodus of Colman and his party from Lindisfarne back to Iona and Ireland. Yet the manner of his life indicates beyond a shadow of doubt that though his head became Roman his heart was emphatically Celtic.

His life was essentially one of self-offering to God and his neighbours: 'Not I but Christ liveth in me'.[33] In the company of the angels he found Christ in the 'stillness of divine contemplation' afforded by the solitude of Inner Farne. He came to love the rugged beauty of the Northumberland coast and to respect, indeed reverence, the forces of nature and the wild creatures of sea and sky. Love of the geographical environment is a timeless concept of the monastic life found equally among the early Desert Fathers of Egypt and monks today, who see that Christianity is essentially sacramental being based on the Incarnation. When 'the Word became Flesh', matter and spirit became one as did the human and natural communities. Benedictines take a vow *stabilitas* expressly to encourage this sense of oneness and belonging.

Cuthbert was no Benedictine[34], though he would have some familiarity with the Rule, yet he 'saw creation' charged with the glory of God but given for the glory of man... he was at home on Farne as Christ was at home in Galilee... creation was a divine masterpiece'.[35]

As he grew more Christ-like, with increasing detachment from worldly affairs, he fashioned within himself a brilliant spiritual synthesis not unlike that of the Lindisfarne Gospels in the realm of culture.[36] Herein lies his real appeal.

In his preface to the *Lindisfarne Life* the Anonymous advises: 'It is in itself a ready virtue to know what he was': in his *Life of Wilfrid* Eddius Stephanus gives identical advice about his saint.

In truth, we can never really know in any detail what manner of men these saints were for they moved in a world in many respects strange and alien to us; furthermore, the hagiographers focus not on the human faults and foibles of their subjects but on their Christ-like qualities and their relationship with God; in so doing, they often reveal more about themselves than the saint. Though Cuthbert only emerges from the mists of legend and hagiography as a shadowy and elusive figure, rather like Sir Galahad of the 'Quest of the Holy Grail' in Arthurian legend, yet we are left with a firm conviction that here was a good and holy man who, more by his deeds than by his preaching, manifested the gospel message to the Northumbrians.

When we explore the region where Cuthbert lived and the places we know he visited we are on surer ground for, in some ways, nothing has changed; sheep still graze on the hills where the Leader falls into the Tweed; the trusting eider still nests beside the path on Inner Farne, and the tide still ebbs and flows twice a day around

Lindisfarne.

A waymarked route of 62.5 miles, St. Cuthbert's Way, from Melrose to Lindisfarne, opened in 1996, has proved to be immensely popular with walkers and a welcome boost to the local economy. The Way crosses magnificent Border scenery of rolling farmland, verdant river valleys and high hills and, even apart from its associations with St. Cuthbert, offers much of historical interest – Iron Age Hill Forts, a Roman signal station and stretches of the old Roman roads of Dere Street and the Devil's Causeway, a medieval castle at Cessford and easy access to Dryburgh and Jedburgh Abbeys. A friend who recently completed the walk described it as delightful; all the more so, I imagine, for those who come armed with some knowledge of the life and times of Northumberland's patron saint.

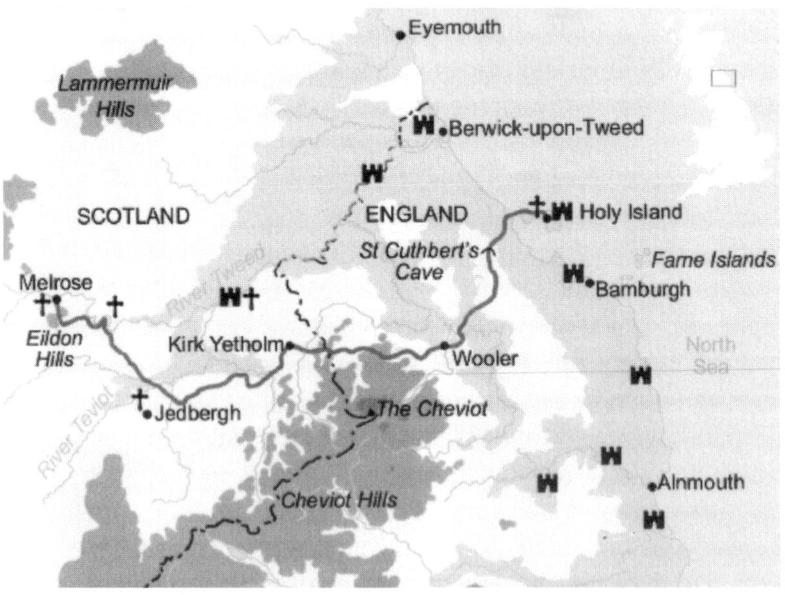

Map of St. Cuthbert's Way - 64 miles
from Melrose to Holy Island.

'For with the flow and ebb its stile
Varies from continent to isle:
Dry-shod, o'er sands, twice every day
The pilgrims to the shrine find way:
Twice every day, the waves efface
Of staves and sandaled feet the trace'.

Sir Walter Scott
Marmion 11.9

Lindisfarne Castle on Beblaw (Bible Hill), and the Ouse, the harbour where the 6th century British war fleet once sheltered.

St Cuthbert, holding the head of St Oswald, from the bishop's throne canopy by Ralph Hedley (1848-1913), St Mary's Cathedral, Newcastle upon Tyne.

NOTES AND REFERENCES

1. Kings, 19.9.

2. HOARE F.R. The Western Fathers. 1954. p.24.

3. The High History of St. Benedict and his Monks. A Monk of Douai Abbey. 1945. p.1

4. ALCUIN. *Bishops, Kings and Saints of York.* ed., trans. P. Godman 1982

5. Vita Sancti Cuthbertii, Auctore Anonymo (VA). Trans. B. Colgrave 1985.

6. See Bede's Matrical Vita S. Cuthbertii, M. Lapidge p.77-94 in St. Cuthbert, His Cult and His Community to AD 1200. eds. Bonner Stancliffe, Rollason. 1989 (I can find no English translation of this poem)

7. Vita Sancti Cuthbertii, Auctore Beda (VP). Trans. B. Colgrave 1985

8. BEDE. A *History of the English Church and People.* Trans L. Sherley-Price 1968 (HE)

9. ADAMNAN OF IONA. *Life of St. Columba.* Trans. R. Sharpe 1995

10. HOARE F.R. OP. CIT. p.28

11. BLAIR P.H. The World of Bede. 1993. p.279

12. BUTLER A. Lives of the Saints 1745. Vol. 1949. ed. p.291

13. See article by M.H. Dodds, 'The Little Book of St. Cuthbert' in A.A. 1929 p.52 where this claim is summarily dismissed: The Irish Life is almost identical with that of St. Molacus of Lismore and originated in Melrose Abbey c.1138

14. BATES, C.J. The Names of Persons and Places mentioned in the Early Lives of St. Cuthbert. Archaeologia Aeliana XVI 1894 (AA)

15. The Spirituality of St. Cuthbert, B. Ward. P.65 – 76. St. Cuthbert op.cit.

16. Cited in Hexham Abbey 674 – 1973 W. Taylor p.52

17. VA op cit. B. Colgrave n.p 322

18. Exodus 1.3

19. At the time of writing the whole Spitsbergen population of pale-bellied Brent geese is overwintering around Lindisfarne as well as a flock of whooper swans from Iceland.

20. See D. O'SULLIVAN and R. YOUNG. Lindisfarne. 1995

21. Job 12.7

22. 22 V.A. op. cit. B. Colgrave p 330

23. Aldfrith, illegitimate son of King Oswin and the Irish Princess Fina, ruled 685 – 705; he proved to be a strong and scholarly ruler, almost certainly our first fully literate King.

24. KIRBY D.F. St. Wilfrid at Hexham. 1974. p.19

25. Waddell.Helen for a charming anthology of such tales see Beasts and Saints, 1934

26. KIRBY D.F. Innes Review XXIV. 1973. p.12 – 13

27. Benedict's Disciples. ed. D.H. Farmer. 1980. Article on St. Cuthbert and St. Wilfrid. Dom. E. Power p.67

28. Some notes on the Benedictine Secret regarding St. Cuthbert's body. Dom. G. Scott. Northern Catholic History No. 25. Spring 1987. p.14-17

29. LINGARD Antiquities of the Anglo-Saxon Church Vol.11 p.49

30. T.D. KENDRICK Journal of the Society of Antiquaries 1937, cited in The Relics of St. Cuthbert. C.F.

Battiscombe 1956, p.58

31. See Sermon by Bishop Lightfoot of Durham Cathedral, 1883, cited by G. Bonner in article St. Cuthbert Soul-friend p.48-49 in Rollason op. cit.

32. D.W. ROLLASON 'Why was St. Cuthbert so popular?' Article op cit. Rollason

33. Galatians 2.26

34. It is interesting to note that the Benedictines claim him as one of their own: in the Book of Saints compiled by the monks of the Benedictine Abbey of St. Augustine, Ramsgate, 1989 p. 143, he is listed as St. Cuthbert OSB (Order of Saint Benedict)

35. HUGH LAVERY, Portrait of a Saint. 1993. p.5. An Epilogue on Tyne Tees Television.

36. H. MAYR-HARTING op. cit. p.161

4

THE FATHER OF ENGLISH HISTORY

THE FIRST GREAT ENGLISHMAN

Bede found in death a fame he never sought in life for he was the humblest of men. Through the centuries saints and scholars alike have sung his praises: for his contemporary Boniface (c.675-754), Apostle of Germany and Frisia, he was 'a candle of the church lit by the Holy Spirit'; the respected monastic historian, Dom David Knowles, considered that 'in his learning, in his candour and in his art Bede is without rival in the Middle Ages … he is the first great Englishman of whom we can form a clear personal picture … a clear cut, living and attractive being'[1]. For Sir Richard Southern, Bede is 'a pioneer, the first Englishman of his type, the first scientific intellect produced by the Germanic peoples of Europe … the most unexpected of all products of a primitive age, a really great scholar'[2]. Universally recognised as the 'Father of English History' by virtue of his best known work, 'A History of the English Church and People' (History or HE), he was the first to conceive the notion of a united English nation rather than some seven separate warring kingdoms.

Bede is also unique among Englishmen in three respects: he is the only Englishman mentioned in Dante's 'Paradiso'[3]; he became the only English Doctor of the Church when in 1897 Pope Leo XIII proclaimed him 'Doctor Optimus', henceforth to be counted among the early Fathers, Augustine, Ambrose, Gregory and Jerome, whom Bede so reverenced; in the following year he became the only Englishman to have an Italian college named after him when the Pope decreed that the English College for seminarians in Rome be placed under the patronage of Bede, to whom he had a personal devotion, and be known as the Beda College.

Bede has never been officially canonised as a saint by Rome: he is a 'vox populi' saint whose cult was established within fifty years of his death, but which never blossomed like Cuthbert's; there are no ancient dedications to Bede in England.

The title of Venerable, first bestowed by the Council of Aachen in 836, is quite rare among the saints. The present meaning of venerable is; one of great age but it originally meant one deserving of the highest honour; in his writings Bede often describes men he greatly admires as venerable.

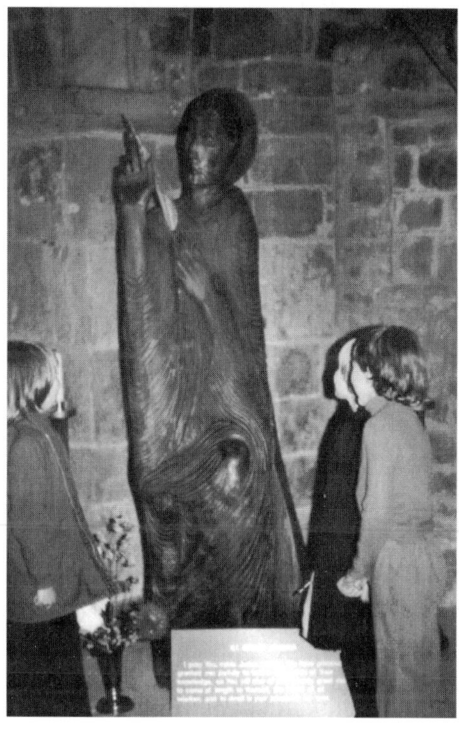

Modern sculpture of Bede carved from elm wood by Fenwick Lawson, based on medieval portrait from Engelberg Codex.
St Paul's Church, Jarrow.

Bede is special in another way; of all famous historical figures of the past he evokes among many who study him at length a sense of friendship and affection, all the more remarkable as we have so little factual knowledge about him. The first editor of the History, Plummer, confessed such a 'personal feeling that I am well content that some trace of my personal feelings and circumstances should remain in what I have written about him … for it is no light privilege to have been for so long in constant communion with one of the saintliest characters ever produced by the Church of Christ in this island'[4]. Knowles considered that the reader of Bede quickly comes to feel that Bede himself is more admirable and lovable than any of his characters. The present writer readily admits he has succumbed to Bede's charm.

Every year in late May about the time of Bede's Feast Day – now kept on 25th May instead of 27th May, the date of his death, to avoid a clash of dates with Augustine of Canterbury – the Bede lecture is delivered by an eminent Bedan scholar in St. Paul's Church, Jarrow. One lecturer wondered how it was that Bede, in the face of difficulties beyond our understanding, was able to achieve so much in that remote, bleak and still barbaric world into which he was born.

This essay seeks some answers to this intriguing question.

Bede did, indeed, live in the darkest hour of European civilisation, as dark as 1940 in recent time. The great Roman Empire had disintegrated from moral degeneracy within and external conquest; half of Christendom had been conquered by the Saracens, as Bede called them, and was not finally saved until 732 in one of the most decisive battles in history when Charles Martel defeated the Moslem army at Tours, an event noted in later additions of the History. Yet in the meantime in a remote and backword province of the old Roman Empire a civilisation grew up without parallel in European history.

In the late seventh century, until the Viking longships began landing at Lindisfarne and Jarrow in the late eighth century, there was a flowering of Christian culture, a Northumbrian Renaissance or Golden Age, when Bede and his contemporaries found themselves living in a time and place ideally suited to their talents for learning and teaching. Redolent of this exciting time are treasures still extant such as St. Cuthbert's Cross, the 'Codex Amiatinus', the Lindisfarne Gospels, Bede's History and the Ruthwell Cross.

BOYHOOD

In a brief autobiographical note at the end of his History Bede tells us all we know about his early life: 'Bede, the servant of God, and priest of the monastery of the blessed apostles Peter and Paul, which is at Wearmouth and Jarrow; who being born in the territory of that same monastery, was given at seven years of age to be educated by the most reverend Abbot Benedict, and afterwards by Ceolfrid; and spending all the remaining time of my life in that monastery, I wholly applied myself to the study of Scripture, and amidst the observance of regular discipline, and the daily care of singing in the church, I always took delight in learning, teaching and writing'.

We know nothing of his parents; the leading monastic figures of the time were all of royal or noble blood but there is no clue as to Bede's family status. It is likely that they were either converts or first generation Christians and that by the time Bede entered Wearmouth monastery they were dead and Bede an orphan child; if it were not so why should Bede use the word '*propinquae*' (kinsfolk) rather than'*parentes*' (parents)? In the Roman tradition, an infant became a boy at seven years, a time for decisions on his future education. Again we cannot know whether Bede was vowed to a religious life until his death or given the option of leaving at seventeen to lead the life of a layman.

He tells us that he was born 'in the lands of this monastery', though we do not know where exactly for the lands were extensive, all we can say with certainty is that he was a Northumbrian, or more precisely a Bernician. There is a Bede's Well at Monkton, Jarrow and there are Bedan Hills above Gibside in the Derwent Valley, but these are only names and no real help in identifying his place of birth.

The name Bede is unusual – we hear only of one other Bede, a servant of Cuthbert on Inner Farne. It derives from an ancient office of the church, the bedesman, whose duty it was to pray for the souls of the deceased. Bede may have been given his name at Baptism, or when he took his religious vows. Anglo-Saxons did not choose biblical names, the only exception being John.

No one wrote a life of Bede presumably because his life appeared so unremarkable: wonder-workers like Columba or Cuthbert attracted hagiographers. He tells of only one miracle relating to himself; while composing the Verse Life of Cuthbert he says he was cured of 'an affliction of the tongue'; whether this was a speech impediment like a stammer or he simply meant he received fresh inspiration through Cuthbert when his mind was blank and his pen run dry we can only guess.

Bede was never an abbot or bishop, his talents would have been wasted in such a role; his name appears in no church documents; he initiated no new doctrines; in all his prodigious output of writing he rarely mentions himself. His abiding virtue is his self-effacing humility: therein lies his charm.

By modern standards the education received by Bede in the classrooms of Wearmouth monastery sounds monotonous and harsh but it served him well for he became the 'ideal monk-scholar' and a leading light among the second generation of monks who fulfilled the literary and scholarly role in the conversion of Northumbria following on the missionary work of that first generation of Aidan, Wilfrid, Cuthbert, Hilda and others.

Armed with talents and texts and a pellucid Latin style, Bede energetically began teaching. He was demanding of himself and his students. Though his pupils at an early stage became '*psalterati*' (literate in reading, memorising and reciting the Psalter), trained in memory and the basics of grammar, Bede's texts challenged these linguistic and intellectual abilities[6]. He was sensitive to their needs. He found that one of his first books *De Temporibus* was too difficult so he wrote a fuller and revised edition *De Temporum Ratione* some years later. The emphasis was on grammar, syntax and Latin as essential tools for studying the Bible and the writings of the Fathers. With few text books available there was much rote learning. Aelfric's Colloquy[7] gives an insight into the rigours of discipline: 'Let not novices be easily moved to laughter, tittering in general is a great disgrace to the gravity of a religious … if any boy offend in psalmody or chant, or fall asleep, forthwith they are to be stripped of frock and cowl and beaten in their bare shirt by the prior with smooth and supple osier rods kept for this single purpose … boys are scourged customarily when there is need during talking hour in cloister, never after vespers'. Aelfric tells of boys in trouble for scrumping apples from the monastery orchard and Alcuin[8] warns against young men who rejoice more in being drunk than in learning or who prefer to spend their time coursing hares or digging out foxes rather than singing the Hours.

It is again Alcuin who, in a letter to the monks of Wearmouth, tells the tale of how Bede, not doubting the presence of angels in holy places, said: 'I know that the angels visit the canonical hours and the congregations of the brothers; what if they do not find me among the brothers? Will they not say: "Where is Bede? Why does he not come to the appointed prayers with the brothers?" ' It seems Anglo-Saxon monks shared with their Celtic brethren a powerful sense of an angelic presence.

An event in the time of Bede's boyhood reveals the terrible sufferings of monastic communities when struck by the plague. An outbreak of pestilence in 686 killed off many of the monks of St. Peter's, Monkwearmouth, including the co-abbot Eosterwine; at the newly-established twin monastery of St. Paul's, Jarrow, all who could read, write and sing the antiphons died; only abbot Coelfrith and a young boy 'nourished and taught by him' were left to recite the psalms without antiphons, except at vespers and matins. After a week of tears and lamentations the abbot could bear it no longer and the full office was not restored until a new choir could be trained. The vision of the abbot with a manly voice and the young boy praising God in an empty church while all around were dead and dying brethren is impressive evidence of their depth of devotion to the singing of the Hours. Psalm 90 would have a special poignancy:

You will not fear the terror of the night
Nor the arrow that flies by day,
Nor the plague that prowls in the darkness
Nor the scourge that lays waste at noon.

A thousand may fall at your side
Ten thousand fall at your right
You, it will never be approached
His faithfulness is bucker and shield.

It is generally believed that the small boy was Bede who had transferred to Jarrow with his former novice-master Coelfrith, the newly appointed abbot of St. Paul's at Jarrow, though there is no real evidence of this – nor indeed of the popular view that Jarrow was Bede's monastic home. Medieval pilgrims came to St. Paul's to venerate the saint at his shrine and were shown the supposed site of his cell outside the north porch. The relic hunter Alfred Westou, sacristan of Durham Cathedral, stole what he considered to be Bede's bones from his tomb around mid 11th century to add to his collection. However, there is no evidence that the bones were those of Bede, nor that the site was his cell.

More convincing is the use by the author of the Life of Coelfrith of the word *puerulus* (small boy) rather than *puer* (boy) in relating the 'touching and beautiful tale of the abbot and lone boy' singing the hours for by then Bede was nearing the age of majority at fourteen years, no longer a small boy. It was unlikely therefore to be Bede.

In his history of The Lives of the Abbots of Wearmouth, Bede focuses strongly on Wearmouth giving detailed descriptions of the buildings and describing such momentous events as the death of Benedict Biscop and the final departure of Coelfrith with the intimacy of an eye-witness. In his History he makes no mention of a move to Jarrow as a boy or at any time in his life. I agree with the conclusion of the two editors of the most recent edition of the History: 'it must be conceded that the association of Bede with Jarrow is poorly grounded'[10]. Bede would consider the issue of no consequence for he was at pains to stress the unity of the twin monasteries; however, it matters greatly to the folks of Jarrow who are extremely proud of their patron saint and of Bede's World, which attracted 70,000 visitors last year, including 25,000 schoolchildren .

Unlike his abbot, Benedict Biscop, Bede was not a traveller. He visited Lindisfarne to the north to submit his Life of Cuthbert for the approval of the community there; towards the end of his life he went to York to confer with Bishop Egbert but was prevented from making a second visit due to illness so wrote a letter instead, of which more later. He did occasionally visit other local monasteries 'with the permission of my abbot', on one occasion to see Abbot Wichted at an unnamed place but otherwise he 'rested within the monastery walls … serving Christ in secure freedom'. Scholars have pointed to the cloistered nature of his life in which he probably never witnessed an act of violence nor suffered the king's anger; yet in the seclusion of his cell he travelled greater distances in time and place 'than perhaps any other major scholar in Christendom'. For his wide ranging studies he had available books brought back by the founding abbot and bibliophile, Benedict Biscop, from his six journeys to Gaul and Italy. At his disposal was one of the finest libraries in Western Europe comprising some two hundred books, theological, scriptural, scientific and literary; a legacy from the old Roman Empire.

THE ABBOTS

The life of a hermit on Inner Farne or Coquet Island was not for Bede:he felt at home in the heart of his community surrounded by an extensive network of friends and correspondents. Most influential in his life were the abbots, 'the Fathers in Christ', under whom he served: he was fortunate in that, without exception, they proved to be men of the highest calibre and we are fortunate in that we have in Bede's Lives of the Abbots of Wearmouth, an invaluable source of information on the character of the abbots and of everday life in England's largest seventh century monastery. Written by our pioneer historian The Lives became a model for future historians and a fitting prelude to the later History of the English Church and People. The abbots were such key figures in Bede's life that they merit some attention.

BENEDICT BISCOP

It was fitting that Bede was chosen to give the eulogy at Benedict's funeral Mass for it was the abbot's life's work that, above all else, made Bede's achievements possible. Benedict was 'a model leader ... who worked so zealously that we are freed from the need to labour in his way; he journeyed so many times to places across the sea that we, abounding in all the resources of spiritual knowledge, can as a result be at peace within the cloisters of the monastery, with secure freedom to serve Christ'.

Even a brief outline of Benedict's life reveals the wealth of experience he brought with him as founding abbot of Wearmouth in 673.

Born in 628 into a noble Bernician family, probably of Romano-British stock, Baducing, as he was first known according to Wilfrid's biographer Eddius, became a thane and warrior-companion of King Oswin. Aged about 25 years he journeyed to Rome with Wilfrid as companion, the first known Anglo-Saxon pilgrims to the Holy City: there they were mightily impressed by the great stone churches and the tombs of St. Peter and St. Paul and succumbed to the attractions of the cultural life of Rome.

Returning from a second visit to Rome, this time with King Oswin's son Aldfrith, a future king of Northumbria, Baducing stayed at the monastery of St. Honorat on the Isle of Lerins off the coast of Provence; here he stayed two years taking monastic vows and the religious name Benedict in honour of the great Benedict of Nursia, whose Rule Book he was learning to appreciate. His companion on a return from a third visit to Rome was the newly appointed Archbishop of Canterbury, Theodore of Tarsus, for whom Benedict acted as interpreter. Inspired by all he had seen and heard in Rome he was moved to found his own monastery on the north bank of the Wear estuary on seventy hides of land granted him by King Ecgfrith.

On at least three future journeys to Gaul and Rome Benedict amassed the resources on which Bede drew for his studies and which played a key role in the Northumbrian Renaissance. Bede fully appreciated and acknowledged Benedict's contribution, praising his zeal in collecting 'a great variety of spiritual treasures for the new monastery of St. Peter's; a great mass of books of every sort … an abundant supply of relics of the blessed apostles and Christian martyrs … many holy pictures to adorn the church'. All who entered the church 'even those who could not read, were able, whichever way they looked, to contemplate the dear face of Christ and his saints' as they saw fixed to the walls a painting of the Mother of God, one of each of the twelve apostles, scenes from St. John's vision of the Apocalypse, Isaac carrying the wood on which he was to be sacrificed by his father Abraham next to a picture of Christ on the Cross. Later, Abbot Coelfrith hung holy pictures collected on his continental travels on the walls of St. Paul's, Jarrow, where incidentally the foundation stone now set as the keystone of the chancel arch gives us our earliest Saxon dating, 24 April 685. Bede's commentaries on passages from scripture often illustrated his reflections on the pictures: Isaac carrying the wood on which he was to be sacrificed showed him as a prototype of Christ whose picture on the cross was adjacent, thus the Old Testament foreshadowed the New.

Abbot Benedict showed wisdom in his decision-making; he

appointed co-abbots to rule in his long absences 'while transacting the business of the institution' and he chose well in men of the calibre of Eosterwine and Sigfrid; on his death-bed he requested that successors should be elected not on rank but on merit alone as was Eosterwine, even though he was a cousin of Benedict's and had been a thane.

He is to be commended too for his enterprise in importing glaziers from Gaul to glaze the coloured glass windows in the new church, in adopting the latest techniques in making cement and using lathes; Bede's detailed accounts of the materials and processes involved in building indicate not only that as a young, active boy he was a keen observer of the busy scene but that he may also have lent practical help.

Benedict's successful request to Pope Agatho to secure the services of John, the chief cantor of St. Peter's, Rome, to be choirmaster of St. Peter's, Wearmouth, was a real coup. John taught the monks the chant for the liturgical year and the theory and practice of singing aloud, all of which was put in writing and preserved in the library. Singers came from other monasteries to learn from John, who received many invitations to sing elsewhere. Sadly John died on his return journey to Rome and was buried at Tours but not before he had been able to reassure the Pope of the orthodoxy of the Church in England. Bede's enjoyment in observing the regular discipline and singing 'the choir offices daily in church' surely owed much to the talents of archcantor John.

Eosterwine, Benedict's cousin and co-abbot, sounds a most attractive figure, though sadly he ruled for only four years before he died in the devastating plague of 686. In that short time one imagines he made a deep impression on Bede and the brethren for 'his discourse was engaging, his aspect agreeable, his mind cheerful and his hand bountiful'. Though he was abbot he slept in the same dormitory as the other monks and happily joined with them in guiding the plough, winnowing and threshing the corn, beating the corn with a mallet and working in the garden, bakehouse and kitchen; in so doing 'he cultivated the habits of a scholar of industry, patience and obedience'. One wonders whether Bede as a scholar was excused any of these physical labours recommended by the Rule of Benedict[11] and essential to supply the needs of as many as six hundred monks with their needs. Few Saxon settlements of that time would have such a population.

Probably the most influential man in Bede's life was novice-master, abbot of St. Paul's and then Benedict Biscop's successor, Coelfrith. He was 'a man of extraordinary diligence and unrivalled piety', he doubled the size of the library, built more oratories and added to the plate and vestments. He was both 'Father in Christ' and a father-figure to Bede who did not hide his deep affection for him in his moving account of Ceolfrith's departure to die in Rome after twenty eight years service as abbot; in the passage we see Bede's descriptive powers at their best: 'Having sung a solemn Mass in the church of the Virgin and of St. Peter's, Coelfrith blessed the brethren and, in a final farewell, begged forgiveness of any he had treated with unjustifiable vigour. The whole convent accompanied him to the river bank when, receiving in tears the last kiss of peace, all knelt while he prayed aloud. The deacons preceded him bearing a golden cross and holding lighted tapers … the skiff glided swiftly across the Wear, Coelfrith reverenced the cross and, springing on his steed, disappeared. The brethren in mournful silence retraced their steps to the church to intone the Psalm of Terce'. Sadly, Ceolfrith never reached Rome but died at Langres in Burgundy one hundred and fourteen days into the journey.

Bede was much affected by Coelfrith's departure, suffering 'anguish of mind … and having completed the third book of Samuel I thought I would rest awhile but that rest has turned out to be much longer than I had intended'. The separation so disturbed him that it was some time before he could recover the peace of mind he needed 'for searching out the wondrous things of the Scriptures carefully and with my whole soul'.

Coelfrith's successor Huetbert was unanimously elected as 'the assembly was pervaded by the greatest concord'. He, like Bede, had been in the monastery since 'tender childhood' and, having studied in Rome during a long residence, was learned in the arts of reading, writing and church music. Huetbert acquired the nickname Eusebius through his zeal for piety and was the writer of a collection of Latin riddles, a genre popular among Anglo-Saxons newly discovering the fascination of the written as well as the spoken word. The riddles often referred to writing:

In kind simple am I nor gain from anywhere wisdom,
But now each man of wisdom always traces my footsteps.
Habiting now broad earth, high heaven I formerly wandered;
Though I seem to be white, I leave black traces behind me.[12]

The answer is a pen whereas the preparation of parchment is described thus:

A life-thief stole my worldly strength,
Ripped off flesh and left me skin,
Dipped me in water and drew me out,
Stretched me bare in the light sun…

Answers to other riddles were as diverse as a whelk, a cloud, a chicken, the moon and an organ. Such puzzles give deep insights into the questing Anglo-Saxon mind. One can readily visualise the scholar Bede having a close rapport with brother 'Eusebius'; indeed he dedicated two of his works to him, his commentary on the Apocalypse and his scientific treatise *De Temporum Ratione.* Huetbert was abbot for the rest of Bede's life.

There is no doubt Bede's achievements owed much to the high quality of the abbots, 'rulers of this monastery in which I delight to serve the Divine Goodness'. Much credit too reflects on a system which brought men of learning and personal sanctity to the fore on a free vote in a time when rank and patronage were the norm.

FRIENDS

Throughout his life Bede was encouraged and supported by a network of friends both within and outside the cloister. Apart from the aforementioned abbots two of the brethren were especially close. Wilbert was a loving brother who took down Bede's translation of St. John's Gospel as he lay dying. Cuthbert, a pupil and later abbot, wrote the most moving account of his master's death very much in the style of Bede himself and felt that 'the whole race of the English in all provinces wherever they are found should thank God for giving them Bede'.

The affectionate manner of Bede's greetings to his correspondents illustrates the bonds of friendship that existed between them. One of his books, *De Arte Metrica*, was addressed, rather curiously, to 'my dearest son and fellow deacon Cuthbert'; Plegwine, monk of Hexham, was 'most loving and dearest brother'. The Verse Life of Cuthbert was written for the bishop John: 'My most beloved Lord in Christ... how much I am moved by your love and delighted by your presence'. In 708 he sent his commentary on the Apocalypse to 'my most beloved brother' Huetbert then studying in Rome. 'Such greetings reveal a warmth and intimacy between early Anglo-Saxon monks of a kind the monks of the twelfth century thought they were pioneering ... the Normans and Cistercians were conscious of their friendships, it seems that the monks of Bede's time took them for granted'[13]. Bede was on close terms with John and Acca, early bishops of Hexham and therefore the leading churchmen in Northumbria.

John, better known as St. John of Beverley, visited Bede's monastery at least twice to ordain him deacon c.691 and priest c.702: it may well have been on these occasions that he told Bede about the school of Theodore at Canterbury and the monastery at Whitby, as related in the History; he had been a student monk in both places until his appointment as bishop of Hexham in 686.

Bede enjoyed a long and fruitful friendship with John's successor, Acca, 'by letter when absent and by converse when present'. In encouraging Bede to write a commentary on Luke, Acca addresses him 'his most reverend brother in Christ and fellow-priest'. Bede refers to Acca as 'the most dear and beloved of all the bishops who dwell in the lands' and mentions him in several works. Acca had trained under Bosa, bishop of York, 'a man of great holiness and humility' and then under Wilfrid whom he accompanied to Rome visiting Willibrord in Frisia on the way. It was probably Acca who gave Bede information on Bosa and the Frisian mission for the History. Bede greatly admired Acca for he was a good musician who enriched Hexham with works of art and a fine library, relics and raised altars. Acca was orthodox in faith and most skilled in sacred letters. When in 731 Bishop Acca was driven from his see in a dispute Bede sent him his tract *De Templo* 'to alleviate daily the present troubles of temporal affairs'.

Bede's relationship with Wilfrid, bishop of Hexham from 705 to 709, was different. The two men did meet when Wilfrid asked

Bede the truth about the virginity of Aethelthryth (Etheldreda), who was the wife of king Ecgfrith but left him to enter the double monastery of Ely.

Bede treats Wilfrid ,not with an active dislike for that would be foreign to his nature, rather as some historians have suggested, coolly, with a curious detachment. His greetings show respect but lack the warmth shown to others; 'most revered Bishop Wilfrid' and 'Bishop Wilfrid of blessed memory'.

The two men had much in common: both were monks zealous for the conversion of Northumbria and thoroughly Roman in outlook; both loved the Gregorian chant and saw the need for order and discipline in monastic life rather than the 'erratic ebullience of Celtic saintliness', Bede preferred the unworldliness of bishops like Aidan and Cuthbert to those like Wilfrid who 'decked out the superb edifice of the finest church north of the Alps (Hexham Abbey) with splendid gold and silver ornaments, precious stones and silks and purples for the altar'[14]. Certainly Bede would feel badly let down by bishop Wilfrid when he failed to support him against a charge of heresy brought by a monk of Hexham. Bede implies criticism of Wilfrid in his Life of Cuthbert when, after the death of Cuthbert, 'so great a blast of trial beat upon the church that many of the brethren chose to depart'. Had Wilfrid so upset the monks of Lindisfarne by imposing his authority in his zeal for order and discipline? When Eadberht succeeded Wilfrid as bishop 'the storms and disturbances were driven away, then was there a vision of peace'.

There is no doubt the warmth Bede felt for John and Acca was lacking in his relationship with the able statesman-prelate Wilfrid, a fascinating and controversial giant in the story of the conversion of Northumbria.

Many of 'the innumerable witnesses' who gave Bede information for his detailed History were monks of his own community; they were now of advanced age but their memories were still fresh as they recalled experiences elsewhere. Bede was thus able to record for posterity a rich fund of stories: the incident of the hostility of the rustics and the prayers of the youth Cuthbert saving the monks being blown out to sea from the mouth of the Tyne was told to him by ‘the holy priest Ingwald from our monastery at Monkwearmouth who had heard the miracle from Cuthbert himself’; the miracle of how Aidan had foretold and calmed a storm by giving seafarers holy oil to pour on the water was ‘no groundless fable for it was related to me by a most faithful priest of our church who heard it from Utta’, later abbot of Gateshead. Incidentally, this reference is the only evidence we have for the existence of an Anglo Saxon monastery at Gateshead. Bede’s account of the Irish hermit Fursey in the fenlands of east Anglia and his vivid visions of heaven and hell came from ‘yet another old brother of our monastery who is still alive and who testifies that he knew a truthful and devout man who heard it from the mouth of Fursey himself’. The final miracle in Bede’s Life of Cuthbert relates how a ‘good priest of this monastery of Jarrow’ witnessed the cure of a disfiguring swelling on the face of Felgild, a hermit of Inner Farne, by the application of pieces of calfskin dipped in water which Cuthbert had fixed to the walls of the cell to keep out draughts.

Bede was friendly with several monks of Lindisfarne who had known Cuthbert personally for he had died only thirty years previously: he heard how the novice monk Cuthbert had been struck down by the plague at Melrose from Herefrith who was there at the time; from Baldhelm, ‘now a priest of the church of Lindisfarne’, he learned how Cuthbert cured the dying servant of one of the king’s bodyguards by giving him water to drink which he had blessed; the tale of the visitors storm-bound on Inner Farne because they neglected to cook the goose as ordered by Cuthbert ‘came to me not from any casual source but from one of that very party, the venerable monk and priest Cynemund who is still alive and renowned for his great holiness and great age’. In his Prologue to the Life of Cuthbert Bede thanked Bishop Eadfrith for ordering ‘our holy brother Godfrith, the sacristan, to put my name in the register of your congregation even now’ therefore ensuring he would be remembered in daily Masses. The Life is written ‘in brotherly compliance with your wishes’ and read for two days before the elders so that ‘what was false could be amended and what was true confirmed’. Bede’s relations with the monks of Lindisfarne seem to be as friendly as those with his community.

Scattered references elsewhere point to information gathered from many sources: the abbot of Partney described Paulinus to him as told by an old man baptised by the first bishop of Northumbria; a monk of the monastery at Dacre related how one of the brothers was cured of a tumour of the eye by applying to it a relic of Cuthbert, some hair from the holy man's head. Two stories came from Pecthelm, Bishop of Whithorn, one about miracles worked by the relics of Haeddi, Bishop of Winchester, and another about a thegn of the King of Mercia who was shown the record of another man's sins before his death yet failed to mend his ways. Bede comments: 'I have told the story in a straightforward way, as I heard it from the venerable bishop, to further the salvation of those who may read it or hear it.'

One visitor to Northumbria in c.703 deserves special mention.

When Adamnan, Columba's biographer and ninth abbot of Iona, came to visit King Aldfrith he presented him with a copy of his book, *De Locis Sanctis*, On the Holy Places, in gratitude for the release of Irish captives taken by the previous King Ecgfrith on his raids into Ireland. It is very probable that Adamnan met Bede in his monastery; in any case, a copy of the book fell into Bede's hands.

Adamnan acquired the information for his book from the Gaulish bishop Arculf, a pilgrim returning from the Holy Land, whose ship was driven north by Atlantic gales, and eventually arrived at Iona. The scholarly abbot at once realised the immense value of Arculf's experiences and recorded them on wax tablets and then in book form for posterity. In such serendipitous ways was knowledge in the early medieval world transmitted.

One can readily appreciate the eagerness with which Bede would study the book for it contained a recent and first-hand account of places intimate to the life of Christ, especially valuable to those who lived so far away from Palestine. Previously, knowledge was scant and derived from earlier historians such as Josephus and Eucharius of Lyons but here Bede could delight in eye-witness accounts of places and treasures visited as recently as his own boyhood: the church of the Holy Sepulchre, the Basilica of Constantine on the site where the crosses of the Lord and the two thieves had been found; the chalice from the Last Supper 'with the measure of a Gaulish pint'; the church of the Ascension where pilgrims could see the Lord's footprints; Jerusalem crowded with people, camels, horses, asses laden with merchandise, where stinking streets were flushed clean by torrents of rain; descriptions of Bethlehem, Nazareth and the River Jordan[15].

Bede later quoted from *De Locis Sanctis* in his Commentary on Acts and in his History where chapters 16 and 17 are respectively entitled: 'The Sites of Our Lord's Birth, Passion and Resurrection' and 'The Site of Our Lord's Ascension'; he thus ensured that the knowledge newly gained reached a wider audience.

Knowledge fortuitously gained thus enabled Bede with his keen intellect and disciplined imagination to travel great distances in his mind while remaining cloistered in his library and cell. His frequent references to the city of Rome and the Mediterranean lands which he saw as the centre of the cultural word point to his fascination with the geography of places as distant and exotic as India, Egypt, Arabia and Judea. In his commentary on the Song of Songs he tells us he learned about the trees and aromatic herbs from 'the books of the ancients', notably Pliny's Natural History; elsewhere, he describes the properties of the cedar tree for book-binding and the ways dark Ethiopians are presented in wall-paintings.

Bede was no traveller; Lindisfarne to the north and York to the south were his farthest journeying. He saw his ministry as essentially literary, winning souls for Christ by faithfully transmitting knowledge of the past about biblical places and peoples and in so doing, revealing a sense of continuity of past and present.

THE SAINTS[16]

Visitors to Bede's tomb in the Galilee Chapel of Durham Cathedral will read the inscription from his commentary on the book of Revelation 'Christ is the morning star who, when the night of this world is past, will bring his saints to the promise of the light of life and everlasting day'.

Bede's lively sense of the communion of saints meant that all saints were 'alive unto God'; those now enjoying the seventh age of heaven were readily available to help, encourage, and edify all who are still in the sixth age of their earthly pilgrimage. Throughout his writings and homilies Bede reveals himself equally at home in the company of holy men and women from biblical times and in his own lifetime. Be they king like Oswald or cowherd like Caedmon they were living proof that the message of salvation actually worked in transforming human beings into likenesses of Christ, often manifest in signs and wonders. Gifted with the insights of a theologian and historian he tells with relish the many tales of the miracles worked by such virtuous men as Aidan and Cuthbert, sure signs of God's blessing on them despite their human frailty, but he also quotes Augustine of Canterbury in warning that these are not occasions for vainglory for 'true disciples ought not to rejoice except in the good they have in common with all the elect whose names are written in heaven'. Especially praised are the virtues found in the Beatitudes as seen in Aidan, 'love of peace, charity, temperance and humility' as well as the 'devotion, chastity, peace and charity … after the example of the primitive church' of Abbess Hilda of Whitby.

Such men and women, along with many others in that golden age of saints, were moved by grace to a degree of sanctity whereby they were able to become key players in God's plan for the conversion of England.

The incorrupt state of the body after death was for Bede a sure sign of the sanctity of the deceased: on elevation from the tomb eleven years after he died Cuthbert's body was intact and whole, the joints of his limbs flexible, 'as if he was asleep'; the body of the Irish preacher and visionary Fursa was found incorrupt after four years; the incorrupt state of the Queen and Abbess Aethelthryth was a sign of her virginity of body; the arm of Oswald was still incorrupt at Bamburgh when Bede was writing. Preservation from the usual processes of decay were seen as a sign that the saints had successfully completed their pilgrimage to the City of God and were now eager to intercede for those still on their journey that Christ be propitious to them.

In his sermons and commentaries Bede refers frequently to the saints of the New Testament. Peter and Paul, patrons of his own twin monasteries and of Canterbury, are dealt with in detail, in both the Lives of the Abbots and in The History. Devotion to these two models of Christian living was encouraged by 'the abundant supply of relics of the blessed apostles and Christian martyrs' brought back from Rome by Benedict Biscop. For Bede 'Peter was a son of the Holy Spirit who followed the Lord with a wise and good simplicity'. In the History Peter is the focus of pilgrimage to Rome, the door-keeper of heaven, who turned the decision of Oswin at the Synod of Whitby: in a commentary he explains 'Bar-Jonah' as 'son of a dove', for the dove is a very simple creature and Peter followed the Lord with a wise and good simplicity. He calls Peter the 'son of the Holy Spirit' who 'affirms Christ as the Son of God'.

Bede's professionalism is revealed in his comment on his translation into Latin of the Life of Anastasius, Persian monk and martyr (d.628): 'A book on the life and passion of St. Anastasius which was badly translated from the Greek and worse amended by some unskilful person … I have corrected as best I could to clarify the meaning'. The monks of Monkwearmouth / Jarrow celebrated Anastasius' feast day on January 22, the day of his martyrdom; thus we see how Bede's work helped to bring an eastern saint, hitherto relatively unknown, into the heart of the monastic liturgy.

The Life of Felix (d.431) who was tortured for his faith but survived, had been well written in verse by his contemporary and admirer, Paulinus of Nola. Bede simplified the text and put it in prose, 'prose is more suitable than verse for untrained readers so it seemed right to make plain the story of the holy confessor in prose for the benefit of many'. Making better known the deeds of good men and women is the motivation for all Bede's works.

Foremost among the saints was Mary, about whom Bede spoke and wrote with warmth and delight in sermons and commentaries. Devotion to Mary was unusual at this time. There is only one place in the History where her name is mentioned, St. Mary's Chapel at Monkwearmouth. No holy Anglo-Saxon women were named in her honour: the Hail Mary was still centuries away. Mary's time really came in the twelfth century, spearheaded by Bernard and the Cistercians.

For Bede, Mary was a second Eve, the chosen Mother of God. In a homily he said: 'Just as sin began from women so too it was fitting that blessings should spring from women and that life which was lost through the deception of one woman should be given back to the world by these two women, Mary and Elizabeth, who rival each other in giving praise'. In a commentary on Luke he rephrases the Magnificat; 'I offer up all the strength of my soul in the thanksgiving and praise. In my joy I pour out all my life, all my feeling, all my understanding in contemplating the greatness of him who is without end. My spirit rejoices in the eternal divinity of Jesus my Saviour'. This same prayer was sung daily in the Office of Vespers, an excellent and salutary custom giving time for quiet reflection on the Incarnation and the example of the Mother of God.

Elsewhere Bede praises Mary's obedience at the Annunciation and her humility at the Purification; in a sermon on the Nativity Mary is 'the steadfast company of spiritual guides, the virginal beauty of the church'. For Bede, the saints are holy through their intimate association with Christ and no one was more intimate than the Virgin Mary who bore Him in her womb.

Bede recommended prayer both for the dead and to the dead who 'having entered in through the right side' are close to Christ and eager to intercede: 'Through the intercession of the saints who shine, not through their own power but from him, Christ will be propitious to the faithful when they raise their minds to heavenly desires and recognise his glory in the words and deeds of the preceding fight'.

To keep the memory of the saints fresh, Bede composed a calendar of saints commemorating the lives and deaths of the Virgin Mary, the apostles, martyrs of the early church and the recent dead like Cuthbert and Benedict Biscop. This martyrology gave the saints a new significance in the history of salvation and made them readily available throughout the liturgical year, most especially on their feast days when we celebrate their heavenly birthdays. He wrote; 'I have carefully tried to record everything I could learn not only of the date but also by what kind of combat and under what judge they overcame the world'.

THE EXEGETE[17]

Bede is known today primarily as a historian but this is not how he saw himself: 'I have spent all my life applying myself entirely to the study of the Scriptures'. The Bible was the focus of his life for it contained the Word of God and he was a servant of the Word. The bible was 'the Bread of Life'. Of the thirty nine books he lists at the end of the History twenty five are scriptural commentaries or homilies where the emphasis is on compiling 'short extracts from the Venerable Fathers on Holy Scripture and commenting on and interpreting their meaning'. From the 8th to the 15th century Bede as an authority on the Bible ranked second only to the Latin Fathers on whom he acknowledged he drew extensively: 'to read the Fathers is to look upon the face of God'.

Fearing that history in its seventh age was reaching its climax and that the eighth age of eternity was about to dawn, Bede wrote with a sense of urgency: it seems strange to say it of an unworldly monk working quietly away in his cell but Bede worked with a sense of tearing hurry ... there was no time to be lost.

It is well to remember that the production of books from pelts and calfskins to be scribed by calligraphers was indeed a labour of love. The Bible had not yet been divided into chapters and verses: there were no indices or cross references or any cataloguing system.

His target audience shifted in his lifetime: at first he wrote text books on grammar, spelling, metre and compilation for the use of the boys in the monastic schools so that they could learn to read and write. Next he turned to commentaries on Acts, Luke and Mark and later to some books of the Old Testament Genesis, Proverbs, Samuel, The Song of Songs and Habakkuk. Finally he focussed on translating scriptures and prayers into English; St. John's Gospel, the *Pater* and the *Credo* for those newly converted who needed instruction and spiritual ministration, an urgent need. He wrote for all who preached the Word of God, 'not only bishops, priests and deacons, or even abbots, but for all the faithful, however small their house may be, are rightly called shepherds insofar as they rule over that house with watchful care'. He deplored the reluctance of the English to learn Latin, they having received the seed of Faith cherished it only lukewarmly so far as reading is concerned; 'I have collected from the books of the Fathers whatever can instruct the untrained reader'.

Sending his friend Acca a commentary on Samuel, Bede explains his fourfold approach to exegesis: it is historical, as when the people of Israel saved from Egypt made a tabernacle for the Lord in the wilderness; it is moral when it gives instruction 'my little children, let us not love in word nor in tongue but in word and deed'; it points to higher things and future rewards, 'Blessed are the pure in heart for they shall see God'; It is allegorical when Christ or the sacraments are represented by mystical words or events, as when Isaiah says 'there shall come forth a rod out of the stem of Jesse and a flower shall rise up out of its root' meaning 'the Blessed Virgin Mary shall be born of the root of David and Christ shall be born of her stock'.

Such interpretations helped to make the scriptural passages relevant and meaningful for both readers and listeners so that Christ might be more fully present in the lives of the people of England in his time.

In his commentaries on the first book of Samuel, Bede reveals both his familiarity with everyday monastic life and his flair for illustrating quite difficult concepts with homely analogies.

We are nourished with food cooked in the kitchen on a griddle when we read superficially, and understand literally, the words of Holy Scripture; upon food cooked in the frying pan when we frequently turn the words over in our mind and reflect on their deeper meaning; and, afterwards, we search in the oven when, by exerting our minds, we lay hold of those mystical things in the scriptures we cannot now see but hope to see in the future.

The analogy of the spiritual kitchen came naturally to Bede whose whole life was devoted to the preparation of spiritual food to feed the souls of people hitherto nourished on a diet of paganism; it was an analogy to be used just as effectively by the 12th century Aelred of Rievaulx, as we shall see.

A recurring theme in all Bede's commentaries is that we are a pilgrim people for 'the saint is no denizen of earth but a traveller and stranger … The Ascension to heaven of the Mediator between God and man shows us that the door to the heavenly homeland lies open … he urges us strive as best we may to speed to the endless happiness of that homeland … in that supernal country where the eyes of the saints behold Christ the King in his beauty, the grace of divine and fraternal love shines throughout and love alone reigns'.

Bede saw the church on earth as God's provisional temple: 'We should rejoice that we have become the temple of God by our baptism … daily being built up by the King of Peace, its redeemer'. As in Vatican II Bede preached the doctrine of the priesthood of all the baptised for it was not to bishops and priests but to all God's children that the apostle Peter was speaking when he said: 'The church is Jacob's ladder pitched between heaven and earth … here and now it shares in the worship of the inhabitants of heaven … we are not permitted to doubt that where the mysteries of the Lord's body and blood are being enacted, a gathering of the citizens on high is present … hence we must strive to be mindful of the presence of angels'.

Bede quoted Peter: 'you are a chosen generation, a royal priesthood (1 Peter 2$_9$).' All the faithful who keep watch over the little ones are properly called pastors. He recognised that some who lived before the era of the Gospel lived the life of the Gospel.

Bede's homilies, from which the preceding quotations are taken, were probably not delivered from a pulpit during Mass but intended as subjects for public reading or private meditation but then, as now, they were based directly on the Gospel reading of the day.

He considered that a spiritual rather than a literal interpretation of the Old Testament would make sense to 8th century Christians. The Old Testament, he concluded was written largely in code. His claim to fame lies not in originality as few of his points are original to him, but as a bridge where, through his unrivalled knowledge of the Fathers, he was able to keep the medieval world, and ours, in touch with the patristic heritage.

The fact that Bede's style of exegesis is no longer fashionable[18] must not make us forget that in his time and for some centuries he was probably the world's leading scriptural scholar, especially knowledgeable on the Old Testament. He was filled with delight and wonder as he discovered the story of redemption; his commentaries were tools for conversion, 'windows through which the eastern light of the early church could fall on the Sacred Page newly opened for the western darkness of Anglo-Saxon England'.[19]

He was filled with wonder and delight as he discovered the story of redemption.

THE HISTORIAN

Bede was primarily an exegist but is best known as a historian for his masterpiece 'A History of the English Church and People': it is 'like one of great dark-age brooches for it combines a certain grandeur and sweep of overall design with the utmost delicacy of detail'. Bede is 'a brilliant example to all who, in dark ages, set themselves the task of handing on the glimmering torch of learning to coming generations, through the Ecclesiastical History he himself lighted a new flame'. The survival of some 160 manuscript copies in this country and on the continent where the book was much in demand, prove its enduring and widespread popularity.

Bede's pioneering work in English history encouraged a growing interest in the subject resulting in King Alfred's Old English translation of the History, in the Anglo-Saxon Chronicles, and the works of William of Malmesbury.

The History was a fitting climax to a lifetime's work in chronology and hagiography which had already produced *De Tempore, De Tempore Majore* (The Greater Chronicle) where he computed time and dates, and the invaluable Lives of the Abbots of Wearmouth; its final form and shape was much influenced by Bede's knowledge and love of the Bible.

Bede viewed history through the eyes of a man of God: it was to be presented for the moral good of the reader or listener. In his preface to the History he makes it clear that he writes to oblige esteemed patrons like the most glorious King Coelwulf, to inform posterity and to give models for behaviour for 'if history records good things of good men the thoughtful hearer is encouraged to imitate what is good; or if it records evil of wicked men the devout religious listener or reader is encouraged to avoid all that is sinful and perverse and to follow what he knows to be good and pleasing to God'.

Bede sees himself as a *verax historicus* whose task it is to relate with simplicity and humility good things and bad. The History uses the lowly style of the *sermo humilis* of men like Gregory the Great, whom Bede so admired and called 'our apostle'; the language should be that of 'our fishermen', the first apostles as Jerome observed. Just as the Gospel writers proclaimed the highest truths with the lowliest words so Bede aimed to clarify and glorify the works of God among men in simple style.[20]

This is not history as it is perceived today where the past is recorded, interpreted and analysed with as much objectivity as possible though some subjective judgements must always be involved.

Bede sees in his charting of the history of the English people from Caesar's invasion in 55 B.C. to his own time as a progression from the darkness of heathenism to the light of Christ's Gospel; it is, in effect, a record of salvation history, evidence of God's providence at work. One consequence of this approach is that life in Anglo Saxon England was cast in a more roseate glow than was the case, there are more holy men and women than rough and barbaric warriors, even the infamous Penda escapes lightly. Yet while God rewards the good he does not fail to punish the wicked. A passionate traditionalist with a moral viewpoint of history Bede records how King Ecgfrith of Northumbria and his army were slaughtered at Nechtansmere fighting the Picts as a punishment for previously terrorising the friendly Irish in his earlier campaigns; he agreed with Gildas that the conquest of the British by the barbaric tribes from across the North Sea was God's vengeance on a people 'corrupted by affluence and luxury and given to envy, drunkenness and crime … even the Lord's own flock and pastors were guilty'. Virulent plagues were 'ordained by the will of God so that evil might fall upon the miscreants'. The twelve hundred monks of Bangor, who refused to yield to Augustine's demands, were killed while praying by King Ethelfrid's army and by divine judgement as 'faithless Britons' who were condemned for failing to convert the pagan English.

Bede has little to say on the nature of paganism and considered that persuasion by teaching and example rather than coercion was the best way to convert folk from sacrificing to the old gods and having faith in druids and amulets.

There was innocence deriving from ignorance about paganism but heresies were utterly condemned. Pelagianism was noxious and abominable and Arianism 'a deadly poison infesting these islands' even though they were endemic in the second and third centuries and therefore no longer live issues, but there was a fear they might raise their head again.

For Bede, orthodoxy, unity with Rome and the universality of the church were all important.

It was for these reasons that Bede seems to some to be obsessed with the issue of the date of Easter when even the views of the Celtic clergy were sacrificed in the interests of unity. At the royal court of Northumbria King Oswin feasted as he observed the Roman dating, while his queen fasted as she followed the Irish tradition. If Christians could not agree on the date of the most important feast in their calendar, it augured badly for unity for 'Bede knew the western church for what it was; a confederation of churches, often fissile, divergent, ignorant and passionately local'.[21]

The focus throughout The History is on the church in Northumbria in a wider English context; scant attention is given to Mercia and the other kingdoms which are as subsidiary to Northumbria as the British and Irish are to the English. However, accepting that this is ecclesiastical and not social, economic or political history it is churlish to criticize, for to gather, evaluate, select and interpret a vast amount of material from a variety of sources and weave it into an orderly, coherent and eminently readable story was achievement possible only to one of Bede's particular genius. His lucid Latin, in contrast to the exaggerated style of his contemporary Aldhelm of Malmesbury, as much as the vivid story telling, with frequent use of direct speech, pleased both the ears of the illiterate listener and the eyes of the educated few who could read. Bede was a literary brother of the author of the epic poem Beowulf which may well have been composed in Northumbria in his time.

Cuthbert's encounters with the otters on the beach at Coldingham, the flight of the sparrow through the darkened and royal hall and Coifi's desecration of the pagan shrine, the illiterate cowherd

Caedmon of Whitby singing of the glories of creation, the visions of Drythelm who prayed waist deep in the icy waters of the Tweed below Melrose, and many other tales are pearls of imaginative story-telling recounted by Bede with obvious pleasure and read today with much delight.

Two further considerations help us to a fuller appreciation of the value of Bede's 'masterpiece of Dark Age historiography' which rightly earned him the title 'Father of English History'.

Without the History we would know little or nothing about our early English history, or the Anglo-Saxon missions to Germany and Frisia led by Boniface and Willibrord, or such early saints as Aidan, Cuthbert, Oswald and Hilda. Our literature would be much the poorer without his wondrous tales and miracle stories.

We know the History was several years in the making, at least six, and was prepared in harsh physical working conditions; light supplied by candles or oil lamps, no spectacles to salve tired eyes, temperatures so low that the abbot Cuthbert apologised to the German bishop Lul for the small number of books he sent for 'during the past winter the island of our race has been savagely oppressed with cold and ice so that the hands of the scribes become sluggish'. With their exposed situation near the mouths of the Wear and Tyne the monasteries were wide open to the icy blasts of winter from the North Sea. One can readily empathise with the scribe who notes informally in the margins of his manuscript: 'the lamp is not very bright' or 'I do not feel very well today' or 'the sailor is not more glad to reach harbour than the weary scribe to arrive at the last line of his manuscript'.[22]

POLYMATH

Bede was a monastic rather than a scholastic educator, whose subjects were chiefly biblical and historical rather than philosophy, abstract theology, medicine or law; his lifetime of study gave him a breadth of knowledge remarkable for his time. In all his writings, especially in *De Rerum Natura* (On the Nature of Things), he showed himself a master of many disciplines, chronology, geography, poetry, natural sciences and computation. His mastery of astronomy and mathematics made him the leading scholar of his time in those fields; for several centuries he was Europe's authority on chronology.

It was the Scythian monk Dionysius Exiguus c. A.D. 500 who first conceived the idea of dating time to before and after the birth of Christ; it was Bede who regularised the custom still with us today of using the BC\AD format.

He sets his history in a geographical context. The Britain he describes is rich in grain and timber, with good pasturage for cattle and draught animals; its rivers and seas abound in fish, seals, dolphins, even whales; the land has rich veins of many metals, copper, lead, iron, zinc, silver with much jet of fine quality. Hibernia (Ireland) is even more favoured for snow rarely lies so there is no need to store hay in summer for winter use or to build stables for beasts. There are no reptiles or snakes, the island abounds in milk and honey with plenty of birds, fish and vines.

From travellers like Arculf and from books Bede learnt that in the summer the sun over the minaret in Jerusalem makes no shadow and that the seas beyond Thule (Orkneys?) freeze in winter. Quoting Virgil he concluded that there were five climatic zones and, good teacher that he was, illustrated his theory with a simple analogy: imagine that you are sitting around a fire in the hall in the cold of winter, if you are too far away you are frozen, if you are too near you burn but between the two are temperate zones where you are warm and comfortable, 'two zones vouchsafed by the grace of God to feeble mortals', he concludes, paraphrasing Virgil in the Georgics.

He knew too that the length of the seasons and the hours of day and night varied according to place and time of year.

Astronomy was a keen interest; from his observations of the sun and stars he deduced that the earth was not a flat circle like a shield but a circle rounded on every side like a ball used in playing games, in fact a globe.

Bede was an authority too on tides and compiled tide-tables, essential for monks living by tidal estuaries like Jarrow slake, and on Lindisfarne, as modern visitors are only too aware. He noted a close correlation between phases of the moon and the strength of the tides; a full moon brought the highest tides at the time of spring and autumn equinoxes whereas a waning moon meant low tides and exposed mud flats. He recognised that 'when the tide is flowing at one point along the shores of Britain it is ebbing at another'. His tide-tables are testament to his powers of observation and deduction and were for many years a valuable navigational guide for sailors.

Noting the scarcity of birds in winter he concluded as he saw gannets and cormorants diving into the water that they hibernated on the bed of the ocean; it was not until the 18th century that the first ideas on bird migration were put forward by naturalists like Gilbert White.

The concept of time held a special fascination: it was divided into moments, hours, days, months, years, centuries and ages. Five ages had already passed into divisions marked by Creation, the Flood, Abraham, David, the Captivity and the Birth of Christ. The sixth age was the present, the seventh the Age of the Blessed to the Second Coming of Christ, the eighth was the eternal bliss of heaven.

THE LETTER TO EGBERT[23]

Bede ends his history c.731 on a hopeful note: the Picts are at peace with the English and 'are glad to be united in Catholic peace and truth with the universal church; the Scots (Irish) living in Britain are 'content with their own territories'; in Northumbria peace and prosperity prevailed for many 'both noble and simple have laid aside their weapons and taken monastic vows rather than study the arts of war'. Bede expresses his deep sense of gratitude for the many blessings God in his providence has bestowed on the nation by quoting Psalm 29: 'Let the multitude of isles be glad thereof and give thanks at the remembrance of his holiness'.

Such sentiments are in marked contrast with the anxieties about the future expressed in his letter to bishop Egbert of York written in the autumn of 734. Bede had visited Egbert in the previous year and intended a second visit but was prevented by illness from travelling. Egbert was a former pupil, a cousin of the king, and the leader of Northumbria's foremost school of learning, yet Bede wrote forcibly and frankly reaffirming the message of his History that God's blessing rested on those like Aidan and Cuthbert who followed the Gospel message and on the example of the apostles rather than self-seeking; the letter was, in a sense, a colophon to The History.

It is a challenging letter laying several charges: too often the clergy were lax and greedy, failing not only to preach the Gospel freely and lay hands on the faithful, but even more seriously, 'after accepting money from the hearers, forbidden by Our Lord, they despise the ministry of the Word which the Lord ordered them to perform'; especially neglected were the villages and hamlets of our people situated in dense woodlands and inaccessible mountains. Instruction in the faith and the sacraments were, after baptism, a matter of chance.

Bede condemned the recent growth of spurious monasteries on land bought from the king where communities of married laymen lived with their families who were exempt from taxes and military service; they even had these privileges confirmed by abbots and bishops. Such places became abodes of sloth and vice and Bede asked for their abolition.

He felt strongly that the pastoral needs of his fellow Northumbrians were being neglected: the bishop should ordain more priests and teachers who would visit outlying villages to teach the unlettered the *Pater* and the *Credo* in their own tongue and behave in an exemplary way: more bishops should be appointed, as many as twelve, within the York diocese, using monasteries as Episcopal seats, thus York would become an archbishopric to balance Canterbury. He criticised existing bishops who were rumoured to be given up to jests, laughter feasting and drunkenness instead of feeding their souls with heavenly sacrifices. He drew attention to the *Regula Pastoralis* of Pope Gregory who advised: 'Hear the Word of God and keep it in good lives. Priests and bishops are spiritual shepherds of the church chiefly ordained to preach the mysteries of the Word of God and to show the wonderful things they have learned in Scripture to the admiration of the hearers'.

In the same letter Bede could write of the 'innumerable blameless people of chaste conduct, boys and girls, young men and maidens, old men and women' who were fully worthy to participate week by week in the observances of the heavenly mysteries.

Bede's letter to Egbert was his last major piece of writing: the fears he expresses for the future of the church in Northumbria are not just the gloomy prognostications of a dying old man, though that may have been part of it, but are genuine anxieties over the success of his life's work, the conversion of his fellow-countrymen to Christianity.

It may well be that Bede's candid letter bore fruit. In 735 Egbert became Archbishop of York and held the office until 766. Alcuin described him as *rector clarissimus* and *doctor egregius*, a worthy successor to Bede as a teacher, and praised him for his generosity and devotion to the poor.

A HEAVENLY BIRTHDAY

As with the deaths of Boisil and Cuthbert, we have a moving account of Bede's 'passing from this world': it was written in language worthy of Bede by another Cuthbert, a pupil of Bede and future abbot, in a letter to his fellow-teacher and friend Cuthwin.[24]

After the First Vespers of the Feast of the Ascension on the evening of May 26, 735, Bede's condition worsened. Despite weakness and breathing difficulties he remained 'cheerful and happy' giving lessons to his students, singing psalms, meditating on the scriptures and thanking God with arms outstretched. Being well versed in our native songs he composed a verse for us in our own tongue on the dread departure of the soul from the body. 'When he reached the words in the antiphon "do not leave us orphans" he broke into tears and wept much … we who heard sorrowed and wept with him'. He quoted St. Ambrose: 'I have not lived so that I am ashamed to live among you and I do not fear to die for the God we serve is gracious'.

Latin and English were by turns on the lips of the dying Bede, showing his faithful love of the Catholic Church in general, and of the English nation in particular.
He persisted with his tasks of translating St. John's gospel into old English and correcting extracts from the words of Bishop Isidore of Seville (560-635) 'for I cannot have my children learning what is

not true and losing their labour on this after I have gone'. Bede knew the end was near.

Cuthbert followed Bede's practice of heightening the drama of a situation by using direct speech in recording the final exchanges between the dying Bede and his scribe, Wilbert: 'I do not know how long I can continue for my Lord may call me in a short while' – 'There is still one chapter missing in the book' – 'It is no trouble, take your pen and write quickly' – 'Dear Master, there is one sentence unfinished' – 'Very well write it down' – 'It is finished, *Consummatum est*', Bede echoed Christ's last words on the Cross.

Summoning the priests of the monastery he distributed his worldly wealth among them, 'the gifts God has given me', pepper, linen and incense. He spoke to each one in turn requesting them to offer Masses for him. They were all sad and wept but heartened when he told them: 'I have had a long life and the merciful Judge had ordered it graciously. The time of my departure is on hand, and my soul longs to see Christ my King in His Beauty'.

Bede asked that his head be raised 'for it would give me great joy to sit facing the holy place where I used to pray' – thus on the floor of his cell he chanted: "Glory to the Father, the Son and the Holy Spirit' to its end and breathed his last as Ascension Day dawned.

Bede spent his last hours among his friends translating the Bible and then, unexpectedly, breaking into the poetic idiom of his ancestors; a perfect example of the range of activity and the unruffled temper of his life and death.[25]

Writing in the late eleventh century Symeon of Durham tells the macabre and unedifying tale of how Alfred Westou, a married priest of Durham Cathedral, stole the bones he believed to be Bede's from the grave at St. Paul's, Jarrow, and placed them beside the bones of Cuthbert, Acca, Boisil, Ebba, Bilfrith and others in the Cathedral to add to his own considerable collection as a relic-hunter. Westou declared: 'the same shrine which contains the holy body of father Cuthbert contains also the bones of the teacher and monk Bede. Let no one seek for any portion of the relics outside this shrine'. In 1370 'Bede's bones' were removed to the Galilee Chapel where they were venerated until the shrine was destroyed at the

Reformation. A marble slab now marks the spot inscribed '*Hac sunt in fossa Bedae venerabilis ossa*'. (In this ditch lie the bones of the Venerable Bede).

Believed to be Bede's tomb in Galilee Chapel in Durham Cathedral

Whether the bones in the 'ditch' are truly Bede's is open to question. We are on surer ground in assuming that Bede's body, unlike Cuthbert's, was subject to the natural processes of decomposition and that the bones were then washed (a procedure described in E.H. with reference to King Oswald's body) to be preserved and venerated as relics. A letter from abbot of Wearmouth/Jarrow in 764 thanks the Anglo-Saxon bishop of Mainz, Lul, for his gift of a silk sheet in which to wrap the relics of Bede.

In his Poem on the Bishops, Kings and Saints of York, Alcuin records a miracle worked through Bede's relics: 'when a sick man was surrounded by the relics of that blessed father he was completely cured of his illness'. Yet there was never a cult of Bede as there was of Cuthbert.

CONCLUSION

Bede was a son of his times, a touchstone of orthodoxy who made no claims to originality, founded no new school nor proposed any new doctrine. He served his fellows best by appreciating, classifying and interpreting the newly discovered literature in a manner harmonious with the traditions of the Latin church, 'it was all at the time his countrymen needed'. In later life he turned increasingly to the needs of the rustics encouraging the saying of key prayers in the vernacular, the local element in liturgy by the giving of homilies on local saints on their feast days, and the daily reception of Communion as on the continent rather than only thrice a year at Christmas, the Epiphany and Easter, as was the custom in England.

Alcuin holds up Bede with his lifelong delights in study, teaching and writing as a model scholar for all students, in all times: 'Consider the noble teacher Bede, what zeal he showed to learn while he was young, and what praises he now enjoys among men … by his example, therefore, stir up those minds that are slumbering; attend on those who teach, consult books, examine the writings they contain, investigate their meaning, that you may find sustenance therein for yourselves and may be able to administer to others the beauties of a holy life'.

There seems to be several answers to the original question: how could Bede achieve so much in the face of so many difficulties?

He was gifted with a disciplined imagination and powerful intellect and lived in a time when zeal for learning in the monasteries of Northumbria was as keen as the winter winds blowing in from the cold North Sea; he served under wise abbots who recognised his talents early as was shown by his ordination as deacon at the age of nineteen, seven years before the usual age of twenty six. He was supported and encouraged at all times, not only by the abbots but also by the brethren of his community and by an extensive network of friends and correspondents. Above all Bede would surely point to the graces he received in his daily Mass and singing of the Divine Office and to the ineffable promptings of the Holy Spirit, without which, he would say, he could have achieved nothing.

Bishop Henson of Durham considered that in Bede two streams seemed to meet and blend, the evangelistic passion of the Celtic missionaries and the disciplined devotions of the Benedictine monks (see note 11)….. he stood at the point of a new departure - a

Benedictine monk in the yet living tradition of Celtic piety, an English student in the rich treasury of Celtic learning, a disciple of Rome inspired by the intellectual passion of Ireland.[26]

Knowles reckons that among the world's great historians Bede has most kinship with Herodotus, the father of Greek history; among famous Englishman he is of the family of Alfred the Great, of Chaucer, of Thomas More and of Samuel Johnson; Shakespeare too has some of Bede's qualities. He displays a ready sense of pathos which has always been a mark of English literature. 'There is no brilliance in Bede but much steady clarity, no overtones or undertones, no subtle intuition, no twilight mystery, no lightning flash of genius. He lives and writes in noonday sunshine … simple, sane, loyal, trusting, warm hearted, serious … falsehood and vanity were quite foreign to him … Bede was a good man who, as he himself said, could live without shame and die without fear'.[27]

The autobiographical note at the end of the History is the only place where Bede writes about himself, yet in his many other works he reveals himself as a man and friend, unlike Aidan and Cuthbert who, while most attractive figures, remain shadowy and elusive. Bede displays an earthiness some may consider characteristic of Northumbrians in musing on such questions as why the ark of Noah did not sink under the weight of the waste from all the creatures it was carrying nor the timbers rot; he expressed admiration for that most manly attribute, the beard; he is warm in his friendships yet constantly critical of the Irish for their dating of Easter; he is angry at a charge of heresy and hostile to heretics; he is emotionally disturbed by Caelfrith's departure, weeps on his death-bed before bursting into a song in the vernacular; above all he finds constant delights 'in singing the daily offices and in studying, teaching and writing'. He really does come alive.

The first line of the spiritual classic: 'The Mirror of Charity', written by the twelfth century abbot of Rievaulx is: 'Genuine and discreet humility is indeed the virtue of the saints'. Bede is an exemplar of that virtue.

Bede was probably the best read and leading scholar of the early Middle Ages yet he was ever conscious of his own fragility and ignorance. He would be familiar with the text: 'A simple and ignorant brother who does the good he knows is better than the one who is famous for his scriptural erudition … if he lacks the bread of love‘. From his reading of Tobit he learnt to pray: ‘My God, illuminate my darkness’. Bede could carry his learning lightly because his heart was in the right place. He was as William of Malmesbury put it: ‘*Uir maxime doctus et minime superbus*’ (the most learned and least proud of men). His blending of sanctity and scholarship remain exemplary for all time.

Saint Peter’s Monkwearmouth
18th Century Sketch

REFERENCES AND NOTES

1. KNOWLES, David. Saints and Scholars 1963 p. 12

2. SOUTHERN, Sir Richard. 1964. Cited in Benedict's Disciples, ed. D.H. Farmer, p.86. St. Bede by Dom Alberic Stackpoole.

3. Dante Paradiso Canto X. 131. trans. Sinclair 1946 (EH)

4. Ecclesiastical History of the English People. A Historical Commentary. J.M. Wallace – Hadrill 1988. Bede and Plummer p.XVI.

5. A History of the English Church and People. Bede. Trans. Leo Sherley-Price 1968. p.336.

6. BROWN, G.H. Bede the Educator. Jarrow Lecture 1996.

7. Aelfric's Colloquy ed. G.N. Garmonsway 1939. Dated to c. A.D. 1000 This dialogue between a schoolmaster and his pupils is one of our earliest English educational documents: such colloquies had long been used in monastic schools, especially for teaching Latin.

8. Alcuin (c.735-804), Northumbrian, probably noble, deacon, master of school at York, adviser to Charlemagne architect of the Carolingian Renaissance, author of text books, saints' lives, commentaries and missals.

9. BEDE. Lives of the Abbots of Wearmouth in Age of Bede, ed. D.H. Farmer, 1988. ed. p. 185-210.

10. BEDE. E.H. 1999. Introduction J. McClure,R. Collins, p.XIII.

11.The monks of Wearmouth / Jarrow were certainly familiar with the Rule of Benedict; though they lived in the spirit of much of the Rule they were not strictly Benedictines for their Rule, Benedict Biscop tells us, was compiled from his experiences of seventeen monasteries. Nowhere in his many writings does Bede mention the Rule. Not until c. 1400 were black monks known as Benedictines; not until the 1890s were all Benedictines united into the loosest of confederations. See D. Knowles. op. cit. p.8

12. BLAIR, P.H. Northumbria in the days of Bede. 1976. Chapter 7. A Treasury of Words, p. 150 – 170. Equally fascinating is the companion volume, The World of Bede, latest reprint 1993, by the

same author.

13. Benedict's Disciples. ibid. p.90.

14. Age of Bede. Ibid. Life of Wilfrid. Eddius Stephanus. p.128

15. Northumbria in Days of Bede. Ibid. p.102-104.

16. This section owes much to the Venerable Bede, Benedicta Ward 1990. Chapter 4. Bede and the Saints. p.88 – 109.

17. My thanks go to Biblical scholar, Bernard P. Robinson, for his help in this writing on Bede the Exegete.

18. In the 1475 pages of the New Jerome Biblical Commentary, Bede is mentioned only once, on page 1155.

19. MAYR-HARTING H. The Coming of Christianity to Anglo-Saxon England. 1972. p.42 on the Gospels Books 1 and 2 1991.

20. Famulus Christi, Essays in Commemoration of the thirteen Centenary of the Birth of the Venerable Bede. Ed. Gerald Bonner. 1976, an invaluable collection of essays. Chapter 8, Bede, the Exegete, as Historian. Roger D. Ray. P.134.

21. E. H. Commentary. Ibid. p.XXIII

22. See the Awakening of Europe. Phillippe Wolff 1968.

23. Letter to Egbert. Bede E.H. 1999 p.341-357.

23. Famulus Christi. Ibid. Bede and the Vernacular. André Crépin Chapter 10 p.179.

24. Bede. E. H. idem 10 p.299-305

25. SOUTHERN R.W. 'Bede' Medieval Humanism 1970 p. 1-8.

26. Cited by A. Hamilton Thompson 'Bede, his Life, Times and Writings', 1935.

27. KNOWLES David. op. cit. p.17-18.

See also Northumbrian History and Identity AD 547 – 2000. Ed. Robert Colls. 2007. Bede, St Cuthbert and the Northumbrian *Folc* p 48 – 67. Joanna Story.

5

‘WHAT MEAN THESE STONES TO YOU?’[1]

From earliest times mankind has sought to find expression in rock art and sculpture: some of the 5,000 rock art sites identified in the caves and rock shelters of the Kakadu National Park in the Northern Territory of Australia are believed to be 50,000 years old: the mystifyingly beautiful cup and ring markings in north Northumberland on the sandstone rocks at Roughting Linn near Wooler and at Lordenshaw in the Simonside hills, the first evidences of man in Northumbria, are dated to c. 5,500 BC.

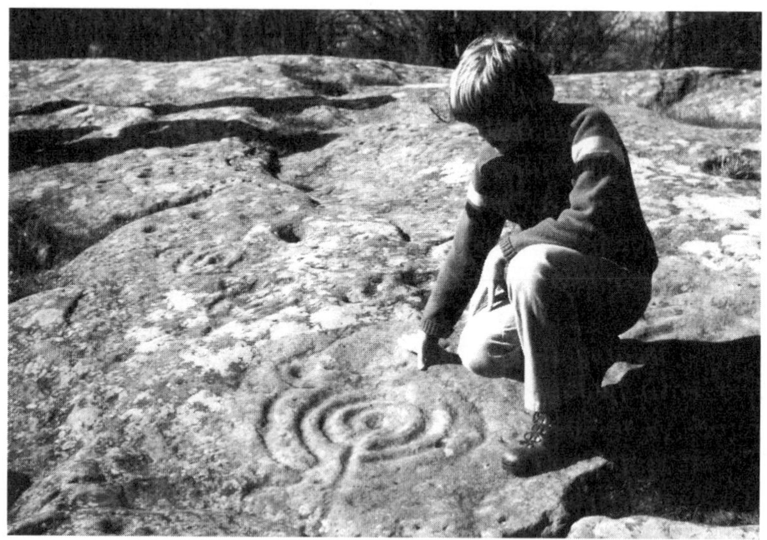

Cup and Ring at Roughting Linn

To religious devotees stones and carvings can be a lasting memorial of their deepest feelings of awe in the presence of the divine.

When Christianity was officially recognised in the Roman Empire early in the 4th century, the way was open for art to be used openly in the service of the Christian God.

There is an annual lecture in St. Paul’s Church at Jarrow by an eminent scholar to celebrate the life of Bede: it takes place around the time of the saint's feast day on 21st May. Professor Rosemary Cramp began her lecture on 'Early Northumbrian Sculpture' by asserting that acceptance of Christianity by the English brought about their conscious adoption and preservation of an antique and contemporary Mediterranean culture. In no more striking way does this manifest itself than in the magnificent, varied and inventive stone carving of the pre-Viking period.'[2] The quality and ornamental versatility of English stone carving from the late 7th to the late 11th century is one of the unexplained phenomena of Early Medieval art-history.

Remarkably, only 20 per cent of surviving material is Anglo-Saxon for it arises in a monastic context and is therefore limited in its geographic distribution. The remaining 80 per cent is Viking-Age dating from the first invasions in the 870's to about the Norman conquest in 1066; it is widely distributed throughout Cumbria, Yorkshire and Teesdale in areas of predominantly Norse settlement, sculpture from this period is more accurately known as Anglo-Scandinavian for the Vikings came with no history of stone carving and built on earlier Irish and English models. Viking sculpture differed in two important respects from the earlier Anglian: the patrons were lay not religious and therefore it had a different function and served a different audience; Anglo-Saxon sculpture was usually Christian in its symbolism and though Viking crosses included some biblical references these were mainly secular and showed scenes from Norse mythology. The number of surviving sculptured stones from the Viking age indicates that the Norsemen were no iconoclasts[3].

Happily for us, more of these pre-conquest carvings exist in Northern England than anywhere else in Britain; moreover these often are to be found *in situ*, in churches and churchyards in wild and remote places in the countryside rather than in museums or libraries. It is a tribute to the skill of the sculptors and the durability of the stone, mainly sandstone, that so many carvings are so well preserved despite the depredations of weather and vandals of the last 1300 years.

At Bewcastle the cross head is missing, at Ruthwell the cross has been re-constructed inside the church. At Rothbury the base of the cross supports the font, in York Minster and in Hexham Abbey pre-Viking sculptured stone was incorporated in the rubble, others as at Gosforth and Irton in Cumbria are wonderfully well preserved and intact in the open. Detailed study by many scholars of these sculptured stones has produced a wealth of literature yielding valuable information on the beliefs, practices and social and political lives of local peoples at that time. Inscriptions at both Ruthwell and Bewcastle are in the runic alphabet, in Old English (Anglo-Saxon), so informing the study of linguistics. The knowledge gained is all the more valuable as the devastation caused by the Viking invasions of the 10th and 11th centuries was so complete that monasteries and monastic culture were virtually wiped out - but not completely, for some schools of stonemasons survived to sculpture crosses to remind us of the strength of tradition and intellectual background of an earlier Christian heritage. Written records are sparse or, in the case of the Gosforth Cross in West Cumbria, non-existent, thus sculpture gives information when records fail us.

So what was the purpose of those impressive stone crosses so splendidly preserved at Bewcastle, Ruthwell, Gosforth and elsewhere? Were they signposts for travellers or preaching posts? Were they cenotaphs or aids for liturgical worship for local monastic communities? What does the stone carving symbolise? Who paid for the crosses to be sculptured and erected and who were the craftsmen involved? Did their function change over the years? There may well be no clear-cut answers to these questions, but here are fascinating fields to explore.

Amongst the oldest of our stone monuments, the Neolithic circles at Castlerigg above Keswick, and in Northumberland at Three Stone Burn south west of Wooler, show no sign of sculpturing. It may be that our pagan ancestors regarded ancient standing stones as symbols of the world-axis just as later Roman Emperors and Popes had the title Pontifex, bridge-maker, between heaven and earth. They may also have been phallic symbols of fertility[4].

The Celts did not carve in stone though they excelled in metalwork; yet, as we have seen, the many epitaphs and inscriptions carved on tombstones and altars yield a wealth of knowledge on the Roman and Romano-British periods in our history.

Early Christian worship had been mainly esoteric and contemplative in nature so felt no great need for pictures, crucifixes and statues and other external aids which many worshippers find helpful today.

A NEW ART FORM

Stone sculpture was a new art form for the Anglo-Saxons. In the late 7th and early 8th centuries the first sculptors concentrated on the internal and external decoration of the new stone churches being founded in the wake of the Synod of Whitby in 664 by Wilfrid and Benedict Biscop at Ripon 671, Hexham 673, Monkwearmouth 674, York and Jarrow 672 – 675. Wilfrid had made three journeys through Gaul to Rome and Benedict Biscop as many as six, perhaps seven, where they saw magnificent churches like St. Peter's in Rome and contrasted them with the humble structures in Northumbria. Bede informs us that the first church on Lindisfarne was made of hewn oak and thatched with reed. Wilfrid and Biscop wished the liturgy to be sung in the monastic churches of Northumbria with the same richness and in as magnificent a setting as in Rome. The relics, pictures, tapestries, and books they brought back from Italy and Gaul served as models for artists in the new monastic schools. Thus the burgeoning art of stone sculpture is best seen as an integral part of that cultural renaissance popularly called 'The Golden Age of Northumbria', where new technologies developed in building using glass, mortar, plaster, and baluster shafts turned on lathes, in the exquisite metalwork of St. Cuthbert's pectoral cross, in illuminated manuscripts, and in the growth of Gregorian chant taught by Archcantor John specially brought over from Rome. The early work of the sculptors can still be seen in the inscriptions in the wall-slab in St. Paul's, Jarrow, with a cross in relief: '*In hoc singulari, signo vita redditur mundo*', 'In this unique sign, life was restored to the world', again an echo of Constantine's vision and reckoned to be the oldest surviving inscription in a church in Britain. The dedication stone of St. Paul's church at Jarrow, now in the apex of the chancel arch, is dated 23 April 685 and is our earliest exact Anglo-Saxon dating. The remnant of a stone lectern from the same church is a good example of early stone furnishing[5].

Outside the porch of the western entrance to St. Peter's,

Monkwearmouth, one can still just recognise in a much eroded stone sculpture one of the first portraits of 'Christ in Majesty'. It is noteworthy that the earliest sculpture in Benedict Biscop's church shows insular (Irish) characteristics in the twisted beasts in the jambs of the western entrance door and in the ribbon animals on a closure screen of the altar where small neat interlace resembles that in the Book of Durrow. These animals come from an earlier Anglo-Saxon repertoire as seen at Sutton Hoo. The influence of Lindisfarne was still then strong for imported Gaulish craftsmen would be at work here as at St. Paul's, Jarrow, eight years later where the architecture and building techniques and materials are entirely '*in more Romano'*.

The earliest inscribed stones are called 'pillow stones' though they are placed beside the body in the grave, not under the head; soon stone coffins were made for the more distinguished members of the community and a grave marker set up in the form of a slab with a cross, either incised, or in relief, giving the name of the deceased. At Monkwearmouth we find one of the earliest inscribed memorial stones, extended, the Latin translates as 'Here in the tomb lies Herebericht the priest in (his) bodily form'.

Six inscribed grave-markers of limestone have been found in the Christian cemetery of the double monastery (for nuns and monks) at Hartlepool, one of Aidan's earliest foundations. Two have incised crosses similar to those on ornamental pages in the Lindisfarne Gospels. One slab bears the name Hilddigyth in runic script and an alpha and omega sign: the other is inscribed in Latin and translates as 'Pray for Vermund, Torhtsuid', a man and a woman's name. A unique inscribed house-shaped memorial stone was found at Falstone in the North Tyne Valley c 1816. The runic inscription can be translated as 'In memory of Hroethberh(t), a monument in memory of (his) uncle. Pray for (his) soul'.

The Anglo-Saxon names are occasionally shown both in Roman letters in insular style and in the runic alphabet. An extant letter dated 674 refers to 'the mysterious writings of the pagans' and states that in Mercia runes were now officially banned from use in the scriptorium. Clearly in Northumbria ecclesiastic authorities condoned, even encouraged, the use of runic letters for they also appear on such a revered object as Cuthbert's coffin where, for example, the name of Mary appears in both scripts. By the end of the 7th century the old pagan Germanic runic alphabet had lost its sinister connotations; it occurs again on the Ruthwell cross whose forerunner is seen in the plain cross-shafts most evident in the main monasteries at Lindisfarne, Hexham and Monkwearmouth/Jarrow in the late 7th and early 8th centuries. These were times of intense and swift experimentation.

The cross had been adopted as the universal symbol of Christianity as early as 312 following Constantine's vision of a cross in the sky with the words '*In hoc signo vinces'* before his great victory in the battle of the Milvian Bridge. Although the cross did not come into general use until the 6th century, yet we know as early as 417 that the Christian emperor Theodosius erected at the site presumed of the crucifixion the Golgotha cross encased in gold and silver, the *Crux Gemmata.* When Bede wrote his *De Locis Sanctis* drawing heavily on Adamnan's record of Arculf's visit to the Holy Land, he described other crosses over Christ's tomb and at the place of Baptism in the Jordan. Bede is quite definite too when he states firmly that 'there was no emblem of the Christian faith in the whole of Bernicia, no church, no altar, until the Christian leader Oswald set up this standard of the holy cross before giving battle'[6]. The site was called by Bede 'Heavenfield', and it was here that King Oswald faced the superior forces of the Cadwallada, probably a Welsh apostate, in 632 and was inspired to victory by a vision of a cross and message similar to that of Constantine. The cross was taken as a sign of victory, just as the cross had revealed Christ's triumph over death. The cross became an annual place of pilgrimage for the monks of Hexham Abbey and miraculous qualities were attributed to its splinters of wood. A recent construction stands at the spot today beside the busy B6318, the old Stanegate, just two miles west of Stagshaw where Dere Street crossed the Stanegate.

Fine crosses mortised in wood and later in stone were very much a Celtic tradition seen at Iona in St. Oran's, St. John's and St. Martin's Cross and one that was introduced by Aidan and his successors into Northumbria. There is no evidence, however, for Irish stone crosses existing before English examples. Before he died Cuthbert expressed a wish to be buried on Inner Farne beside the (stone?) cross, probably a simple stone slab of the type found on island hermitages off the west coat of Scotland. A surviving fragment of an early cross perhaps from the original is kept in Durham Cathedral. More celebrated is the cross Aethelwold had made c. AD 740 in honour of Cuthbert as the saint's cult was being promoted. Though damaged in the Viking raid of 793 it was mended with lead and later carried by cart along with the saint's body, the Gospels and other relics during the community's seven year wanderings throughout Northumbria. Wherever it went the cross was 'honourably regarded by the people of Northumbria, out of regard to these two holy men'. By planting Aethelwold's cross at Durham 'the hard pressed community of St. Cuthbert proclaimed their heritage… so that the light of the Lindisfarne tradition burnt brighter through time as other competing illuminations flickered and died'. Both abbots Coelfrith and Hwaetberht of Jarrow / Monkwearmouth were in Rome in 701 when Pope Sergius encased a relic of the True Cross in a silver casket to be kissed and venerated and kept in a Vatican sacristy, one of the most important events in history, according to Bede.

After the landmark Synod of Whitby, in 664, European influences were evident in refined classical cutting techniques with high relief and curving planes. The new schools of stonemasons based on the monasteries gradually grew in confidence and became less imitative of the late antique Mediterranean style of decoration and more imaginative and adventurous as Gallic, German and native English influences came to bear. This was an aesthetic crossroads where new ideas met with old classical Celtic, Germanic and Gallic traditions not only in stone sculpture but also in manuscript illuminations and other art forms. Yet the dominant influence remained that of the Eastern Mediterranean, including Byzantium; one reason may have been the rule of the renowned Archbishop Theodore of Tarsus in Asia Minor from 668 to 690 but, more importantly, the monks of the Northumbrian monasteries drew heavily for inspiration on the lives and examples of the Desert Fathers, notably Paul and Antony of Egypt, where the third and fourth centuries had experienced a 'Golden Age' of monasticism. The Anglo-Saxons felt as though they lived on the edge of the known world, which indeed they did. Having settled in the north-west fringes of the old Roman Empire, the Irish monks on Iona shared these sentiments. The civilised world centred on the Mediterranean Sea, as the name implies, and its cultural foci were in such ancient towns as Rome, Jerusalem, Damascus, Antioch and

Alexandria.

Bede considered he lived on the 'misty edge of civilisation'. It should therefore come as no surprise to see that Eastern Mediterranean culture was a strong influence in western art and found expression in the burgeoning art of stone sculpture.

Vine-scroll was the first decorative feature to appear on Northumbrian stone crosses. Popular on the mosaic floors of villas in Roman Britain as at Hinton St. Mary the vine was much used in 6th century Mediterranean art. Grapes to yield wine 'to gladden the hearts of men' had been grown since earliest times and the vine was the most characteristic Mediterranean plant along with the olive. The vine was soon adopted by Christians for it figured frequently in the scriptures and was rich in scriptural and eucharistic significance; in John 15 1-7 we read: 'I am the vine, you are the branches'. The psalmist sings of the trees as the refuge of birds and beasts, hence later vines are inhabited by a range of mythical creatures feeding off the word of God which, like the tendril of the vine, has no end. The vine became the symbol of Christ in union with His Church and of His sacramental presence in the Eucharist. On the apse mosaic of one of the oldest churches in Rome, St. Clemente, is a vine scroll with the inscriptions 'The Church of Christ is for us like a vine which the Old Law made wither and which the Cross made green, once more true'.

HEXHAM

Nowhere is the early vine scroll better seen than on the so-called Acca's Cross in Hexham Abbey, "the finest stone church north of the Alps", according to Eddius Stephanas, Wilfrid's biographer. Bailey argues that while the rich variety of the leaf and plant forms of the carvings date the cross to the time of Acca's death in AD 740 there are no historical or epigraphic reasons for associating this impressive cross with the celebrated Bishop Acca, Wilfrid's successor and friend of Bede for whom he is 'a man of great energy and noble in the sight of God and men'. The mistake arose chiefly from a misreading of the letters A E T O as A C C A whereas the letters are now seen as forming part of an article of faith from the Nicene creed UNIGENITO FILIO DEI. Thus is scholarship being constantly revised and updated[7].

Hexham was an important episcopal centre and the finely executed scroll of the vine of double leafed form, interlacing stems and trumpet endings well illustrate the high quality of the workmanship and the willingness of the sculptor to try out new forms. There is a total absence of figures in the panels but clearly master sculptors were appearing who showed how quickly the art was developing.

The theme of the vine will reoccur in our study of our three outstanding and best preserved crosses at Bewcastle, Ruthwell and at Gosforth in the west of Cumbria.

Hexham Abbey is also the place to find a fine example of Anglo-Saxon stone furniture, possibly as early as the late 7th century. Originally set in the wall, though now on the floor of the choir, is the Frith Stool, 'Peace Chair', sometimes referred to as St. Wilfrid's chair. The chair has been scooped out of a solid piece of sandstone and has a back the same height as the arms which are decorated with a plait and triangular knot pattern. The Frith Stool seems to have served two purposes, as the centre of an area of sanctuary reaching out for one mile wherein anyone apprehending a fugitive would be heavily fined by the church; and as the 'cathedra' seat of the see of Hagustald, as Hexham was then called, wherein the bishops were consecrated and early Northumbria kings crowned.

Hexham Abbey is indeed a treasure house of Anglo-Saxon sculpture for Cramp lists as many as 45 pieces found there including cross shafts, cross heads, grave makers and the Frith Stool[8].

It seems that by the mid 8th century major monastic sites with stone churches such as Jarrow, Monkwearmouth, Hexham, Whitby and Lindisfarne were the centres for stone sculpture and supported teams of highly skilled masons while smaller monastic communities or local nobles hired the services of workmen with specific commissions in mind.

The Museum of Antiquities houses a fine collection of Anglo-Saxon and Viking carved and inscribed stones with particularly impressive exhibits from Alnmouth, Rothbury and Nunnykirk but the three crosses selected here are each to be found in their original location.

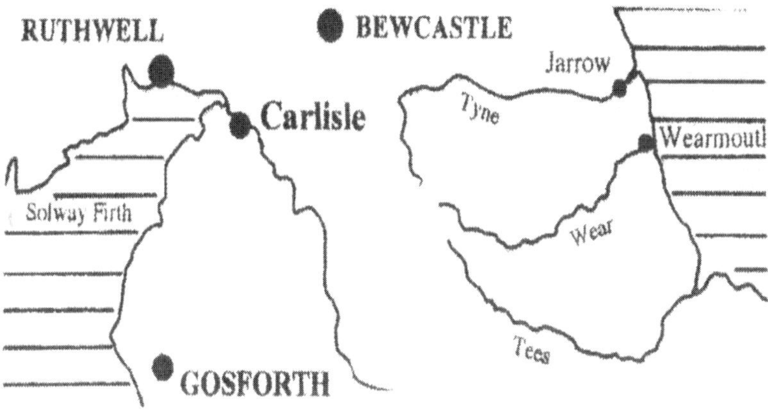

<u>**BEWCASTLE**</u>

The isolated hamlet of Bewcastle is a place of much historic interest. It is the site of a Roman outpost fort some 10 miles north of Birdoswald on Hadrian's Wall where a cohort of 1,000 men was stationed in the 2nd and 3rd centuries. In an angle of the old Roman fort a castle was built soon after 1092 using stone from the old fort, and then rebuilt c. 1350 by John the lord of Bewcastle; it remains an impressive ruin. Most impressive, however is what no less a judge than Pevsner considers is one of the two most perfect crosses of comparable date in Europe; the other is at Ruthwell.

The cross was clearly meant to be seen for it still stands 4.4 metres high; its slender tapering form gives it an upward dynamic thrust pointing to the skies like a church steeple. Only the cross head is missing. It would have been a conspicuous landmark in a frontier region between the northern Angles and the Celtic sub-kingdom of Rheged north of the Solway Firth. The place was much less isolated then than it is now for it lay on the Maiden Way across the hills north into Scotland and on the Roman road from Banna south to Catterick and York; it was also only a short distance from the ports of the Solway Firth and from the main east-west route to Ireland where Bede tells us there was much traffic.

The first impression is that this is a cenotaph set up in the memory of a deceased person by perhaps three others. The runic inscription of the west face has been so eroded by weather and changed by misguided antiquarians that it is virtually indecipherable. There have been many attempted translations; one displayed in the nearby stone barn now used to stage an attractive exhibition reads: 'This slender victory sign set up (by) Hwaetred, Wothjar, Ollfwolthu in memory of Alcfrith, the king and son of Oswin. Pray for his soul'.

Another barely legible name may be Cyneburg, daughter of Penda and wife of Alcfrith. It is quite possible that the dedicator is Wilfrid himself or Acca and that the Bewcastle cross was fashioned in the same mason's yard in Hexham Abbey as that formerly ascribed to Acca for both are dated c. A.D. 740 .

The panelled format and geometric interlace on the cross have much in common with Insular manuscripts and therein reveal strong Celtic influences; indeed one of the five panels of fine stranded interlace on the south face of the cross is identical to one found in the Lindisfarne Gospels. Plant scrolls are not part of early Irish art-forms but the decoration here shows sculptors growing still further in confidence and imagination for new varieties of forms have been carved with complex stem patterns inhabited by a variety of birds and beasts, one with a foliate tail linked to the vine. Innovative too is a sundial in the foliage, a reference to Luke 21 25-33 where we are told that 'there will be signs in the sun, the moon and the stars' to herald the coming of the 'Son of Man', a theme also taken up by the scene on the Judgement Stone on Lindisfarne.

Vine scroll with mythical birds and beasts.

Perhaps the sundial on the south face was intended to assist with the daily routine of religious worship as the Divine Office was sung at the major hours: a sundial on the wall of one of our finest earliest Saxon churches at Escomb near West Auckland in County Durham served the same purpose. One commentator on the artist's portrayal of the leaves of the vine remarks rather unkindly that they resemble more closely the leaves of hops or our native clematis.

The iconography of the west face is most striking and much debated. Three separate panels seem to show in descending (and in chronological) order, John the Baptist, Christ in Majesty and John the Evangelist.

The Baptist panel is straightforward, John points his right hand at an Agnus Dei, 'Lamb of God', cradled in his left arm. It may be no coincidence that the prayer '*Agnus Dei, qui tollis peccata mundi….*' was introduced into the Eucharistic Liturgy at the very end of the 7th century by Pope Sergius and therefore the scene was a reminder and a visual aid in the daily celebration of Mass by a local monastic community. In his commentary on Luke Bede mentions the new '*Agnus Dei'* prayer six times. Clearly it was a prayer of profound significance[9].

Christ in Majesty in the middle panel was a popular image in contemporary iconography; it occurs on the Ruthwell Cross and in manuscript illustrations.

The suffering Christ on the Cross is rarely seen at this time, only appearing once in the Lichfield Gospels. People associated kingship with power and victory and the idea of victory through suffering and death was difficult to accept.

Christ in Majesty is shown between two adoring beasts, a reference to the Book of Habbakuk, 'You will be known between two adoring animals' and to Psalm 90 (Vulgate).

The crossed paws of the animals, each with three pads, form a chi-rho, the earliest Christian symbol, and well placed for viewing at eye level five feet above ground. A runic inscription reads: '† *gessus Kristus'*, 'Jesus Christ'. Christ is shown raising his right hand in blessing with the correct finger raised and holding a book in his left hand symbolising strong links with Rome and the unity of the church.

Closer inspection of what used to be recognised as John the Evangelist raises several questions: Why is St. John in secular clothes? Why does he not have a halo as do all the evangelists in the portrait pages of the Lindisfarne Gospels? Does the bird of prey being held not resemble a falcon rather than an eagle, John's traditional symbol? It seems more probable that the figure in fact represents a memorial portrait of a local secular nobleman for whom the falcon would be an appropriate symbol of status whereas church authorities at the time frowned on hunting with hawks. The distinct arching frame of the panel may represent the protecting heavens above. This portrait is unique in Hiberno-Saxon art.

Bewcastle Cross – west face

On the west side there is the runic inscription which seems to read: 'this victory sign was set up by …' and to have ended with prayers for souls. Bewcastle is only one of nearly a dozen crosses like the one from Lancaster bearing the inscription 'pray for the soul of….' In the 8th century Life of St. Willibold we read that it is the custom of the Saxon race 'on the estates of many nobles they have, not a church, but the standard of the Holy Cross --- lifted up on high so as to be convenient for the frequency of daily prayer'[10] It is significant that the Anglo-Saxon word for a cross is *becun*, meaning a conspicuous symbol, a visible reminder of an unseen world rather than marking a burial site. Beacons on hill tops were for centuries set alight to warn of foreign invasion; today planes are guided along safe flight paths by radio beacons.

Though Bewcastle Cross may have served several purposes as a conspicuous landmark and signpost for travellers, as a meeting place for country folk to gather to hear the Christian message, as an aid to the daily worship of local monks, yet it seems evident that our first impressions were correct; the primary function was a cenotaph, a memorial calling for prayers for the deceased. The cross at Bewcastle reflects the diversity of the models and motifs circulating in north Northumbria in the early 8th century.

Bewcastle deserves to be better known for it is a place full of rich history spanning many centuries. The cross at Bewcastle has much in common with the sister cross at Ruthwell some thirty miles to the west but there are major differences.

RUTHWELL

Approaching the small church of St. Ruth along a narrow country road just south of the busy A75 route from Carlisle to Dumfries it is hard to appreciate the strategic location of the place when the cross was first erected, c.750. Only a mile to the south is the Solway Firth, the main sea route from the port of Carlisle to Ireland; it stands astride the main land route from Northumbria through the Tyne Gap to Whithorn and the shortest sea route to Ireland; nearby was the important Minster of Hoddom where Kentigern was once bishop and where Irish crosses have been found; here too is the sandstone quarry providing the materials from which the cross was made. Unlike Bewcastle it seems the cross was always within the church and thus preserved from the elements, but not from the Covenanters who despoiled it in 1642 after the General Assembly of Scotland had declared it an idolatrous monument.

The monument is first recorded in history around 1600 when Reginald Bainbrigg sent a note to the Elizabethan traveller and writer Camden for inclusion in any future edition of his 1586 Britannia, the note reads; 'unexpectedly I encountered a cross of wonderful height which is in the church at Ruthwell. It has on it beautiful images telling the story of Christ. It is wonderfully decorated with vines and animals and on two sides, ascending from the top to the base and then opposite, descending from top to base, it is incised with strange and unknown letters'.

Between 1802 and 1823 the fragments were unearthed and put together by the Reverend Henry Duncan into the cross we now see. Duncan notes that the lower stone which he calls the column is a different sandstone from the upper cross where figures and inscriptions are cut differently. An excellent replica of the cross has been erected at Bede's World in Jarrow on a prominent headland overlooking the river Tyne. Jarrow is an appropriate site for the replica as it seems many of the details on the original might come from there. The story of the Ruthwell Cross is one of 'evangelical vision and veneration, followed by destruction, neglect, reconstitution and obscurity reflecting what has happened to the religious imagination in Britain over two millennia.'[11]

Bainbrigg's 'strange and unknown letters' we now recognise as the runic characters of the Germanic alphabet seen earlier in the memorial slabs marking Christian graves: this form of writing was much in favour by sculptors from the third century to the Conquest as it uses oblique, horizontal, vertical or straight lines and is therefore much easier to cut in stone than rounded letters. The Runic alphabet was revived by the Vikings who used a modified and expanded version.

Uniquely the author of the poem The Dream of the Rood invests the Rood in his dream with a personality and the voice of the True Cross. The artist of the Ruthwell Cross by his choice of verses from an earlier version of this poem similarly identifies his own monument with Christ's Cross so that any reader of the runes 'shares in this dynamic and didactic relationship between reality and imitation and between word and image'. The subject of the poem is Mediterranean-Christian and 'the vernacular language, poetic idiom, metre, alliteration and runic letter forms belong to the Germanic heritage of Anglian Northumbria'[12]. The legible fragments of the poem read as follows:

> He stripped himself there, God Almighty, when he willed to climb the gallows, bloody in front of all the people. I did not dare to give way….
> I raised up the powerful King, the Lord of Heaven. I did not dare to topple. They humiliated us both together. I was soaked with blood, poured forth…
>
> Christ was on the Cross. But diligent and noble men came there from afar to the lonely one. All this I witnessed. I was sorely oppressed by anxieties, nonetheless I bowed….
>
> …..wounded by sharp points. They laid down the man weary of limb. They stood at his body's head. There they gazed upon the Lord of Heaven….

By allowing the cross to tell its own story of how it was cut down, taken from woods, and made into gallows and shared Christ's embrace and his suffering, the poet evokes the empathy of the reader as 'all creation wept, keened with the King's death.' The poem reinforces the essential message of the Ruthwell Cross, by his terrible yet glorious victory on Good Friday Christ triumphed over death and Satan even in this heathen wilderness, a struggle enacted many times by later saints. The dreamer prays to the Tree of Victory: 'I saw the glory-tree shine out gaily, sheathed in yellow decorous gold and gemstones made for their Maker's Tree a knight mail coat'.

The belief then was that victory was achieved on Good Friday whereas on later medieval and modern crucifixes Christ is the suffering servant, a Man of Sorrows, glory does not come until Easter day[13].

Both Ruthwell and Bewcastle crosses share the complex stem patterns of vine scroll with a variety of birds and beasts symbolising the sustenance and protection offered by Christ and His Church. There are only three figural scenes at Bewcastle, each one is mirrored at Ruthwell. Scenes from the life of Christ predominate in marked contrast to the High Crosses of Ireland and Iona where stories from the Old Testament figure prominently. The high crosses of Monasterboice, Durrow, Castledermot, Clonmacnoise and St. Martin on Iona are rightly called 'the crosses of the scriptures'. Typically it is the story of Daniel in the lion's den, Jonah and the whale and Abraham's sacrifice of Isaac that we see illustrated, scenes notably absent from our northern crosses.

Again prominence is given to the *Agnus Dei* panel with John the Baptist cradling the Lamb of God in his left arm while pointing to it with a finger of his right hand. The context is plainly Eucharistic for the panel is placed next to that showing Paul and Anthony sharing the bread of the Eucharist in the desert. Clearly the newly introduced *Agnus Dei* prayer before the distribution of Holy Communion was again being highlighted.

Also figuring here is the panel of Christ adored by the beasts recalling two biblical texts; Habbakuk 3.3 from the old Latin canticle sung every Friday at Lauds and at the ninth hour on Good Friday, Psalm 90 sung every evening at Compline, 'You will walk on the asp and the basilisk, and tread down the lion and the dragon'. At both Ruthwell and Bewcastle these two dangerous creatures are transferred into anonymous good beasts with crossed paws, a pun on the symbol of the cross.

There may well have been a rich symbolism in the placing of Christ between two beasts for was He not the bridge between the Old and the New Testaments and did He not die between two thieves and appear between Moses and Elijah at the Transfiguration?[14]

A theme of the cross is clearly penance, reconciliation and conversion as in Celtic spirituality and this is perfectly illustrated in the Paul and Anthony scene, desert monks widely regarded as the 'Fathers of Western Monasticism'. The fame of these two hermits who lived a life of self-imposed exile in the Egyptian desert soon spread westwards aided by two of our earliest hagiographies, 'The Life of Anthony' by Athanasius translated into Latin by Evagrius of Antioch c.360 and 'The Life of Paul of Thebes' by Jerome about the same time. Both lives became influential throughout western Christendom and provided the basic texts of Celtic monastic wisdom. They were known both to the unknown author of Brendan the Navigator for in his monastic odyssey on the seas Brendan encounters Paul, and to the architect of Ruthwell Cross who portrays Paul and Anthony sharing bread in the desert, a reference to the passage in Elisha where the prophet is fed bread by a raven, though no raven is shown, so that the focus is on the bread. Christ is recognised in the breaking of bread, equally at the end of the road to Emmaus, in the deserts of Egypt or in the wilds of Northumbria. Ruthwell celebrates here the great symbolic riches shared by the Roman and Irish traditions besides which differences in the dating of Easter are of no great significance. In the early church the Communion bread was one loaf and shared among the people; the sharing by Paul and Anthony demonstrates the importance of communal liturgical worship, the great achievement of Christian culture in the early Middle Ages. This panel epitomises the message of the cross as a whole in celebrating both the universality of the Church in time and place and a lively liturgy worked out by a small community of monks with only limited resources. Mary does not feature strongly in the illustrated manuscripts or in the iconography of the early Middle Ages, her cult was to burgeon later in the 12th and 13th centuries – yet, in contrast to Bewcastle where the only reference to women is the name Cyneburh, at Ruthwell, both Mary and Martha figure prominently. Mary is central to the Flight into Egypt scene and, in a scene as simple in outline as it is pregnant with meaning, Mary Magdalene is shown washing the feet of Jesus. Again the kneeling figure of Mary Magdalene, the ideal penitent, sums up the significance of the cross.

Ruthwell Cross

Left. - Mary Magdalene washes the feet of Jesus.
Right - Replica, Bede's World, Jarrow.

Recent scholars believe that the panels at Ruthwell celebrate the four major Marian feasts inaugurated by Pope Sergius c.700, Candlemas or the Purification on February 2, the Annunciation on March 25 inscribed with a verse from Luke 1 28, the Assumption on August 15 and the Nativity of the Virgin on September 8 shown by the Visitation. It says much for the awareness of the community and their close contact with distant Rome that these innovative feast days should be incorporated in the liturgy and commemorated so soon after their inception.

Though it was probably some local aristo who financed the community initially and the setting up of the Cross the inscription '*Iesus Christus, index aequitatis'* is a clear warning to anyone who deems nobility of birth and political power to be important as God judges all men equally. Mayr-Harting calls this 'monastic classlessness' where true nobility arises from a growing spiritual and sacramental relationship with Christ for membership of the communion of saints is open to all. At the same time the patron, almost certainly an Anglo-Saxon, was demonstrating that Anglo-Saxons controlled this debatable region.

Scholars are united in their admiration for the degree of intellectual sophistication seen on Ruthwell Cross. The inscriptions and iconography are closely related to a fast changing 8th century Roman liturgy with a new cycle of feasts. The daily routine of communal acts of worship at set times, the Divine Office, is greatly aided for a monastic community with scant resources of books and heavily dependent on rote learning and chanting of prayers like the *Kyrie, Gloria* and *Credo.* The cross synthesises in stone the Gregorian ideal of blending Roman and Irish traditions in a diversity within a unity, an ideal stressed by Bede. Local needs are met yet there is no provincialism, but a sense of the universal church as East meets West and Heaven meets Earth; participation offers all Christians, living or deceased, membership of the communion of saints and a share in the fruits of the Incarnation and Resurrection. Ruthwell is 'a great contemplative monument of universal significance' and has 'the most complete theological programme of any surviving cross'.

GOSFORTH[15]

Gosforth is an attractive village a few miles from St. Bees (Bega) Head on the Cumbrian Coast: in the churchyard of the parish church of St. Mary's stands a remarkable and, in some respects, a unique Viking-Age stone cross. Standing in its original socket and constructed from a single block of local red sandstone, with the base stepped like a market-cross. Five meters high it is taller and slenderer than Irish crosses and is classed as a ring cross, a form used before the Norse invasions of Western Scotland and Ireland and picked up by settlers moving across the Irish Sea to England. There are as many as eleven crosses of similar design on or near the Cumbrian Coast indicating that the main lines of communication were by sea and that it was on the fertile coastal plain rather than the difficult hilly hinterland that the more prosperous farmers and landowners lived. It may well be that the very shape of Celtic crosses like Gosforth was richly symbolic as the square base represented the earth, the shaft the earth-axis and the wheel head the encircling heavens above. A bark-like pattern on the lower cylindrical part of the cross enhances its tree-like appearance. One wonders if the artist had the Tree of Life in mind, a recurring theme of the Dreamer of the Rood and others. The 6th century poet Venantius Fortunatus wrote: 'Oh faithful cross, the only noble tree among all the trees. No forest produces a tree like you in leaf, flower or seed.'

Gosforth Cross - Viking age sculpture

A Holy Week preface reads, 'Death came from a tree, life was to spring from a tree'. At Sherburn in Yorkshire the arms of the cross actually sprout leaves. If this was indeed the intention of the artist then he has succeeded nobly. Though the cross cannot be dated precisely it must be pre-conquest as some of its carvings were re-used as rubble in the Norman church.

The four faces of the cross all have ornament, both figural and zoomorphic, and shows strong Scandinavian influence with no divisions between the panels unlike Anglo-Saxon crosses. However, as with the Ruthwell cross, the approach seems to be contemplative and again poses the question: 'What does this mean?'

The only explicit Christian illustration on the Gosforth cross is a readily recognisable Crucifixion scene, by the ninth and tenth centuries a popular theme among English figural sculptors. The later medieval portrayals of Christ on the Cross as the Suffering Servant with twisted and tortured body had not yet reached the remote and conservative north and Christ at Gosforth is shown as reigning from the tree, head erect, eyes open, limbs straight, legs uncrossed so avoiding any hint of suffering or death. Blood issues from Christ's right side but no cross is shown so no nails are seen; the emphasis being on the spear.

Two other figures are shown, on the left is Longinus holding a spear and at the foot of the cross a female with what appears to be a horn, in style she is purely Scandinavian with hanging pigtails, trailing dress, horn in hand, yet she stands where Mary stood beneath the Cross and where in a typical crucifixion scene Stephaton, as partner to Longinus, the sponge-bearer would have stood. We see the more typical scene at Hexham, Penrith and Bothal. Is she in fact Mary Magdalene in Scandinavian guise carrying ointment and, if so, is she as at Ruthwell representing penance and conversion? Equally she could be seen as a Valkyrie who welcomes heroes to Valhalla.

At the foot of the panel is a double-headed snake symbolising triumph over the devil.

Gosforth Cross - Christian and Norse iconography

All the other panels show scenes from Norse mythology about which little is known in Britain. Our main source derives from the 13th century Edda written by Snorri Sturlusson where he records tales of a dying Norse pagan tradition reminding us that 'these beliefs of theirs have changed in many ways as people drifted apart and their tongues became separated one from another.' The Gosforth sculptor therefore offers us a unique glimpse of how Norse myths were seen and interpreted in the 10th or 11th century.

On the same face as the Crucifixion scene we see Vioarr, son of Odin, avenging the death of his father by breaking the jaws of the wolf who had swallowed Odin, 'Vioarr shall avenge him, he shall rend the cold jaws of the Beast and kill him!' Odin's son was one

of the innocent gods who survived the Ragnarok, the holocaust, where the gods of Norse mythology were overthrown and destroyed led by the evil god Loki. The juxtaposition of the two scenes is unmistakeably a reference to Christ who lived through the Crucifixion to rule the world after his great struggle against evil, the scenes comment on each other.
Another scene shows the watchman god Heimdallr holding back two advancing beasts with a spear in one hand and a horn in the other to awaken the gods to the impending doom of Ragnarok, a tortured Loki, father of many of the monsters, who is held, legs and arms pinioned beneath the venomous fangs of a serpent whose poison drips onto his forehead. Loki's faithful wife attempts to collect the venom in a bowl. Loki's terrible fate epitomises the fates of the evil gods.

The Gosforth cross introduces for the first time into sculptural art the figure of the armed secular warrior familiar in pagan tradition since earliest times.

Ragnarok with its darkness, wars and earthquakes echoes Doomsday still believed to be near (at the end of the millennium A.D.1000?) and sounds an apocalyptic theme. The graphic scenes described all spell out clearly a message of the triumph of good over evil and may well have been chosen both to celebrate the myths of a rich pagan Norse folk-lore and some central truths of the new Christianity. With the final defeat of the forces of Loki the innocent gods who survived the chaos of Ragnarok rule a new cleansed world where 'the fields will grow unsown'.

Other scenes show threatening monsters and horsemen riding out to battle and point to the eternal struggle between good and evil and the end of three worlds; the pagan world of Odin; the world Christ redeemed by His death on the Cross and resurrection; and the world ending in Doomsday as portrayed by the artist of the Lindisfarne Judgement stone.

Two panels of a wall frieze, perhaps continuous in the 10th century church, show the same commentary on Viking myths and Christian beliefs. In the upper panel a snake curls around the feet of a beast with horns, interpreted as a hart. The Roman writer Pliny considered the snake and the hart traditional enemies. In early

Christian imagery the hart is shown as a symbol of Christ and the serpent equated with the devil; an Anglo-Saxon homilist names serpents 'among the eleven pains of hell' for did not the Lord say to the serpent who tempted Eve to commit the first sin, 'Cursed are you among all animals and among all wild creatures, upon your belly you shall crawl all the days of your life'.
The upper frieze panel is known as the Fishing Stone and features Thor, a god of great strength and limited intelligence, struggling with the World-serpent. Thor is in a boat and holds a hammer and a fishing line with an ox head for bait from one of the giant Hymir's oxen. Hymir is also out fishing and when Thor hooks the World-Serpent, whose coils encircle the world, Hymir cuts the line with an axe enabling the serpent to escape until the final battle of Ragnarok. Has the artist of this 10th century church wall-frieze chosen this colourful episode from Icelandic folk-lore to remind his audience of the passage in Isaiah XXVII I: 'On that day the Lord with his cruel and great and strong sword will punish Leviathan the fleeing serpent and will kill the dragon that is in the sea'? Again in Job XLII we read 'Canst thou draw out Leviathan with a hook?' Bede describes Leviathan as a sea-serpent. Stories of struggles between men and serpent-like monsters are popular in both Scandinavian and Christian tradition. Grendel, the dragon of the Beowulf saga, is described as the 'progeny of Cain'.

Another interesting sculptural feature described as a 'hogback' only emerged during 19th century restoration work among the rubble used as foundation material by a Norman mason. It is a small solid structure with end-beasts as gables and a curving ridgeline reflecting the shape of contemporary Viking-age houses. The hogback developed into a shrine tomb in which Christian relics were housed. Two examples can be seen in St. Mary's church at Gosforth and another in Hexham Abbey, possibly hinting at Scandinavian settlement in the Mid-Tyne valley.

Cumbria can boast of more Viking age carvings, some 120 in total, than anywhere else in the country and nowhere are they better seen than at Gosforth. Here is craftsmanship of the highest quality where artist and patron with access to a wide variety of ideas and much skill produced a programme of pagan iconography and Christian beliefs. Pagan narratives are used to celebrate Christian truths in line with the advice of Pope Gregory three centuries earlier, not to deny immediately pagan traditions but from time to time to compare their superstitions with our Christian beliefs. The cross illustrates the remarkable conversion of settlers achieved by a Church stripped of resources, deprived of its monastic centres and with its upper organisational echelons disrupted and impoverished. Its patron may well have been a rich land-owner with Scandinavian origins.

CONCLUSION

The Northumbrian crosses are then an integral part of the spiritual, cultural, and intellectual renaissance that flourished in the old Britannia Inferior in the late 7th and early 8th centuries. New heights of excellence were scaled by talented individuals and competing monastic communities in a range of disciplines. It was 'an immense achievement for the English to step outside their tradition of abstract non-monumental decorative art and to produce.... 'a premature variety of Romanesque art'. Regretfully, although skilled sculptors were in high demand and their artistry much appreciated, no name has come down to us. Wilfrid and Benedict Biscop are famous as church builders, travellers and book-lovers; Bede we at once associate with history and scriptural commentary; Caedmon with poetry and John the Archcantor with singing; Eadfrith is celebrated as the artist of the Lindisfarne Gospels and Bilfrith, the anchorite, as its bejeweller; Ultan was so revered as a scribe that he was regarded as a saint whose relics reputedly wrought miracles.

However, the name of the artist of the exquisite vine-scroll on what was considered Acca's Cross or of the sophisticated iconography of the Ruthwell Cross or of the Gosforth Master remains unknown. The only exception is the late 9th or early 10th cross shaft found near the ruins of the old 'Woden's Church' at Alnmouth which bears the runic inscription 'Myredah (Old Irish Muiredach) made me'; it shows a crucifixion scene with the sun and the moon on either side of Christ's head and the figures of the lance-bearer and the sponge-bearer below. It is now in the Museum of Antiquities.

As with passages from scripture the crosses can be interpreted at different levels. For the pagans, illiterate country-folk gathering around the cross to hear the word of God in remote regions where there were no churches, the figures and scenes portrayed on the Cross illustrated key events in the life of Christ and central beliefs of Christianity; in this respect they served the same purpose as the pictures collected in the journeyings of Benedict Biscop and hung on the walls of St. Peter's, Monkwearmouth and St. Paul's, Jarrow. Nowhere is this didactic role better seen than on the three surviving parts of the Rothbury Cross. The foot of the shaft base of the font in All Saints Church in Rothbury shows Christ rising into Heaven surrounded by the apostles, the earliest portrayal of the Ascension known in Britain; adjoining is a graphic representation of the Damned in Hell with deformed figures struggling in the coils of beasts, their genitals threatened by the jaws of the creatures. Sockets in the limbs of fragments of the Rothbury Cross, again in the Museum of Antiquities, were probably meant to hold candles and it is none too difficult to imagine the effect of such a vision of Hell, originally painted, on a simple soul viewing it in a darkened church lit only by flickering candlelight[16].

An incomplete sandstone cross-head was found when the walls of the Rothbury church were dismantled during restoration in 1849. A face of the cross-head shows a crucifixion scene though only the right arm of Christ survives. The central roundel may be interpreted as a bust of Christ with figures offering symbols of imperial Roman authority in submission, rods (*fasces*), a laurel wreath and a white handkerchief.

Profound canonical beliefs are also demonstrated by the scene at the top of the Rothbury cross formerly considered to show the Healing of the Blind Man and now recently convincingly reinterpreted as the Raising of Lazarus from the Dead[17]. Three figures are shown; crouching in the foreground is the model penitent Mary Magdalene, above her is Christ touching the forehead of Lazarus. The grave clothes fall away as Lazarus is awakened from the darkness of death and, freed from entombing sin, enters the light of the living world redeemed by Christ's Resurrection. Interpretation is made no easier as the whole scene is turned through 90° to accommodate the three figures on a narrow tapering stoneface at the head of the cross. The iconography of the Rothbury cross was orthodox and informed, the product of a literate and skilled artist and a sophisticated Northumbrian milieu, yet its key note biblical scenes illustrated the power and glory of Christ and the importance of faith in winning salvation. This message was readily comprehensible to a wide audience, learned and illiterate alike.

The Bernician stone-crosses of the 8th and 9th centuries have many similar motifs and symbols which hint strongly at a common centre of production, probably Jarrow/Monkwearmouth or Hexham; the vine-scroll decoration and the figure of Christ in Majesty are typical recurring themes. However, these crosses were not mass-produced or based on one model for there are marked differences well seen at Rothbury, where, unlike Bewcastle and Ruthwell, Christ in Majesty has a youthful face and is shown only in a half-length figure. Rothbury also illustrates the majestic pomp of the Ascension and a vision of the writhing torment of Hell.

Rothbury may well be the oldest stone-rood in England and, in its original intact state, dramatic and impressive as any Northumbrian rival. In the complexity of its theological programme it stands second only to Ruthwell.

For educated laity and members of monastic communities who knew Latin and were familiar with the Bible the sculptures on the crosses were clearly aids to both daily and seasonal liturgical worship and to personal meditation; certainly this was the main function of the Ruthwell Cross whereas Bewcastle was predominantly a commemorative obelisk with religious significance. We can only speculate on the relative importance of other roles as signposts for travellers in difficult, unmapped territory, as statements of the power and prestige of the local lord or as celebrations of both old and new traditions and beliefs; probably they all played some part.

While scholars interpret crosses differently they unite in praising their significance for the people of the time and the artistry of the sculptors who displayed such high quality workmanship. Bewcastle is 'impressive' yet is 'puzzlingly eclectic', the geometric interlace and intricate vine decoration of the south face is 'a masterpiece of 8th century ecclesiastical sculpture'.[18] Ruthwell is the cross which best illustrates 'the intellectual background of Northumbrian Christianity' and is 'a litany of penance for those who pray before it'[19]; 'its synthesis of Roman and Celtic ideals is the embodiment in stone of the Gregorian ideal of diversity within unity'.[20] Gosforth cross is simply the best piece of stone carving of the Viking Age surviving in Northumbria.

Individual items of sculpture produce endless speculation: does the triangle within the circle on the reconstructed Ruthwell Cross symbolise the unity of the three persons of the Trinity within one Godhead? Are the five bosses at the head of the Irton Cross representing the Five Wounds of Christ? Is the figure at Bewcastle John the Evangelist or a local noble? Are the 18 awe-struck figures in the Rothbury crowd scene souls in heaven or Israelites listening to Moses?

There is an explicit answer to the question posed in the title of this essay from the Book of Joshua: 'one man from each of the twelve tribes of Israel was to take a stone upon his shoulder and place it in the middle of the River Jordan to mark the eventual entry of the Israelites into the Promised Land at the place where the waters were cut off before the Ark of the Covenant of the Lord passed. These stones shall be to the people of Israel a memorial for ever'.[21]

The purposes of the stones set up in Northumbria from the 7th to the 11th century are complex and far from clear, but what is not in doubt is 'the love of earlier Christian culture… that so early brought Christ and His Saints out of the surroundings of the Church and majestically mounted them in the wild open places of Northumbria'.[22]

Any visitor today to these fascinating stone crosses who spends a few moments in silent contemplation will find the experience richly rewarding.

'What mean these stones?'

Bewcastle Cross

REFERENCES

1. JOSHUA 46 Bible R.S.V.
2. CRAMP R. Jarrow Lecture 1965
3. LANG J. Anglo-Saxon sculpture 1988. Chapter 3
4. BRYCE D. Symbolism of the Celtic cross 1994, p.11-28
5. MAYR-HARTING H. The Coming of Christianity to Anglo-Saxon England 1972. Chapters 3,4
6. BEDE History of the English Church and People. Penguin.1968.p143
7. BAILEY R.N. England's Earliest Sculptures. 1996. p44
8. KIRBY D.P. ed. Saint Wilfrid at Hexham. 1974. Chapter 5 Early Northumbrian Sculpture at Hexham. R. Cramp.
9. HAWKES J., MILLS S. ed. Northumbria's Golden Age 1999. Chapter 16 Imitatio Romae and the Ruthwell Cross. E. O'Carragain.
10. MAYR-HARTING H. ibid. p247. It was at the foot of one such cross that the parents of St. Willibald offered him as a boy to God.
11. ALEXANDER M. Ancient Witness to the Crucifixion. Article in Tablet April 6 1996.
12. BRADLEY S.A.J. ed. Anglo-Saxon Poetry 1992. p5
13. ALEXANDER M. ibid.
14. O'CARRAGAIN E. ibid.
15. BAILEY R.N. ibid. This section draws heavily on England's Earliest Sculptures.
16. HAWKES J. ibid. Anglo-Saxon Sculpture: Questions of Context.
17. HAWKES J. A.A. 5th Series Vol. 17. p207-210
18. HIGHAM N.J. The Kingdom of Northumbria AD350-1100. 1993. p163
19. MAYR-HARTING H. ibid. p261
20. O'CARRAGAIN E. ibid. p201
21. JOSHUA ibid. 4 2-7
22. CRAMP R. ibid. 1965

For more detailed study:
Catalogues of Anglo-Saxon Sculpture 1982 Cramp R. Miket, R.
Corpus of Anglo-Saxon Stone Sculpture 1984. Cramp R. Vol. I, covering Northumberland and Durham.

SON OF HEXHAM: ABBOT OF RIEVAULX.

Though the many illustrious figures who illuminate our early Christian history in Northumbria have unique personalities and differing roles they complement each other to a remarkable degree. The stooping figure of Paulinus was a pioneering Roman bishop; Aidan from Iona, and Cuthbert of the Farnes, were missionary bishops in the ascetic, evangelistic Celtic tradition (though Cuthbert was of Anglo-Saxon stock); the dynamic Wilfrid of Ripon and Hexham, a spiritual giant in his time, was thoroughly Roman in outlook, almost a prince-bishop; the book-loving widely travelled Benedict Biscop, the founding father of Monkwearmouth monastery and the provider of many of the resources for the Northumbrian Renaissance; the humble monk Bede, the ideal scholar, making full use of those resources; Hilda, the inspirational abbess of Whitby abbey: yet of these holy men and women, and many others, it is the twelfth century Cistercian Aelred, abbot of Rievaulx from 1147 to 1167, who impresses as 'pre-eminently the abbot of England'[1] and the most attractive religious figure in that time of spiritual renaissance.

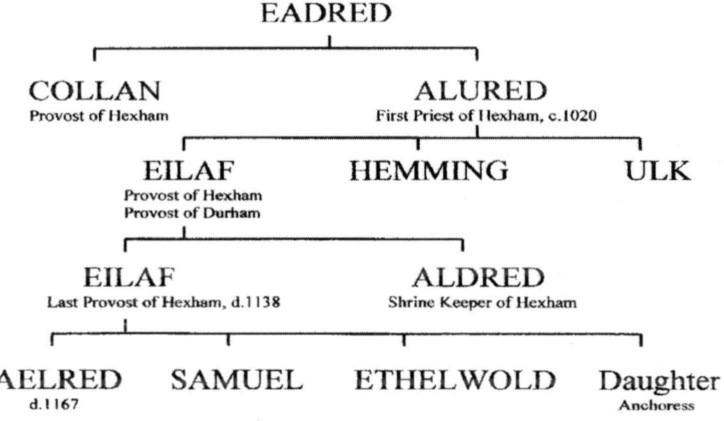

In a letter to Maurice,[2] abbot of the Austin canons of Kirkham Abbey, Walter Daniel, Aelred's biographer, reveals some details of the Hexham family into which Aelred was born in 1110. Walter was told at first hand by William, son of Thale, a kinsman of Aelred who was very fond of the child's father and mother, that as Aelred was lying in his cradle 'he saw his face turned to the likeness of the sun … it shone with the radiance of solar light so serene was the countenance'. All present, father, mother, and brothers, agreed with William 'the shoots of felicity sprouting in the soil of Aelred's infancy' showed he would become a man of virtue. It seems that Aelred was the youngest of three brothers and that his sister, who became 'a chaste virgin and a recluse', was born later as she is not mentioned in William's tale. Walter does not deem it worth mentioning that the father of the family was the priest of Hexham, perhaps because it was usual then for parish clergy to be married men.[3]

The family's close links and pride in their Anglo-Saxon heritage are very evident in the chronicle of Reginald, a monk of Durham and a contemporary of Aelred.[4]

Reginald records details revealed to him by Aelred of the experiences of the bearers of the coffin of St. Cuthbert in its journeyings in the 9th and 10th centuries known only by custodians indicating that one of his forebears may well have been a bearer. Cuthbert was still a powerful presence in the north of England and a key figure in Aelred's life: in all his many travels he entrusted himself to the care of Cuthbert.

His great grandfather was that eager hunter of relics, Alfred Westou, sacristan of Durham Cathedral, who stole from Jarrow what he believed to be the bones of Bede to add to his collection in Cuthbert's shrine. Relics were much prized for they were visible reminders of the continuing presence of saints, by whose intercession petitions could be granted, help given to those in need and transgressors punished.

Aelred sprang from educated stock for both Alfred, and his son Eilaf, were *larwa,* teachers in the cathedral school at Durham, who instructed boys in letters and in music for the liturgy.

Aelred's early life and his family fortunes were inextricably bound up with the events in Northern England following the Norman Conquest some four decades earlier.

In 1069 Norman forces were cut to pieces outside Durham, causing Bishop Aethelwine, fearing retribution, to flee with the body of Cuthbert to the safety of Lindisfarne. Retribution came with a vengeance in 1080 when, after the murder of Bishop William of Durham by a mob in Gateshead, King William devastated the northern 'counties' in the 'Harrowing of the North', a region labelled 'wasteland' in the Domesday Book.

The new Bishop of Durham, William of St. Carilef, a man of action, installed a house of canons and gave the older clergy, many of whom were married men, the chance of becoming monks or leaving. All except one chose to leave, including Aelred's grandfather Eilaf, who took up the family living of Provost of Hexham (see family tree). Eilaf, in his turn, passed on the position to his son, also called Eilaf, a strong protagonist of Celtic and Saxon traditions, who found it difficult to adapt to Norman ways. Late in life this Eilaf, Aelred's father, made a profession of faith to the community of canons of Durham Cathedral and died, seemingly reconciled, in the presence of the abbot and Aelred.

The magnificent new church arising on the rock at Durham 'to honour God and Saint Cuthbert' was a powerful expression of Norman dominance in the land and stood in marked contrast to the ruinous state of what had been 'the finest stone church north of the Alps', according to Wilfrid's biographer, Eddius Stephanus. In the year of Aelred's birth, when the relics of St. Cuthbert were being translated to his new shrine in the Cathedral at Durham, Eilaf found 'everything deserted' in Wilfrid's old church at Hexham, which had been burnt down by Halfdene, the Danish leader, in the invasion of 875. 'The walls of the roofless church were clogged with grass ... a sorry sight on account of the dirt, the rains and the storms ... it had no trace of its former beauty left'; a sad reflection on the glorious past of Cuthbert and Wilfrid's time. For two years Eilaf kept himself and his family only by hunting and fowling as they began the painstaking work of restoration.[5]

Firstly, an altar was built at the east end where Eilaf celebrated his priestly duties. Then a new sanctuary floor was laid, and the roof repaired with tiles. The relics of the local saints were enshrined in a casket. One visualises the boy Aelred helping in this work wherever he could: at this time he formed a friendship with a bearded lay brother, Hugh, who had just been cured of a hernia.

THE KING'S STEWARD

Quite how Aelred at age fourteen years came to be adopted into the royal household of King David of Scotland (1124 – 1153) at Roxburgh and brought up with Prince Henry and two stepsons, Simon and Waldef, we can only surmise. Ties between Scotland and Northumbria were close. Roxburgh was only a day's ride north of Hexham, perhaps the arrangement was made between Eilaf and a member of the Scottish court visiting Durham.

Roxburgh, along with Stirling and Dunfermline, was a regular meeting place of the royal household. Strongly sited at the confluence of the rivers Teviot and Tweed, only massive earthworks and a curtain wall of the castle remain to hint at its former status.

Aelred, and indeed the Cistercian Order, owed much to King David and his patronage of monasticism in his kingdom. During David's long reign of three decades four of the eleven eventual Cistercian monasteries in Scotland were founded, as well as houses of Benedictines and Augustinians. Aelred was fulsome in his praise of the Scottish king. In his lamentation on the death of David he wrote: 'he adorned you with castles and cities … he filled your ports with foreign merchandise … he changed your homespun for fine clothing … he tamed your wild manners with the Christian religion'. Raised in the English court of Henry I and the sophisticated Queen Matilda David 'had rubbed off all the rust of his Scots barbarity and knew well the value of education'. The young men in the royal household at Roxburgh were almost certainly tutored by the monks from Tiron in Northern France who had established a house at Selkirk in 1113, and later a school at Kelso, next to Roxburgh. At court French was spoken and Norman ways followed.

It was a strange, new and exciting world and an ideal learning environment for the eager, intelligent and sensitive priest's son from Hexham. Here as Nicholas, a monk of Rievaulx, states in a poem, for nine years Aelred 'prospered as a youth under the Scottish king'. He formed friendships which would last a lifetime with Simon and Henry, and most especially with Waldef. There was time for play; Simon built castles with branches, Waldef built churches, while Aelred escaped the royal hunt by hiding up a tree with a book.

Recognising the tact and natural charm of Aelred, the king gave him the post of steward of the royal household, a position held to be of such importance that it gave its name to Scotland's best known royal family. In later life Aelred would say he knew more about catering than anything else, and earned the soubriquet 'graduate of the kitchen'.

It seemed an idyllic existence; 'the charm of my companions pleased me very much. I have my whole soul to affection, nothing seemed sweeter than to love'. Yet for Aelred, a young man of strong emotional sensibility, the friendships he formed 'at once dearer to me than all the delights of life, were also a source of torment, for some offence was also to be feared and a parting, some time in the future, a certainty'[6]. He was caught between ideals he strove for and imaginings he could neither gratify nor transform.

He wrote later, 'those about us said. "How well it is with him," little knowing how ill it was with me … I am no other than the prodigal son. Selfishly I clung to my inheritance. Serve thee I would not. I went to the far country, the land of unlikeliness, of misery, darkness and want'. He revealed that he was even considering a desperate remedy, as his turbulent emotions drove him into a suicidal state of mind.[7]

Providentially, as he reflected later, he was given an opportunity to work out a solution to his problem. He came to see that his time at the royal court taught him valuable lessons where he experienced human weakness at first hand in the worldly life of the King's court. He became sensitive to the doctrine of charity he was soon to find among Cistercian monks.

His close friend Waldef was the first to break the circle of friendship, his intimate companion journeyed south to join the newly established community of canons at Nostell Priory in the woods of North Yorkshire who had adopted the Rule of St. Augustine. Waldef's decision pointed the way Aelred was soon to follow.

RIEVAULX AND THE EARLY CISTERCIANS

About 1134 King David sent Aelred on an errand to York to visit Archbishop Thurstan in an attempt to solve a dispute between Thurstan and Bishop John of Glasgow who refused to recognise York as the Metropolitan See. Aelred may well have taken the opportunity to visit Waldef, now prior of the abbey of Kirkham on the river Derwent, just a few miles north east of York. Perhaps it was at such a meeting that Aelred first heard about monks 'white by name and white also in vesture', who had been granted land by Thurstan and settled on the banks of the river Skell to found the new abbey of St. Mary of the Fountains. He would hear how, after a stormy meeting in the chapter house of St. Mary's Abbey at York, a group of monks, dissatisfied at the laxity of life in St. Mary's, resolved to follow a more austere life in the spirit of the first apostles by following strictly the 'ancient Rule of our Blessed Father Benedict'.

His imagination fired by such news Aelred resolved to visit a similar colony of White Monks who had settled by the river Rye in a deeply wooded valley on land granted to them by Walter l'Espec, the Norman lord of Helmsley Castle, with whom Aelred stayed on the first night of his return journey, probably with a letter of introduction from Thurstan. It seems likely that Walter had already met Aelred's family when visiting his patrimonial estates as Lord of Wark in the north Tyne valley. Walter had earlier founded the nearby Augustinian priory of Kirkham. Rievaulx was a text book Cistercian foundation planned from Clairvaux with the detailed precision of a military operation.[8]

CISTERCIAN ABBEYS IN NORTHERN ENGLAND AND SOUTHERN SCOTLAND WITH DATES OF FOUNDATION.

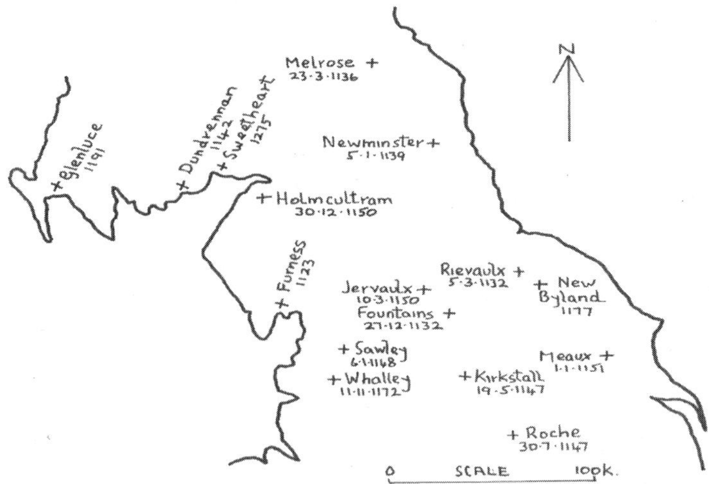

In fanciful language Walter, Aelred's biographer, describes the location of the new monastery, a typical Cistercian site: 'The spot was by a powerful stream in a broad valley. High hills surround the valley, encircling it like a crown. These are clothed by trees of various sorts and maintain in pleasant retreats the privacy of the vale, providing for the monks a kind of second paradise of wooded delight … waters wind and tumble … branches rustle and leaves flutter to the earth … the happy listener is filled with a glad jubilee of harmonious sound … his ears drink in the feast prepared for them and are satisfied.'[9]

Some selected lines from a poem *Rievaulx: St. Aelred*,[10] by the Cistercian writer and poet, Thomas Merton, who died in a tragic accident in Bangkok in 1968 aged only 53, capture the atmosphere of the early days:

Who were the saints who came to claim your peacefulness
And build a valley's silence into bowers of permanent stone?

So Rievaulx raised her white cathedral in the wilderness
Arising in her strength and newness beautiful as Judith.

The sun that plays in the amazing church
Melts all the rigour of those cowls as grey as stone

The choirs fall down in tidal waves
And thunder on the darkened forms in a white surf of Glorias
And thence we see the tribes, the tribes go up
And find their Christ, adore Him in his blazing Sion
While the great psalms are flowering along the vaulted stones.

The beauty of the location and the impressive remains of the monastic buildings still delight visitors today.

Yet it is well not to be beguiled by the natural charm of the sites chosen by the early Cistercians for their monasteries, as perhaps Wordsworth was in his poem on Tintern Abbey in the Wye Valley. Not all locations were so attractive as Rievaulx, Tintern, Fountains or Newminster. A contemporary writer describes the site of the mother house of Cîteaux among the reedy swamps of Burgundy as a 'place of horror and vast solitude': Isaac de Etoile, abbot of the monastery on the Isle de Ré in the Bay of Biscay wrote: 'here in this remote, arid and vile solitude … cast far out into the sea, destitute of all human and worldly consolation you have become totally silent from the world … you have no world left at all except this poor island, the last extremity of the earth'.[11]

Sites were chosen for their solitude where, following the precept of St. Benedict, the monks 'could become strangers to the business of the world' and pursue their search for God in contemplative silence by reading, praying and meditating. *'O beata solitudo'* was the cry: the only conversation was to be between God and the soul.

Thomas Merton believed that the grace of the Spirit of God was there, forming souls in monasteries hidden in valleys and woods to a life of charity and deep contemplation.

Contemplation lies at the heart of the Cistercian spirituality and is a concept most difficult to comprehend for a layman deeply involved in the concerns of family life and/or stressful work and living in a secular, materialistic, sex-mad society in a much troubled world. Perhaps we catch a glimpse, albeit a fleeting one, when we find ourselves totally absorbed and lost to the world in reading a fine book or listening to beautiful music. Contemplation, I surmise, is a gift given to a few who by dint of persevering long and hard in fasting, prayer and worship find God in the centre of their lives and are so able to empty self of self that they find themselves lost in the beauty and wonder of a living and loving creator and in His Divine Revelation. But here I enter deep water, so I leave the final word to Bernard: *What is God? He is at once the breadth and length and depth and height. Each of these four attributes is an object for your contemplation.*

In a Bull approving the new order Pope Paschal II ordered them to 'be free from the disturbances and pleasures of secular life that you may the more eagerly strive to please God with all the powers of your mind and soul.' Confessing that he had acquired much of his wisdom from the oaks and the beeches of the forest St. Bernard urged Henry Murdoch, the schoolmaster of York, to visit Clairvaux where he would learn something from the woods he would not find in books.

Walter Daniel writes of Aelred's meditative approach to nature leading to a knowledge of God: 'In meditating on the harmony among the variety of essences and substances in the created universe he realised how wonderful he must be who created all these ... there is apparent in nature an immensity in which divine power is seen to be impressed as a footprint ... If you closely contemplate every creature, from first to last, from highest to lowest, from the loftiest angel to the lowliest worm, you will surely discover divine goodness – which we call by no other name than his love. This love contains all, embraces all, and penetrates all ...' Aelred sees all creatures are infused with God's love and are worthy of meditative contemplation for they reveal his power, wisdom and goodness.[12] The beautiful surroundings of Rievaulx, no less attractive today, called out for meditative contemplation.

The names the Cistercians chose for their monasteries reveal both their awareness of the spiritual possibilities of their surroundings and their knowledge and love of the Scriptures: Rievaulx (Valley of Rye), Clairvaux (Valley of Light), Mellifont (Fount of Honey), Aiguebelle (Beautiful Water), St. Mary of the Fountains, and many others, 'all ingenuous yet full of meaning, bearing witness to a deep spiritual ideal'.[13]

Many names of houses reflected the importance of the imagery of water in the spiritual thinking of the White Monks who found 'intoxication in the waters of contemplation'. They drank the waters of peace not of bitterness and contradiction. They reflected on Christ's words to the Samaritan woman at the well of Siloe when He spoke 'of water that would become a fountain springing up to life everlasting'. Above the gates of Fontenay (swim upon fountains) were inscribed the words from Genesis I.2. 'And the Spirit of God moved over the waters'.[14] Such was the physical and spiritual context of the life Aelred encountered when he first visited Rievaulx, 'he found peace and a marvellous freedom from the tumult of the world … such unity and accord was there among the brethren that each seemed to belong to all and all to each'.

After Waverley in present Surrey, in a remote corner of England, Rievaulx was the first of 68 Houses of White Monks founded in England and Wales by 1150; by then some 350 had sprung up throughout Western Europe from the Ural Mountains in the east to the Iberian peninsula in the west, and from the Baltic to southern Italy. It was a time of explosive vitality when as one observer remarked: 'it seemed the whole world is turning Cistercian'. The refugee monks led by Robert of Molesme who left what they saw as the laxity of the monastic life of the famous abbey of Cluny to find solitude in the forest in 1098 could never have foreseen the consequences of their flight for, in the womb of time, Cîteaux was destined to become the mother-house of the world's first ever universal, integrated religious order and the spiritual centre of Europe.

The Cistercians became the most powerful force in Christendom inspired by the rugged determination of Alberic and Stephen, the clear sight of Isaac, the sympathy of Aelred, the dynamism of Bernard, and many other 'Fathers in Christ' to their communities.

The peace and concord Aelred found when he first walked through the gates of Rievaulx showed that the ideals set out by Stephen Harding in the charter, *Carta Caritatis,* were bearing fruit; 'we must keep the Rule (of Benedict) with complete sincerity, fidelity and openness … we have freely promised, we must keep our vows … our profession restores the divine image in the human soul and makes us Christlike, much as baptism does. It makes those who live it and love it stand out from other men as rivals of the angels and as hardly men at all'.

It is clear though that the Cistercians did not see themselves as living in an age of great Christian faith for Aelred, in a sermon later in life, referred to the fervour of the Desert Fathers, Antony, Macarius and Hilarion, and observes: 'when I think of their lives I blush greatly for us pitiable ones who live now. I am confounded seeing our torpor and sloth ... since iniquities abound the love of many grows cold'.

Deeply impressed, Aelred returned the next day to seek entry, along with one companion, while the rest of the party returned to Roxburgh. The founding abbot William, who had been secretary to Bernard of Clairvaux, welcomed the newcomers who spent the customary first four days in the guesthouse before beginning life as novices under the care of novice-master Simon, a future abbot of Rievaulx's first daughter-house at Wardon in Bedfordshire.

At the age of twenty four years Aelred found his heart's home.

EARLY YEARS AT RIEVAULX

Aelred played his part in the heavy work of constructing the monastic buildings: 'he did not spare the soft skin of his hands but manfully wielded with his slender fingers the rough tools of his field tasks. Weak though he was in body, his splendid spirit carried him through the labours of stronger and strenuous men'.[15] The new abbey church, the first priority, was oriented north-south rather than the usual west-east, because of the contour lines of the steep sides of the river valley. With typical Cistercian energy the Rye was diverted so that blocks of brownish-yellow sandstone cut from Pennypiece quarry half a mile upstream could be transported by rafts to near the building site.[16] Already, as early as 1140, on major feast days the church was so crowded with brethren that it resembled 'bees in a hive compacted into one angelic body'.[17]

Aelred's spiritual life was transformed no less than the physical landscape in which he spent some four novitiate years. In a community united in a spirit of fraternal charity 'there was no moment for idleness or dissipation' in a daily routine of singing the psalms and hymns of the liturgy, and in intensive reading of the Bible and the writings of the Fathers.

Abbot William recognised Aelred's spiritual progress by appointing him novice-master to replace Simon, who was elected abbot of daughter house Wardon in Bedfordshire in 1135. William saw in Aelred the qualities of tact, gentleness and discretion needed to assist new recruits to overcome their initial problems in settling to the disciplines of monastic life and in revealing its hidden possibilities of spiritual growth.

Further evidence of William's confidence came with his choice of Aelred as representative of the Cistercian monasteries in Yorkshire to travel to Rome in a disputed case over Thurston's successor as Archbishop of York where a kinsman of King Stephen had been appointed. Passing through Burgundy it is very likely that Aelred called at Clairvaux, Rievaulx's mother-house, to consult with Abbot Bernard, his Father-Immediate. Bernard was already emerging as an energetic and charismatic leader in the Cistercian Order, though he was never the head. Clairvaux herself became the fruitful mother of the astonishing number of 64 daughters.

At such a meeting Bernard, impressed by the humility and zeal of the young monk, asked him to put in writing his early experiences, suggesting the title *Speculum Caritatis, 'The Mirror of Love'*. Aelred's objection that he was only 'a graduate of the kitchen' and therefore inadequate for such a task was countered by Bernard recalling his time as steward to King David; 'the dispensing of carnal food was committed to you in the royal household, that, in due course, you might concoct spiritual things in the household of our King and refresh the eaters with food of the word of God'.

Bernard's confidence in the young monk Aelred was amply justified in the spiritual classic *The Mirror of Love.*

In 1147 Aelred's talents were further recognised when he was elected to take the place of Maurice who, 'irked by the uneasy burdens of pastoral care', resigned as abbot of Rievaulx after two years in office' to resume his seat in the cloister. Maurice was successor to the founding abbot William who died in 1145. A monk of Durham Cathedral, Maurice was a distinguished scholar who joined Rievaulx as early as 1132; he earned the soubriquet 'a second Bede' for his pre-eminence in learning; according to Walter

Daniel, Maurice was a man 'of great sanctity and of outstanding judgement'.

The only surviving medieval illustration of Aelred.
M.S. Douai 392
Opening words of Mirror of Love: 'Genuine and discreet Humility is the indeed the Virtue of the Saints.'

DEVOTIONAL WORKS

The Mirror of Love

The theme of *The Mirror* is the place of love in man's growing personal relationships with God and his fellow-men; it deals with the nature of love, its joys and rewards, and the hardships of contrary ways. A true Christian is a complete lover whose soul has an infinite capacity for love of friend and foe alike.[18]

The human person as created by God in His image is happy, unmarred by sin; that image is disfigured but not destroyed by sin and can be restored by our active participation in the grace flowing from Christ's death and resurrection. Perfect happiness will finally be achieved only in the life to come.

The Mirror deals at length with our present situation in this life, where charity, the true goal of monastic observance, co-exists and competes in the soul with self-centredness. Love resides in the will and the intellect as well as in the emotions. We are free to choose the way of charity, humility and self-denial leading upwards to God or the way of self-love, pride and lust dragging us down to earth and eternal damnation.

In true love the soul is freed from the anguish of sin and, inwardly at peace, can love itself in total serenity; only then is the monk able to extend his love to others in that spirit of fraternal charity which is the goal of monastic life. Thus by stages the capacity for love is increased to embrace friend and foe alike and ultimately God Himself, the source of all love.

Aelred distinguishes three Sabbaths, love of self, love of fellow-men, love of God. Love is the soul's true Sabbath bringing peace and a realisation that love is his reason for creating, guiding and planning all things from beginning to end. Crucial is the observance of Christ's new commandment that his followers love one another.

In *The Mirror* the young Aelred reveals himself not only as a monastic theologian and a philosopher who could rival the scholastics but as a young monk with an exceptional capacity for friendship who speaks to God in sublime prayers and meditations. Aelred bares his soul and eloquently expressed the very heart of Cistercian thinking on the complex subject of love.

'When Jesus was twelve years old'

Aelred's brief work, an Exposition of the Gospel reading on the above text, was addressed to a young friend Ivo, a monk of the daughter-house of Wardon. In it Aelred uses Luke's account of the visit of the boy Jesus to the temple to symbolise the growth of a life of devotion. Jesus goes before us as our leader and teaches as we grow from youth to manhood through times of darkness and light. Just as the Lord Jesus is conceived and born in us so he grows and is nourished in us until we attain perfect manhood, to the measure of the stature of the fullness of Christ. Ivo is urged, like the prodigal son, to return from the land of unlikeness and is encouraged to reflect on the nature of Jesus and the 'sweet abiding memory of his name' by asking graphic questions: 'Where were you those three days, good Jesus?' 'Who set food and drink before you?' 'Who took your shoes off?' Ivo is advised that devotion grows through tears of joy and sadness: 'What are you doing, O my soul, O my wretched, sinful soul? Why do you hold back? Break forth sweet tears, let nothing impede your course'.[19]

Aelred, like Bernard and later Ignatius, recommended inserting oneself into the Gospel story as a profitable way of meditation.

The Life Of Recluses

The Life of Recluses is a long letter to his sister by Aelred, 'a brother in the flesh and in the spirit'. It is primarily intended as a guide to beginners in the eremitical lifestyle, the most highly esteemed form of religious life, very much in the tradition of Cuthbert on Inner Farne. A good friend of Aelred was Godric, the hermit of Finchale, whose neighbour was his sister Burchwen, an anchoress.

The letter gives advice on everyday practical matters; diet, dress, daily routine and advises the recluse either to support herself by the work of her own hands or by receiving enough for her daily sustenance from some benefactor. Her life should be one of poverty and simplicity where silence is the norm: "Let her lips be silent that she may speak in the spirit, let her belief she is not by herself when alone, for then she is with Christ. Let her then sit and hold her peace, listening to Christ and speaking with him. She should be as a dead woman buried in a cave with Christ to rise again to a new life through baptism pleasing to God in body and soul as a true bride of Christ."
Relieved of all worldly cares let her find peace of mind and spirit; she is to behold the evil and weep with them, rejoice in the good and in the riches of divine grace, her heart to be a Noah's Ark embracing all.[20]

Aelred wrote this loving and mature letter late in life when, crippled with arthritis and in much pain from gallstones, he was himself a recluse spending much of his time alone in a cell next to the infirmary. In advising his sister to guard against the temptations of the flesh he revealed his own inner struggles as a young man: 'My God, what crosses, what tortures that poor wretch suffered, until at last the love of chastity was granted to him. Now a sick man he is growing old yet even so he does not flatter himself that he is safe'. By regular prayer and meditation on the scriptures Aelred's sister will rejoice in the riches of divine grace whereas 'upon me lies the burden of making whole again what was broken, finding what was lost, mending what was torn'.

Walter describes how Aelred had a small chamber of brick built under the floor of the novice-house into which water flowed from hidden rills. Its entrance lay beneath a broad stone so that nobody would notice it. When he was alone Aelred would enter and 'immerse his whole body in the icy cold water, and so quench the heat in himself of every vice'.[21] He clearly found it helpful to follow the ascetic practice of monks in the Irish tradition like Drythelm and Cuthbert of bathing in cold water though he does not go so far as to recommend it for his sister.

The letter ends with the thoughts of eternal bliss in the vision, knowledge and love of God. Filial love and a warm and gentle piety tempers the austerity of the Cistercian rule to make Aelred's loving letter to his sister, whose name and location is unknown, a charming composition where he displays a special genius as a teacher and pastor of souls. In setting out an easy and practical guide on how to pray in '*The Life of Recluses*' Aelred unwittingly discovered something that would survive in the life of the Church at large even when the anchorholds he knew fell into disuse.[22]

Aelred's *Pastoral Prayer*

This is his most intimate and personal work: in it his weaknesses and sufferings are placed in the context of divine providence and seen as instrumental in his own sanctification and in his service to the community. He is at one with fellow abbot Guerric of Igny: 'I am the handmaid of Christ, be it done to me according to thy word … I am a mother in love and concern … all of you are indeed mothers of the Son who is given to you and in you whereby you have conceived in fear of the Lord – take care then, holy mother, take care of the new-born child, until Christ be formed in you.'[23]

His deep love for the brethren is evident: 'You know, Lord, my intention is not so much to be their superior as to lovingly help them and humbly serve them, to be at their side, be one of them … may they live at peace, each and all … give me wisdom, Sweet Lord, that I may rule thy people well … Teach me, Holy Spirit, to spend myself on their behalf.' Aelred prays that his good fortune, his health, his sickness, his death 'what I am in any way, the fact that I live, feel, perceive, let it all be available for them and all be spent for them for whom thyself didst not disdain to be spent.'

This he believed to be God's will for him where he found personal fulfillment after so many personal struggles. Aelred is first and foremost an abbot at the service of his brethren.

Spiritual Friendship

Spiritual Friendship[24] was written between 1164 and 1167, in Aelred's final years. Along with the *Mirror of Charity*, it is ranked as a minor spiritual classic and is a sequel to the *Mirror.* Drawing heavily on the Confessions of St. Augustine and Cicero's *De Amicitia* which he 'seasons with the salt of holy scripture' the ageing abbot combines his spiritual and historical concerns for his own community and for those in the world outside the cloister.

The book is in the form of a Socratic dialogue, where Aelred as abbot is the central figure answering questions from fellow-monks Ivo, Walter and Gratian on 'the rules of a pure and holy love'.

Spiritual Friendship is an original work in the sense that, traditionally, monastic friendship was reserved for God alone, as human friendship in a closed community could be divisive and lead to factions, even homosexuality. Aelred took a rather different view. 'If you shut out the sunlight of human friendship … they are no better than beasts who give the name of life to living without friendship, without loving and without being loved … our friend Gratian I rightly call friendship's child for he spends all his energy in seeking to love and being loved'. Aelred tells us that true friendship is enduring, disinterested, open, sure sign of spiritual health, of a soul growing in genuine Christian love; it touches the sweetness of Christ and is a foretaste of heaven where 'no one hides his thoughts or disguises his affections … it is easy to pass from Man's friendship to God's for he who abides in friendship abides in God and God in him for God is friendship'. He advises that the

surest way of learning about the nature of God is to study the divine image in man.
In human friendship we talk and laugh together, serve each other, study together and share things trifling and serious: sometimes we disagree, but without passion, we teach and learn from one another, feel the want of our friends when absent and welcome their home - coming with joy; these are the signs of heartfelt affection which are as tinder to the fire and make of many one mind and heart.

As we grow in the religious life, Aelred continues, and in spiritual understanding, together with the gravity of mature years, such friendships of the flesh and the young pass easily into higher regions as the affections become purified.

This is Aelred at his best, characteristically outspoken in his humanism yet serenely optimistic: the rich spiritual fruit of friendship begins to touch the sweetness of Christ and we begin to feel and taste how sweet he is. Friendship is thus poured out upon us all and returned by all to God, when God shall be all in all. It is even claimed that Aelred's treatise on friendship leading to love is 'perhaps the most complete and sophisticated in the history of Christian thought'.[25]

Knowles does well to remind us that Aelred's immense literary output – as well as *The Mirror* and *Spiritual Friendship* and his other devotional and historical writings, some sixty letters are extant and no doubt there are many which are not – is all the more remarkable when we reflect that he was not a philosopher, writing at ease on his terrace, untroubled by the hard realities of life, nor even an Augustine among his pupils in peaceful, sunny Cassiciacum, but an infirm, tireless Abbot, the ruler of a vast household, the counsellor of bishops and kings, who snatched time between his solitary prayer and the visits of those who needed his help, to add a few sentences to the roll in his bare and comfortless cell.[26]

Nor indeed, with a few notable exceptions like Bernard, was writing in the Cistercian tradition where the focus was on contemplative prayer, study and manual labour.

Aelred's last work, '*De Anima*', 'On the soul', probably unfinished, is his least satisfactory. Aelred was a pragmatist, not a Plato or Augustine; perhaps the philosophical nature of his inquiry was too complex for him as his health failed.

AELRED AS HISTORIAN

Aelred's historical writings, unique among his Cistercian contemporaries, all point the way to spiritual advancement while, at the same time, revealing the political anarchy prevailing in England following the death of Henry I in 1135 when the throne was contested between his nephew Stephen of Blois and Matilda. The strife and famine in secular England at the time was in stark contrast to the peace Aelred found at Rievaulx, yet Aelred's historical writings focus more on people than their times: he addresses Henry II praising the virtue of his ancestors and urging him to emulate them: he exhorts all men and women, the great and the humble, whether within or without the cloister, to follow the example of the saints in virtue and faith, most especially the saints of his native Northumbria.

The Battle of the Standard fought in 1138 was 'one of the greatest - yet unheralded - battles in British history, the first major collision between the nascent kingdoms of England and Scotland':[27] Aelred's account,[28] written in 1158, so graphic that he may well have been an eye-witness, was complementary to Prior Richard's earlier account and illustrated the conflicting loyalties of the time. When the Scottish army under King David, Aelred's much loved patron, invaded England in support of Matilda it was routed by the English, one of whose leading barons was Walter l'Espec, the Norman ruler of Helmsley Castle and patron of Rievaulx. Aelred's account describes the valour and piety of Walter and in a lament following the death of David wrote: 'there was no prince like him in our day, beloved of God and men, supporter of churches and monasteries, of the poor and the oppressed, whose only sin was to invade England with a savage and undisciplined army'.

Drawing on a variety of sources including Simeon's History of the Kings and Asser's Life of Alfred, Aelred's *Genealogy of the Kings* aimed to reconcile the Anglo-Saxon past with the Norman present. He affirmed the claim of Henry, son of King David, to the throne of

England by showing his blood descent from Edward I. In fact, the Genealogy reaches back to the pagan Woden, from whom the Saxon kings claimed descent, and eventually to Adam, the father of the human race. Thus, whether in pagan or Christian times, the royal house was invested with a divine sanction. In charting the fortunes of the Saxon kings from Alfred to the Conquest a constant note struck is church reform and devotion to the Holy See. The roles of temporal and spiritual rulers are different yet complementary.

Preaching to a Synod at Troyes on the royal aspect of priesthood Aelred said: 'You are kings, and as much higher than earthly kings as the heavenly kingdom is above the earthly. They rule the bodies of men, you rule their souls. They bear the material sword, to you is committed the spiritual one. It is theirs to give temporal goods to their subjects, yours to grant the eternal'.

Aelred's reputation as a writer was confirmed when Lawrence, a kinsman and abbot of Westminster Abbey, invited him to write a Life of Edward the Confessor. Edward, the last of the Saxon kings, had died on the 5 January 1066 and his body was elevated to a new shrine in the abbey on 13 October 1163. Edward had already been declared a saint by Rome, the first English saint, along with Thomas à Becket, to be officially canonised. Numerous miracles were later reported at his tomb. Aelred may well have been the preacher at the great occasion of the translation. His new *Life,* superseding an earlier *Life* by Osbert of Clare, was most successful and popular in this country and on the continent throughout the Middle Ages. As in the Genealogy he aimed to reconcile the past and present. Alfred had been consecrated King by the Pope himself, according to Aelred's account, whereby divine sanction had been bestowed on the royal line, now represented by Henry II, 'the cornerstone joining the English and Norman nations'. Aelred's enthusiastic biographer Walter Daniel considered the new Life of Edward 'brilliant for its literary excellence'.

Latin hagiography was fashionable again in the twelfth century when Aelred wrote his Life of Ninian at the invitation of Bishop Christian of Galloway. In rhythmic Latin this fine literary composition stressed Ninian's close connection with home and personal acquaintance with St. Martin of Tours: he portrays Ninian as a simple missionary founding the diocese based on Whithorn and drawing attention to the close similarity of the church at Whithorn, the Candida Casa, to that of St. Martin, from whose region Ninian had brought his masons. This polished work emphasises the rich Christian traditions and the catholicity of the twelfth century Scottish church: it was also a justification for King David's re-organisation of the Church in Scotland.[29]

Less accomplished and rated one of his poorer works where 'the arrangement is faulty and confusing and the style often turgid and weak' is Aelred's treatise 'On the Miracles of the Holy Fathers who rest in Hexham church'.[30] Yet the account is of immense local interest. Describing the ritual and ceremony of the translation of holy relics committed to the care of his father and uncle, Aelred reveals the pride the community had for their illustrious predecessors and the reverence in which their bones were held; 'just men live in everlasting remembrance, whose bones, even though dead, burgeon with frequent miracles from their resting place, and whose memory which the years had buried or negligence destroyed does not fail to continue with manifest signs'. The deep sense of the presence of great and holy men was felt so directly and physically as to be shocking to our own very different sensibilities.

Aelred may well have been the preacher when the bones of old Saxon holy men, Acca, Alchmund, Fredenbert, Eata, Tilbert, were translated in the church of Hexham on 3 March 1154. Aelred's account captures some of the colour and solemnity of the great occasion; for him it was especially joyful for the rededication marked the completion of the restoration work of the ruined abbey church begun by his grandfather Eilaf I, and continued by his father Eilaf II, both now dead, work in which he had actively participated as a young boy. The prior and the canons entered the church with bared feet, prostrated themselves before the altar and, with psalms and responses, sang the praises of the saints; the coffer containing the relics was placed on the altar and from it arose an odour as if 'sent from Paradise'. The precious relics were carefully unwrapped and placed in separate caskets set on a richly ornamented table beside the high altar.

Thus, as former glories were relived, the holy men were canonised, to be recognised henceforth as saints.

The earliest written lives of the saints were lost in the Danish invasions when the fine libraries built up at Hexham by Wilfrid and Acca had been burnt down. If the story of these lives were to live on it fell to the pen of Aelred to preserve their memory, drawing on family history and the legends of local folklore. In the second part of the Saints of Hexham he records tales from a past very different to his own time.

The army of King Malcolm of Scotland was encamped on the north bank of the Tyne opposite Hexham on one of his several raids into Northumbria, while the citizens of the town crowded into the prior church praying that they would be saved by the right of sanctuary, for there was no castle or town wall to protect them. However, when some soldiers from Galloway were killed by local brigands, Malcolm deemed the right of sanctuary forfeit and sought retribution. That night the priest of Hexham had a vision when two bishops in white rode up, announcing they were Wilfrid and Cuthbert come to save their people and the resting place of the saints. In the morning a thick fog enveloped the valley of the Tyne so that the Scottish army could not see their way. Three days later such a flood poured down the Tyne that a crossing was impossible. Perceiving the hand of God at work Malcolm withdrew and the people and priory were spared the fate suffered in Halfdene's invasion with the Danes.

A sacrilegious soldier from Galloway, who tried to break the lock to raid the round church dedicated to the Blessed Virgin Mary by Wilfrid, was punished by a devil and died, leaving his body as food for beasts and birds.

A youth accused of theft could find no friend to pledge for his good conduct and was therefore to be hanged: as the gallows were being erected the youth prayed to Wilfrid to save him. The crowd laughed until two horsemen rode up as sureties and the youth's life was saved; thus did the local saints marvellously punish evil-doers and protect those who earnestly sought their intercession.

Aelred was anxious to keep the memories of local saints alive in the consciousness of the people for he saw clearly how rapidly Saxon traditions were disappearing as the Normans increasingly dominated the spiritual and political life in England. Only two decades after the Conquest the only Saxon bishop in office was at Worcester, the names of Wilfrid and Acca had disappeared from the Martyrologies, only the reputation of Cuthbert saved him from a similar fate. Aelred invited his contemporaries to help him in his mission: thus Reginald of Durham was encouraged to write his Little Book on the Miracles of Saint Cuthbert and the Life and Miracles of Saint Godric of Finchal.[31]

LIFE AT RIEVAULX

The ideals inspiring Aelred's writings were more than fine words as the doctrine of salvation he preached and his own personality became increasingly imprinted on the daily life of the monks and lay brothers of the community of Rievaulx Abbey.

All who knew Aelred remark on his compassion; Jocelin of Furness describes him as a 'man of the highest integrity, of great practical wisdom, witty and eloquent, generous and discreet ... he exceeded all his fellow prelates in patience and tenderness. He was full of sympathy for the infirmities, both physical and moral, of others'. In seventeen years, Walter Daniel knew of no one who was turned away: 'wanderers in the world to whom no house of religion gave entry came to Rievaulx, 'the mother of mercy', and found the gates open ... all, strong and weak alike, find here a haven of peace, a spacious and calm house'. Who was there, however despised and rejected, who did not find in it a place of rest? It is the singular and supreme glory of the house of Rievaulx that above all else it teaches tolerance of the infirm and compassion with others in their needs.[32]

While many of the newcomers were for the most part unlettered, stolid and hardworking men, 'pious oxen of Christ', whose labour with the material side of the monastic life, and on the fields and farms, freed the choir monks for their spiritual disciplines, Aelred also found himself surrounded by young novice monks, eager of mind and heart to learn the Cistercian way of a life of prayer and study of the scriptures and the Fathers.

As abbot, Aelred continued the practice he had begun as novice-master of holding frequent, informal dialogues with his monks; twenty or thirty at a time came to talk together of the delights of

Holy Scripture. 'No one said: "Away with you", they walked and lay about his bed and talked with him as children chatter with their mother', they still came even in his last years when he was confined to bed by the infirmary. 'What more homely and delightful picture of Aelred as father and teacher of his monks could be found?' Yet he saw that each vocation was unique, every one an individual; some, like Simon, made a deep impression; 'The Rule of our Order forbade us to speak, but his face spoke to me, his bearing spoke, his silence talked'. His deep love for the brethren is evident in his 'Pastoral Prayer', 'You know, Lord, my intention is not so much to be their superior as to lovingly help them and humbly serve them, to be at their side, one of them … may they live at peace, each and all … give me wisdom, Sweet Lord, that I may rule thy people well … teach me, Holy Spirit, how to spend myself on their behalf'.[33]

Individual problems brought before Aelred were many, varied and very human. One novice found life very difficult; 'I am crushed down by the lengths of the vigils, I often succumb to the manual labour. The food cleaves to my mouth, more bitter than wormwood. The rough clothing cuts through my skin and flesh down to the very bones … my will longs for the delights of the world'. Another was worried because before entering the monastery he had often been reduced to tears as when reading the legends of King Arthur but now he felt no such deep emotions. Another is 'sad and awaits comfort from a father's care' … yet another defeated by depression running round now here, now there, to find someone to talk and consult'; acedia, or general weariness, was a common psychological problem.

In an eloquent passage he describes the joy he experienced in the beauty of nature and in the company of the brothers: 'When I was going round the cloister site sitting with the brethren in a loving circle, as though amid the delights of paradise, I admired the leaves, the flowers and the fruits of every tree. And in the whole of that throng, I could not find one whom I did not love, and by whom I was not loved, and I was filled with such joy. I felt my spirit was transfused into them and their affection was flowing back into me, so that I could truly say with the prophet 'Behold how good and pleasant it is for the brethren to dwell together in unity'.[34]

Aelred used vivid imagery to illustrate his prime duty of leading back to God fallen men who had chosen life in the cloisters rather than in the world. The exodus theme was especially apt. Egypt was the land of bondage to pride and cupidity; self-renunciation came with the crossing of the Red Sea; the desert was a place of trial, of suffering and temptation, but also of purification and generous self-giving, here were oases where the Holy Spirit was encountered and where 'wolves became lambs', the desert was a place to pass through, not to settle in, and in God's appointed time, with Benedict as their Moses, the monks would come to the Jordan, beyond which stretched the lands of silence, solitude and peace, where joy and contemplation reign, 'Be quiet, still, enduring, quietly speaking to God and speaking with Him.'[35]

Again, the monks were engaged in spiritual warfare against Satan; it was the struggle between Crusaders and Saracens elevated onto a higher plane. Cîteaux provided 'strong castles where the battlements are our poverty, the moats are charity, silence is our towers. Let each one keep to his place and defend it well ... you must know that from the day you entered here and began to serve Christ you entered a battle-ground; stand firm, prepare the soul for temptation. This is the fight, so be strong in battle'.[36] To an audience many of whom would be, like Bernard himself, former soldiers and in a landscape dominated by Norman castles, usually the home of the founding baron, this was indeed powerful imagery. Elsewhere, Aelred compares the hard task of salvation to crossing rough seas; 'The sea that keeps us from God is the world that passes ... some drown in this sea, others cross it'; marriage provides only 'a rather fragile vessel but the monastic way of life is a fine seaworthy ship'.[37] At times Bernard goes further and seems to say the Cistercian way of life is the only sure, safe ship.

Throughout Western Europe at this time there was a burgeoning devotion to the Virgin Mary in which the Cistercians played a leading role. All houses of White Monks were dedicated to Mary through whom, according to Bernard, all graces flowed. Aelred shared in this veneration of the Virgin Mary but was ever pragmatic. In an eloquent sermon on the Feast of the Assumption, he advised his brethren that 'you should in no way neglect Martha for Mary or again Mary for Martha. If you neglect Martha who should feed Jesus Christ? If you neglect Mary what use is it for

Jesus to come to your home when you taste nothing of his sweetness?'

'OUR FATHERS ARE GREAT MIRACLES'

In his *Vita* Walter Daniel compares Aelred explicitly with biblical and saintly personages of the past in the supreme model of the Master. Aelred is presented as a second Daniel, a new Joseph, David, Lot, his staff, like Noah's, worked wonders; he was Noah making his body an ark for the faithful. However, it was not the miracles Aelred worked that were of central importance but rather his virtues of charity, his austerity, his patience in suffering – marks of 'outshining sanctity'.

Aelred saw miracles in the same way as Bernard, the most renowned preacher of that age; they were signs to implant or strengthen faith, a means of bringing men to God, of little interest in themselves. God requires faith, not miracles. Is it not better, Aelred asks, to seek the gifts of humility, patience and charity? Where these are present they will be confirmed by miracles. The Cistercian preachers focused on the miracle of the Incarnation rather than the more popular theme of the Creation, for this was when, according to Bernard, 'He joined together God and man, mother and virgin, faith and the human heart ... new things, unheard of and wonderful, which exceed nature'.[38]

Walter Daniel maintained that it was the miracles Aelred worked in his monastic life, especially in his later years, that best reveal the depth of his charity; 'for I deem it unjust to show to the readers of this work the brick, wood, iron and brass in which the father abounded in external things and to be silent about the silver, gold and precious stones in which his spirit exceeded'.[39]

Aelred's miraculous powers were evident in his first few days in the monastery while he was still in the guesthouse even before becoming a novice. Walter describes how grief and desperation seized the monks as a fire flared up, threatening to burn down the buildings and all efforts to extinguish the greedy flames by water failed. Aelred remained unmoved as all were proclaiming, 'Woe to us, all is lost.' He then threw a tankard filled with cider, the native English drink, into the midst of the flames which were extinguished ‘as though the sea had flooded in’ … Oh how the brothers exulted! Oh the solemn praise of God, and thanks of praise to Aelred!

The power of his prayer is seen in the story of the emotionally unstable monk who three times tried to leave the monastery but was prevailed upon to stay; on one occasion, Aelred’s prayer raised a wall of air against his departure. The monk ‘ended his life clothed in his sacred habit, his head cradled in the abbot’s hands’ as Aelred exclaimed: ‘Saint Bernard pray for him’. The tale illustrates Aelred’s loving care for each individual brother of his community.

It is this same deep, mutual love between abbot and the brethren that was the basis of Aelred’s ability to heal.

At Revesby Aelred ordered the sub-prior who was wasting away with illness: ‘In the name of the Lord, make your way to the church and take your place with the choir, sing with them, and pray to God and through him, I believe, you will be well’. Walter records that the sub-prior was cured and clung ‘in ever growing affection to holiness, proved for his sake, of the father’. Aelred had the wisdom to see that the best remedy for one who had given up on life was to return to the daily routine of work, prayer and worship, thereby regaining health of body and spirit.

Walter records how another monk of Revesby, a craftsman crippled by an injury to his arm, was cured by the merits of Aelred when he passed his abbatical crozier three times around the injured arm.

A few examples illustrate Aelred’s growing power to effect miracles of healing as the abbot and brethren of Rievaulx grew in mutual charity.

A monk who suffered from a painful stomach complaint, and who lost his powers of speech, was restored to perfect health when the abbot put his forefinger on his mouth and ordered: ‘Speak my brother in the name of the Lord.’ A lay brother who served as a shepherd was similarly cured after days of dumbness when the abbot touched his lips saying: ‘Speak I command you in the name of Christ’. It is interesting to note how often cures involve physical contact.

A young monk fell desperately ill with heart failure, ‘his end was drawing rapidly near as he seemed to be drawing his last breath’. The abbot was summoned from the orchard and by the time he reached the ill monk ‘his pulse had ceased to beat’. Hurrying to his little oratory he gathered some relics of the saints, and the text of St. John’s Gospel, and placed them on the sick man’s breast, exclaiming with tears, ‘Beloved son, may the Son of God make you whole’. Immediately he was relieved of all his trouble.

Walter tells the bizarre tale of the young man who inadvertently swallowed a tadpole when taking a drink of water. When Aelred riding towards Rievaulx chanced upon the man his belly was frightfully swollen, his head shrunk into his monstrous body, his appearance was that of a very fat ox or sheep for the tadpole had grown into a frog, eating away the entrails of the man’s stomach day by day. ‘Oh how truly wretched is the race of humankind’, exclaims Walter. Aelred put his finger in the man’s mouth praying: “Lord God Almighty, I beseech you, by your Son the Lord Jesus, look upon this your creature, and do to him as you will and know’. At once the frog issued from the door of the mouth and fell to the ground. By next day all swelling and pain had gone and the youth gave thanks to God with all joy and praised the father Aelred ‘by whose kindly intervention he had earned the grace to be healed’. Walter stresses Aelred’s remarkable charity rather than his powers of healing and, in his tale, contrasts his revulsion at the disgusting sight of the monstrous body of the youth, a terrifying object to everybody, with the gentle and compassionate way Aelred dealt with the situation.

OUTSIDE CALLS

Outside demands made heavy calls on Aelred’s time and energy. As the most powerful and best-known Cistercian in the land, renowned for being thorough and fair-minded, he was frequently called upon to arbitrate in all manner of disputes, political as well as ecclesiastical. He arbitrated on the question of prior of Durham’s precedence and in the dispute between Furness and Savigny for jurisdiction over neighbouring Byland Abbey. He was present at a council at Westminster; he was adviser to hermits, bishops, abbots and to Kings David of Scotland and Henry II of England.

Aelred's counsel was sought in some strange cases.

He was called by St. Gilbert of Sempringham to one of the Gilbertine double monasteries at Watton in Yorkshire where a young nun, who had been entrusted to the community from the age of four, found herself totally unsuited to convent life as she grew up. She became pregnant by one of the canons who was forced to mutilate himself, while she was beaten and her feet clapped in irons. Aelred advised waiting upon the Lord. In a dream the nun was told to recite psalms, the fetters fell off, the pregnancy disappeared. In his account Aelred focused on the devotion of the nuns to their spiritual duties where they were 'visited by heavenly contemplations' rather than the unsavoury details of the case.

Aelred's success as a diplomat and negotiator owed much to the experience he had gained as a young man in the royal court of Scotland where his responsibilities as steward taught him obedience to superiors and to be at ease in the presence of those in high places. When Aelred became a monk he did not forget what he had learned in and about the world. The reputation his diplomatic abilities gained for Rievaulx as he acted in affairs of Church and Crown contributed to the renown and prosperity not only of that house but of the Cistercian order in England.

As an abbot he was required by the Constitution to undertake the long and arduous journey to Cîteaux every September for the Annual General Chapter and to make annual pastoral visits to Rievaulx's five daughter-houses of Wardon (1135), Melrose (1136), Dundrennan (1143), Revesby (1143) and Rufford (1146). Though the order later allowed abbots of far distant abbeys to attend Cîteaux every fourth year, and allowed Aelred discretion as his health failed, in carrying out his duties both within and outside the monastery, the evidence is that he did not spare himself.

As late as 1165 Aelred visited the daughter house of Dundrennan[40] where, twenty three years after its foundation, he slept 'in a small dwelling where no part of the roof, not even the space of a couple of feet, was free from the penetration of the rain'. Miraculously, Aelred in his bed stayed dry. Either the buildings were not yet finished or they had quickly fallen into a state of disrepair.

On the same visit Aelred celebrated the feast day of St. Cuthbert, patron of his journeyings, at Kirkcudbright, the fishing port in the Solway Firth which bears the saint's name.

These arduous journeys were broken by visits to good friends in the north, Reginald of Durham and Godric of Finchal: it seems likely that he would also visit his contemporary Robert, the saintly abbot of Newminster in the vale of Wansbeck, the subject of the next chapter. Just months before his death Aelred was enjoying the company of his old and dear friend, Waldef, now abbot of Melrose Abbey, Scotland's equivalent of Rievaulx as a powerhouse of prayer.[41]

For a man racked with the pain of gallstones and crippled with arthritis, such long and difficult journeys on horseback, along bumpy roads, through a forested and hilly landscape where wolves still roamed and Border affrays were frequent, represented devotion to duty on a heroic scale.

Knowles has calculated that Aelred was away from his monastery for three to four months in the year. One wonders if the appointment of co-abbots, as Benedict Biscop did at Monkwearmouth to cover the long absences, was ever considered.

THE SABBATH OF SABBATHS

Not surprisingly, there were times when the responsibilities of ruling such a large and varied community weighed heavily on the ailing abbot. 'All is turned to weariness; everything I see a burden. If someone speaks I scarcely hear, if someone knocks I am hardly aware of it. My heart is like a stone, my eyes dry'. 'It is a great persecution to know the weaknesses, the sorrows and the burdens of many, to suffer for everyone, to be sad with the sad'. At these times he turned to the Scriptures, 'when suddenly thy grace, good Jesu, like Rebecca running up, disperses the darkness with light, breaks my hardness. Sighs give way to tears and heavenly joy comes with tears'. He found strength too in the singing of Divine Office in the great abbey church where 'their praise rises to heaven as one single flame in which we all are united'. 'This is the testimony of our conscience, that this house is a holy place because it generates for its God sons who are peacemakers'.

As his health failed the Chapter-general allowed Aelred to use his discretion in his duties as abbot. When he retired for spells to his cell by the infirmary, there were mutterings of 'glutton, wine-bibber who gives his body to baths and ointments'.

One disturbed monk was moved to violence, rushing into his cell, he seized Aelred as he sat on an old mat by his hearth rubbing his painful limbs, and threw him on the cinders of the fire. Those present seized the assailant and would have beaten or expelled him, but Aelred embraced and blessed him, saying 'He is my son and he is ill'. When he told the monks in a homily that, 'I love you all as I love myself and truly as a mother after her sons', he clearly meant it.

Hagiographers invariably conclude their work with a detailed account of the death of the saint; we have already seen this in the final hours of Boisil at Melrose, of Cuthbert on Inner Farne, and of Bede at Monkwearmouth \ Jarrow. Walter Daniel, Aelred's long-time companion and biographer, served as his infirmarian as he lay dying in his cell; 'an awe-inspiring experience' he calls it.

For a whole year he had suffered greatly with bodily pain, a racking cough, burning thirst, and difficult breathings; on Christmas Eve he began 'to depart and be with Christ. I said to him: "Of a truth the Lord Abbot now suffers much" … He gazed on me fondly; "Yes, my son, yes, yes just as you say, I am greatly vexed by the agonies of this sickness, by the will of the Lord Jesus Christ there will soon be end to all this trouble".'

Very weak in flesh yet very strong in spirit, on 3 January he summoned all the monks to seek their permission to leave, 'to go hence from exile to the fatherland, from darkness to light, from this evil world to God'. All present wept as he concluded: 'God who knows all things knows that I love you all as myself and, as earnestly as a mother after her sons, I long after you all in the bowels of Jesus Christ'.[42]

Fortified by the Viaticum of the most sacred mystery of the Body and Blood of Our Lord and anointed with holy oil by Roger, the venerable abbot of nearby Byland, his face looked brighter and fuller. He was now in truth 'a living soul in a withered body; as his time drew near he said to the company assembled in his cell: 'Silver and gold have I none, hence I make no will for I possess nothing of my own; whatever I have and myself are yours'. He then distributed his glossed psalter, his 'Confessions of St. Augustine', his text of St. John's Gospel, a few relics, and a much loved cross, a present from Henry Murdac, Archbishop of York. 'I said to him in a low voice; 'Lord, gaze upon the cross, let your eye be where your heart is'. He replied, 'My lord, my God and my Saviour, my glory and hope for evermore … hasten for Christ's love'. At the fourth watch of the night before the Ides of January in the year of the Incarnation 1167, in the 57th year of his life, he died; his whole life had been a novitiate for this day, his Sabbath of Sabbaths.

'OUR FATHER IS DEAD'

'Our father is dead, he has vanished from our world like the morning sunshine, and may hearts long that this great light should flood with brightness the memory of generations to come.' In an eloquent lament for the man who 'sought me out, formed me, established me, cherished me, nourished me, taught me and loved me,' Walter grieves as he has been abandoned by his leader and feels gravely wounded, depressed and tearful; yet he convinces himself that 'lamentation is not the best course, instead to live well is best' for Aelred, 'equal in soul as well as in body to many a great saint' has now passed from 'the light of the world to the lustre of Paradise, from mortal life to everlasting life, from this changing world to the stillness of heaven.'[43]

Walter concludes with a prayer, begging God to make him 'happy in the future, in the company and in the sight of beloved Aelred'.

After Mass and the funeral rites observed, Aelred's body was taken for burial in the chapter-house next to his predecessor William, the saintly first abbot of Rievaulx, who had welcomed him as a youth when he sought entry a lifetime ago.

Aelred has been called the 'Bernard of the North'. It is true that both men were zealous monks and gifted abbots in the golden early years of the Cistercians and that both successfully combined the active and contemplative lives to a remarkable degree, yet surely there were marked differences in character. Aelred could be scathing of monks who were indolent, who in their meditations mixed Virgil with the Gospels, and Horace with the prophets, or who kept does, fawns, cranes or greyhounds, yet he was a mild disciplinarian, courteous with friends, compassionate to those in need. Bernard, on the other hand, could be 'provocative, violent and uncompromising'.[44] He was the fiery preacher of the Second Crusade; his language was, at times, acerbic as when he was describing what he saw as the excesses of the Black Monks of Cluny. Aelred was altogether a gentler person.

Believing that knowledge was sterile unless it leads to love, Aelred's simple, direct, intuitive mind saw that there was wisdom to be found among trees and stones that could not be found in books; he would tell his monks; 'Christ came not to teach grammar or rhetoric but charity, meekness and humility'. He practised what he preached. Proud of his local heritage and aware of the value of ascetic practices and the supreme importance of the Rule, he was full conscious of changing times and spoke directly as a monk to monks with an authentic evangelistic voice.

Discretion, described by Cassian as the mother and nurse of all virtues, was one of Aelred's abiding virtues. Walter Daniel says the monks were able to be as open with Aelred as children with their mother. Reginald of Durham's dedication to Aelred in the Little Book on the Wonders of St. Cuthbert similarly has maternal connotations: 'we have often drunk the milk of refreshment and consolation from the breasts of your motherly compassion. For from the three fingers of your paternal rule hangs the regulating vessel of discretion'.

In an age when the concept of love was explored as never before, he became a doctor of spiritual love where his sincere and candid Christian humanism charted the soul's progress from human to divine love, the return of the prodigal. Life for him was all about redemption, recreation and the re-discovery of our divine image. He impresses 'by his sensibility to emotions shared in some degree by all civilised mankind and by reason of a vivid power of self expression'. With his intense love of fellow men, he was a man ahead of his time, 'a harbinger of the Franciscans'.

Aelred was not a mystical theologian who probed deeply into the mysteries of the faith but his position as a monk and writer, wholly unique in England and abroad, is due partly to the limpid sincerity with which he laid bare, in his wish to help others, the growth and progress of his own mind and heart from the human to the divine, and partly to the candid humanism of his most characteristic pages.

Rather like Bede, Aelred reveals himself in some completeness through his writings so he lingers in the memory more than other English monk of the twelfth century. Of the 2,100 professed White Monks and some 3,200 lay brothers in England and Wales in that golden age of monasticism, it is Aelred who stands out as he speaks to us directly from the heart: as we read Walter Daniel's Vita we catch a glimpse of Rievaulx in its first eagerness, at once real and yet alien to our habits of thought.[45]

THE SEARCH GOES ON

From the twelfth century right through to the Dissolution in the 1530's there were as many as sixty-eight Houses of White Monks in England and Wales, and eleven in Scotland. Although one in three monasteries moved sites for a variety of reasons none ever failed. At the beginning of the twenty-first century there is only one Cistercian monastery in each of England, Wales and Scotland: Mount St. Bernard in Leicestershire, Caldey Island off the coast of Pembrokeshire in Wales, and Sancta Maria Abbey at Nunraw in the Lammermuir Hills of Lothian in Scotland.

The community of Sancta Maria Abbey: the same habit and the same Rule as the Founding Fathers of the Cistercian Order.

However, the aims and ideals of Cistercians have not changed since Aelred's time as a monk of Mount Saint Bernard reminds us: his spiritual sons have a deep desire to interpret for their own times the traditions and spirituality which Aelred and his contemporaries in the Order of Cîteaux first lived and then handed on … the search for God was the soul of the Office in choir, their reading, and their work. The environment was poor, penitential and apart; but it was intended to form a community of love suffused with the joy of the Holy Spirit in nearness to God. The call and the mission are the same today as in the twelfth century.[46]

A key influence in the life of Aelred was the Rule of Benedict composed in the mid 6th century for a small community of monks living in a cave at Monte Cassino in Southern Italy. The Rule is short - no more than 10,000 words - and is a mine of human and spiritual wisdom: an invaluable guide for all time, not just for monks, but for parents, headteachers, or anyone in authority. Benedict is well chosen as the patron saint of Europe for his Rule has been influential in the growth of Christian civilisation in Western Europe. A visitor to a Cistercian monastery will be received with the same warmth as at Rievaulx in Aelred's time and will experience the spirit of the Rule in his reception: 'All visitors who call are welcomed as if they were Christ, for one day he will say: "I was a stranger and you took me in" (Matthew 25)'… it is in the welcome given to the poor and the strangers that special attention should be paid, because in them Christ is more truly received'.[47]

NOTES AND REFERENCES

1. PENDRICK B. Reflections on St. Aelred of Rievaulx. Chronicle 14. Buckfast Abbey 1944.

2. DANIEL WALTER. The Letter to Maurice p.147 – 158 in The Life of Aelred of Rievaulx, trans. F.M. Powicke. Cistercian Fathers Series 57.

3. In the first three centuries there was no law requiring priests to be celibate; The law, introduced c.306 by Council of Elvira in Spain, fell into abeyance in 'Dark Ages'; reaffirmed by Pope Gregory VII (1073 –1085); written into Church law by Second Lateran Council in 1139; regarded as a law of the Church not of God.

4. REGINALD of Durham. Libellus de Admirandis Beati Cuthberti Virtutibus Surtees Society (S.S.) Vol.1. 1835.

5. The Priory of Durham, ed. J. Raine. S.S. 1863, Vol. P. 191.

6. Speculum Caritatis. The Mirror of Charity. AELRED . Cistercian Fathers. Series 17. Kalamazoo 1900. 1.28.

7. Ibid.

8. BURTON JANET The Monastic Order in Yorkshire 1069-1215. p. 101. 1999 In these years an astonishing number of religious houses was founded in the county of Yorkshire: 16 Benedictine; 17 of regular canons, mainly Augustinian and Premonstratensian; 2 Cluniac; 8 Cistercian; and 25 nunneries.

9. DANIEL WALTER. Vita A. p.57. Walter's life is written in an exuberant and fanciful style but is the best first hand account of monastic life in the early Cistercian years.

10. MERTON THOMAS. Collected Poems. St. Aelred. 1977.

11. ISAAC DE L'ETOILE, Sermon XIV cited by T. Merton in The Silent Life, p.98.

12. SOMMERFELDT JOHN R. Aelred of Rievaulx. Pursuing Perfect Happiness. 2005. p.48.

13. MERTON T. The Waters of Siloe 1976. p. 273.

14. Ibid p.272.

15. Vita A.p.105.

16. Dept. of Environment. Rievaulx Abbey HMSO. 1967. The River Rye was later diverted from the east to the west side of the valley to solve a boundary dispute with nearby Byland Abbey and to give Rievaulx access to water meadows, a typically radical Cistercian solution to a problem. The two abbeys were so close that each could hear the other's bells at all hours of the day and night 'which was not fitting and could not be endured'. Old Byland moved to New Byland, near Coxwold, several miles away and out of earshot.

17. Vita A.p.119.

18. SQUIRE AELRED. Aelred of Rievaulx. A Study SPCK 1969 p. 25.

19. Ibid p.67 – 70

20. Ibid p.118.

21. Vita A.p.108

22. SQUIRE ibid p.128

23. Pastoral Prayer of Aelred of Rievaulx. Dacre press. Westminster 1955.

24. Spiritual Friendship. Aelred of Rievaulx. Cistercian Series 5. 1977.

25. SOMMERFELDT. ibid. Endpiece.

26. KNOWLES DAVID. Saints and Scholars. 1963. p.45.

27. ROSE A. Kings in the North: The House of Percy in British History. 2002. p.55

28. For probably the first full translation from the Latin of Aelred's account see Northern Catholic History No. 48. 2007. p.42-52. Translated by Anthony Storey. The battle takes its name from the holy rallying point of the English army – a ship's mast was fixed to a four wheeled cart; at the top of the mast was a silver casket, a pyx, containing a host, the Blessed Sacrament.

29. MACQUARRIE ALAN. The Saints of Scotland. Essays in Scottish Church History. AD.450 – 1093. Edinburgh 1997. Chapter 3, p.50.

30. The Priory of Hexham, ibid S.S. ed. 1863. Vol 1. p 1 XXV.

31. SQUIRE. ibid. p.113.

32. Vita A. p.118

33. Mirror. ibid 1.34

34. Spiritual Friendship. ibid p.112.

35. 36. 37. HALLIER AMEDEE. The Monastic Theology of Aelred of Rievaulx. Cistercian Series 2. 1969.

38. WARD BENEDICTA. Miracles and the Medieval Mind. 1982. p.25.

39. Vita A. p.22 et seq. for miracles cited.

40. Dundrennan, founded in 1142 by King David in Galloway 'in wild country where the people are altogether barbarous'; a fine example of an abbey showing the austere yet graceful beauty of Cistercian architecture. Mary Queen of Scots was a guest there on 15 May 1568, her last night on Scottish soil, before she sailed to Workington into a nineteen year exile and eventual execution. The O.S. Map bears the name Port Mary.

41. Melrose, founded from Rievaulx in 1136, herself the fruitful mother of four daughter abbeys at Kinloss in Moray, Newbottle in Midlothian, Balmerino in Fife and Coupar Angus in Perth. Aelred would have been as impressed as modern visitors by the grandeur of the abbey buildings and the location beside the Tweed beneath the three volcanic cones of the Eildon Hills. One wonders if Aelred made a pilgrimage to the site of St. Cuthbert's old Saxon monastery two miles downstream. His noted veneration of the Saint makes this very likely.

42. ita A. p.136.

43. Ibid. Lament for Aelred p.140 – 146.

44. KNOWLES DAVID. Christian Monasticism. 1969. p.79.

45. KNOWLES DAVID. Saints and Scholars. p.34. 1964.

46. DIENIER PAUL. St. Aelred of Rievaulx. Essay in Benedict's Disciples. Ed. D.H. Farmer 1980. p.194.

47. The Rule of Benedict. Chapter 53. Ealing Abbey 1969

7

‘ALL NOW IS SILENCE HERE’

Visiting the ruins of Newminster Abbey early in the 19th century the Reverend John Hodgson wrote: ‘All now is silence here – the keepers of the tombs and the servants of God have long since gone, and the destroying hands of time and man have levelled its altars with the earth.’[1]

Northumberland is known more for its castles than its churches. Some five centuries of intermittent Border warfare and raiding was more conducive to the growth of fortified buildings than the places of worship. Yet some medieval religious houses in the county remain to impress today: Wilfrid’s restored abbey at Hexham, the Augustinian priory of Brinkburn in mid-Coquetdale, and the priory on the headland overlooking the mouth of the Tyne at Tynemouth, to name the best. Sadly, one of Northumberland’s foremost abbeys was listed by English Heritage recently among important buildings in the region in danger of disappearing altogether into the landscape such was its ruinous state. Few people outside the locality, apart from those interested in monastic history, have ever heard of the abbey of Newminster and the Blessed Virgin Mary, in ‘one of the loveliest vales in all England’, on the south bank of the River Wansbeck, a mile upstream from Morpeth. However, for four centuries from its foundation in 1136 to its dissolution in 1535 it was a busy house of White Monks, the only Cistercian House between the Rivers Tees and Tweed.

In 1830 Hodgson wrote in his History of Morpeth: ‘scarcely a stone appears above the ground but several feet upwards of the walls, especially of the chapter house and domestic apartments, still remain buried in the rubbish of their upper parts. Ivy, tree roots and grasses wind through the walls of deserted buildings and as effectively level them as any work of man. Large ash trees, hawthorns and abundance of wake-robin thrive on these ruins.’[2] Now, almost two centuries later, the site is even more overgrown with brambles, dog-roses, ivy and, in places, an impenetrable tangle of undergrowth; however, the shelter and protection this affords together with innumerable holes, nooks and crannies attracts a variety of wild life, birds in plenty, deer, rodents and foxes.

The ruins have long been plundered for building stone; the Newcastle Courant of 25th October 1878 reported that there was scarcely an old building in Morpeth that did not contain abbey stones; the Carfax, the old clock tower and former gaol overlooking the market square is reportedly built of stones from the abbey.

The many empty coffins found beneath the chapter house and the church show that treasure seekers have been at work; indeed the excavations of the 19th Century in 1800, 1836 and 1878 were more in the nature of treasure hunts and only served to confuse the most recent explorations of archaeologists whose findings were published in 1964.[3] The present cloister arcades and the chapter house entrance are reconstructions dating from the years 1912 to 1928 when Sir George Renwick owned the site. As the ground has never been ploughed or built upon, it is quite possible that much remains undiscovered but it is unlikely that there will be any digs in the future, so that Newminster will remain the only major monastic site in the country without a detailed plan; it remains one of our least known medieval abbeys.

On some more celebrated sites such as Fountains and Rievaulx, careful removal of weeds and creepers and skilful conservation work has restored much of the original appearance of order, elegance and purity but it seems that the fate of Newminster is to return to Nature.

The site is privately owned but genuine visitors are welcome. Access is from a public footpath, across a stile and a bumpy field, swampy after rains, for here were once the monastic fish ponds. First impression on arrival is of tangled thickets unless the visitor comes armed with some fore-knowledge or accompanied by a guide. I have been here many times over the past fifty years, alone and with parties of pilgrims, and the place never ceases to fascinate for there hangs over it an aura of sanctity as unmistakeable as it is indefinable. Sitting alone on one of the foundation stones of the chapter house, with only the birds for company, it is none too difficult to visualise the spectral figures of white-robed monks moving quietly yet purposefully about the place and to hear the tolling of the bell in the church summoning the monks to worship.

Questions flood the mind: when and why did the monks first come here? How did they order their daily lives? Who was their leader and why did they and countless others of their generation decide to leave all and become monks? And why choose especially the austere Cistercian Order? What was the impact of their life on the local people of Northumberland? What was the ultimate fate of the monastery and its community? Answers can only be sought by putting these questions into their historical context.

THE NORMANS IN NORTHUMBERLAND

'They said openly Christ and His Saints slept'. Anglo-Saxon Chronicle.

There is no evidence of Northumbrians being involved in the Battle of Hastings but the years following the Conquest brought no happiness to the people of Northern England where the Normans struggled to establish their rule. Rebellions by northern earls with bases in Scotland, at times aided by Danish fleets, were invariably followed by swift and brutal retaliatory attacks by Norman soldiers. King William's revenge for the killing of Robert de Commines and seven hundred of his men in Durham in 1069 was to devastate 'the whole country north of the Humber where corn and cattle, the tools of husbandry and all provisions were set on fire … many died in the famine which lasted nine years. The Domesday Survey dismissed the north of England as 'wasteland'. The turbulent north was not finally subdued until William's eldest son, Robert, built the New Castle at the lowest bridging point of the Tyne in 1080. In 1093 Bishop William St. Calais began the reconstruction of the old White Cathedral at Durham in Norman Romanesque style 'to honour God and St. Cuthbert', then a visible and powerful expression of Norman dominance and permanence, now a world heritage building.

The aim was to rule by the sword and by the spirit. Talented reforming primates Lanfranc, Anselm and Eadmer ensured that almost all clerical vacancies were filled by Normans; within twenty years of the Conquest the only surviving Saxon bishop was Wulstan of Worcester and the only Saxon saint left in the calendar was St. Cuthbert, though St. Edmund of Bury was still venerated.

By the mid-12th century Northumberland was firmly in the Norman hands of some twenty-one barons, all new men loyal to the king, holding some sixty-four knight's fees with their men-at-arms, probably no more than some 400 foreigners. All baronial lands were held on condition of maintaining men-at-arms in the king's service to enforce the king's rule and keep the Scots at bay.

MONASTIC NORTHUMBERLAND IN THE MIDDLE AGES
FROM O.S. MONASTIC BRITAIN. 1975.

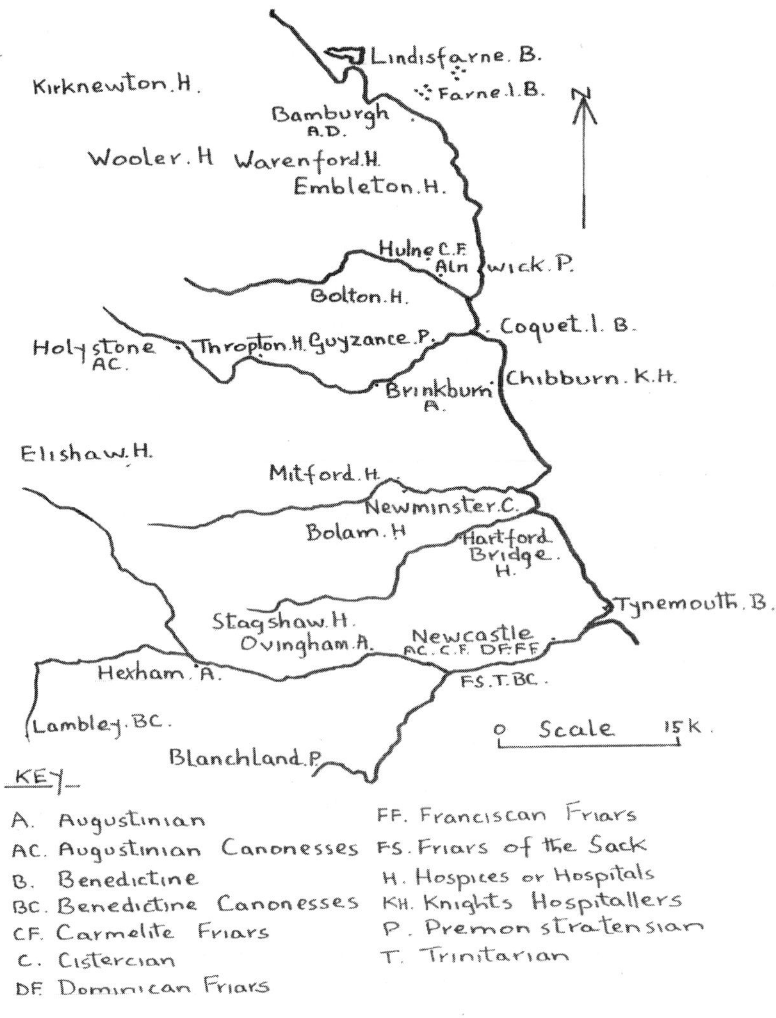

Noble Norman families were installed in their castles to rule in their lands, the Umfravilles at Prudhoe and Harbottle, the De Vescis at Alnwick, and the De Merlays at Morpeth.

The ancestral home of the De Merlays in Normandy is not known but it seems likely that the barony of Morpeth was instituted early by the Earl of Northumberland, Robert de Mowbray, for William de Merlay, Ranulf's father. The De Merlays rarely held positions of importance in the Borders and were never summoned to parliament and are mainly known for their generous benefactions to Newminster. Ranulf married well for his wife Juliana and was a daughter Gospatric, Earl of Lothian, a descendant of the Saxon Earls of Northumberland and through them of the English and Scottish royal families; an early example of Norman lord marrying Saxon noble lady. Juliana's dower consisted of the manors of Longhorsley, Stanton, Witton, Ritton, Wingates and Learchild, several of which figure in grants to Newminster.

It was while visiting the recently founded monastery of St. Mary of the Fountains in North Yorkshire that Ranulf de Merlay conceived the idea of establishing an abbey near to his own castle at Morpeth: as the Memorials of Fountains Abbey record, 'beholding the conversation of the brethren pricked to the heart, under the inspiration of God, he assigned a certain place in his paternal estate in order to build a monastery for the redemption of his soul'.[4] All monasteries kept a cartulary, a form of log-book where deeds conferring and confirming grants of land with the rights and privileges that go with them were meticulously recorded. Occasionally we are given glimpses of life within the walls. Fortunately, the Newminster Cartulary is preserved in its entirety and is our main source book. The first deed records: Ranulf de Merlay, to all sons of the holy church, French and English, clergy and laity present and to come, health: Know ye that I, with the common consent of my wife and sons, have given in fee and free alms to the monks of the abbey of Newminster, which I have built, for the health of myself, of my wife, my sons, my lords, and all my friends, and for the souls of my father and mother, my fore-fathers and friends, and all the faithful that are dead, Rittuna, and whatever belongs to it, in wood or open ground, and part of the wood of Witton, and all the valley between Morpada and Heburn, as the rivulet called Fulbecke, runs and falls into Cottingburn.[5] In all, this was some 200 – 300 acres.

Newminster, first daughter of Fountains, took its place among the 211 monasteries of the Cistercians, the Black Monks and the Carthusians in England and Wales founded in the reign of Henry I, 1100 – 1135, and the following decades: there were also 272 Houses of regular canons, chiefly Augustinian, Premonstratensian and Gilbertine. This was an astonishing growth for, at the time of the Conquest, there were no religious houses in England north of a line from the Humber to the Mersey, except at York and Durham; it was 'a field ready for sowing ... still virgin soil'. The spiritual renaissance in 12th century England was all the more remarkable as the conquerors were sprung from a race who, only two centuries earlier, had crossed the North Sea in their longships to sack Jarrow and Lindisfarne and struck terror into the hearts of the Saxon people; only in the previous century Rollo had invaded Normandy from Norway to rule as the first Duke of Normandy from 911 to 931.

By then the Norman conquerors had experienced only a short period of contact with French and Italian churchmen in which they could acquire a thin veneer of culture so that it is a paradox that these recent barbarians should initiate such an age of religious, cultural and intellectual growth. Ruthless as warriors, eager as tradesmen, energetic and efficient as administrators, the Normans displayed a talent for assimilating existing cultures, as they had already shown in Sicily. William I portrayed himself as the natural successor of Edward the Confessor: the coinage he adopted in 1066 was virtually indistinguishable from that of Harold, a design meant to show political unity.

Behind Norman patronage of monastic houses lay both political and spiritual motives: the prestige and power of the barons were enhanced by the foundation of an abbey in their lands and Norman influence spread more effectively into outlying regions; the abbot might prove a valuable ally at Court; grants of land for abbeys invariably included a clause promising the prayers of the monks for the salvation of the soul of the patron, his ancestors and successors. At the same time the widespread patronage fulfilled a seemingly genuine desire to recreate the golden age of Saxon monastic they read about in the pages of Bede! Such may well have been the motives Ranulf de Merlay had in mind when, prior to the arrival of the founding party of monks, he instructed his workmen to begin erecting the first building of the new abbey. The site would already have been thoroughly explored and the proposal to establish a new monastery there approved by the General Chapter in Cîteaux. It was a well-chosen site raised above the flood-plain on a slight plateau of post-glacial alluvium deposited by the Wansbeck when it flowed at a higher level, and in a deep steep-sided wooded river valley, a typically Cistercian location. Sir Arthur Bryant comments that the White Monks had an instinctive genius for blending the works of God and man yet they sought not a beautiful place to live out their monastic lives but solitude 'away from the comings and goings of men'. Time would show that in this respect Newminster was not a wise choice. The name chosen for the new monastery, *New Minster and the Blessed Virgin Mary,* sounds prosaic. The New Minster was named in honour of the mother house of Cîteaux for the Cistercians had a strong sense of family. New Minster was the first-born of the seven daughter abbeys of Fountains.

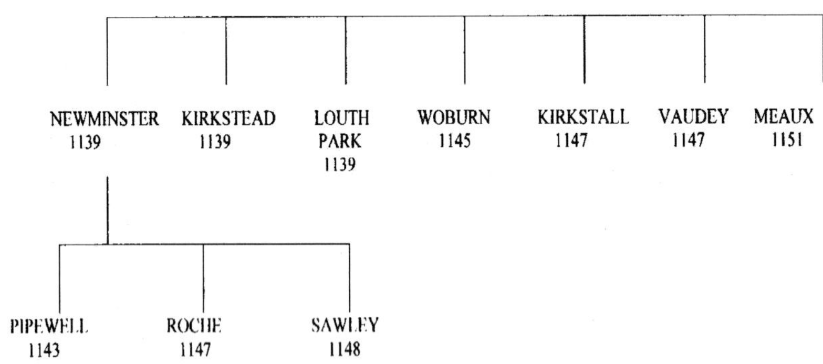

THE FOUNDING ABBOT.

'A man modest in demeanour, merciful in judgement, gentle in companionship, exemplary in holy conversation'.[6]

Few details are known about Robert's early years: indeed throughout his life he remains a rather shadowy and elusive figure. He was born c.1100 in the village of Gargrave in the Craven district of north-west Yorkshire. His parents were 'honourable and eminent in their Christian faith'. Their choice of the name Robert for their son suggests Norman sympathies. Sensing a vocation for the priesthood Robert progressed to university in Paris where he excelled in his studies and developed a life-long love of the Psalms. Sadly, a commentary he wrote later on the Psalms is no longer extant. Perhaps his choice of Paris was influenced by the presence there of one of the leading scholars of the time, the scholastic Peter Abelard.

On ordination, he was sent to his home parish of St. Andrew's at Gargrave but soon felt unfulfilled with parish work and was drawn to join the Black Monks at the recently refounded abbey of St. Mary's at Whitby, former home of St. Hilda and scene of the famous Synod of 664. Again though, after a short while, he felt life was too easy so he hastened, with fellow monk Adam, to join a band of refugee monks from St. Mary's Abbey, York, on land by the River Skell granted by Archbishop Thurstan. At York the community lived honestly but fell far short of the perfection enjoyed by the Rule; after much tumult the prior Richard, like Robert of Molesme, led the party forth in all the nakedness of winter where in pathless woods under a ridge of rocks Robert joined them in cutting down trees to build a chapel, in making huts with hurdles roofed with turf, eating coarse food, at one stage roots and berries but with no sign of sadness, no sound of murmuring, all blessing God with fervour, poor in worldly goods, rich in faith … Through all these hardships and tribulations the spirit of holy joy pervaded their life of devotional exercises alternating with hard, manual labour; pre-eminent among them stood Robert![7] In this bitter cold and extreme poverty Robert found his heart's home.

With a warm recommendation from Archbishop Thurstan, the infant community of Fountains applied for counsel to Bernard, Abbot of Clairvaux, who sent an aged and experienced monk Geoffrey to instruct the brethren in the customs and ways of the Order of Cîteaux. Their struggling fortunes received a real boost when Richard, Dean of York, rode in to join the community with men and books; events at Fountains bore a remarkable similarity to those in Cîteaux in the first difficult days when the Burgundian nobleman, Bernard, entered the gates to join the Order with a company of thirty brothers, uncles and nephews, and with riches and books.

Robert was not alone in answering the call of Cîteaux; others who entered the Cistercian novitiate in the north of England in this time included Henry Murdac, master and teacher at York; Aelred, steward of King David of Scotland; Maurice, scholar and sub-prior of cathedral monastery of Durham; Waldef, nobly-born prior of the canons of Kirkham Abbey and future Abbot of Melrose. Many others too, less celebrated and less gifted, responded to the question: *Good Master, what shall I do to inherit eternal life*? By accepting the invitation: *Enter here, live as we do, this do, and thou shalt live.*

Stained glass window of St Robert, Catholic Church, Catforth, Lancashire.

Benedict in his Rule set out clearly the procedures for choosing an abbot: he should be chosen 'for the merit of his life and for his learning in wisdom, even though he be the last in order in the community … for he is believed to hold the place of Christ in the monastery'. The Rule was followed strictly and paid rich dividends.

Many reasons may be advanced to explain the phenomenal success of the first decades of the Order of Cîteaux: the quality of the constitution; the appeal of Cistercian austerity, especially to men in the north schooled to a stern Celtic piety; the welcome given to uneducated men to serve as lay-brothers, *conversi*; the generous patronage and grants of land and rights by Norman barons; most important, however, was the calibre of the men elected as the first abbots, some forty of whom have been acclaimed saints, *vox populi*. The dynamism of Bernard, the genius of Stephen, the determination of Alberic, the warmth and sympathy of Aelred 'flesh out a picture that cannot fail to attract and hold'. When the monks of Fountain elected Robert to be the founding abbot of Newminster he joined an illustrious company.

If we include Robert and Adam from Whitby in the original founders of Fountains even though they may well have joined later, then no fewer than seven were destined to become abbots; Richard prior (Fountains), Richard the sacrist (Fountains), Robert (Kirkstead), Gervase sub-prior (Louth park), Walter the almoner (Kirkstead), Ranulf (Lyse), Alexander (Kirkstall), Adam (Meaux) and Robert (Newminster).

FOUNDATION

In mid-winter, late December 1137, Robert and twelve monks, the usual number in a founding party, representing Christ and the apostles, left Fountains for the journey north. They called in at Durham Cathedral, now nearing completion, to receive the blessing of Bishop Geoffrey, spent Christmas with the De Merlay family in Morpeth Castle, then moved onto the newly constructed buildings of the monastery on January 6, the Feast of the Epiphany.

John, prior of Hexham, records: *In 1138, a certain powerful man in Northumberland received on his property at the castle called Morpeth on the nones of January eight monks of Fountains who built the monastery called Newminster; for whom on the Feast of the Epiphany in this year, Geoffrey, Bishop of Durham, consecrated as abbot the holy man, Robert. Them Ranulf de Merlay gladly favoured.*[8]

Four centuries later the itinerant Tudor chronicler Leland recorded: *a quarter of a mile out of towne on the hitherie side of Wanspeke was Newe Minster, Abbey of the White Monks, plesaunt with water and very fayre wood about it.*[9]

The new abbey had an unfortunate beginning, for within a few months it was burned down by the demoralised Scottish army straggling north badly defeated at the Battle of the Standard near Northallerton on 22 August 1138. It was an irony that the leader of the Scots was King David who ruled from 1124 to 1153 and became renowned for his patronage of new monasteries, especially those of the Cistercian Order.

The first buildings, an oratory, a refectory, dormitory and guest house, being built of wood and wattle, would burn easily but were soon replaced by more permanent structures of stone by local men who were offered indulgences by Robert as an inducement.

Fear of Scottish raids was never far away. On the north bank of the river, opposite the monastery, is the ominously named Scot's Gill, while a few miles upstream is the village of Scot's Gap. The fear was well-founded: the Augustinian canonesses of Holystone Priory petitioned Rome for help to restore the ravages of Scottish raiders; Hexham Abbey was burned down as was Eggleston Abbey in Teesdale; fellow White Monks of Holm Cultram in Cumbria had to evacuate their monastery in 1216 and again in 1316 while Scots plundered their lands and at neighbouring Calder the community was forced to leave permanently. One abbot of Newminster was taken hostage by the Scots and we know nothing of his fate.

At Hulne Priory near Alnwick there was a curtain wall, Blanchland Abbey had a tower house, Tynemouth Priory a castle protecting the only landward approach but at Newminster there were no defensive features.

Newminster under Robert was so successful in the first decade that three daughter abbeys were established with the mother house providing the founding community of the abbot-elect and twelve monks. The foundations were at Pipewell in Northamptonshire (1143), patron William de Batevilyn; at Roche in South Yorkshire (1147), patrons Richard de Bulli and Richard Fitzturgis, and at

Sawley (1148), patron William de Percy, on the bank of the river Ribble, near to Robert's native village of Gargrave in North Lancashire.

Perhaps the founding patrons of Roche and Sawley turned to Newminster rather than the more illustrious and nearer Fountains, or to Rievaulx, for the practical reason that Fountains had already sent out seven colonies and Rievaulx three, and therefore they were unable to supply the thirteen monks required by the Cistercian Statutes to start a new monastery.[10] Within fifteen years the family of Fountains was into the third generation.

EVERYDAY LIFE

For White Monks fasts were long, and vigorous. Meals were frugal; fish, eggs or white meat and bread eaten in silence in the refectory. In penitential seasons the single meal would not be taken until after Vespers in late afternoon. Robert's fasting was especially severe: one Passiontide he became so weak that the brethren feared for his life; 'if I had a little buttered oat cake I might eat it', he said to the attendant monk. When it came he ordered it to be given to the first poor man at the gate. Robert gave *unstinted time to prayer and meditation* reciting the beloved psalms daily; a book recording his daily prayers and spiritual exercises *collectaneus sancti Roberti* was produced but is sadly no longer extant. Once in prayer, it was revealed to him that two *conversi* had lapsed to the world, not long afterwards they died a miserable death. One night at Nocturns he saw the devil, clad like a peasant, his long shanks bare, a basket on his back. Straining his neck he appeared between the abbot's and the prior's stalls rolling his eyes round and scrutinising each face. The abbot alive to all this, prayed the more earnestly exhorting each to vigilance. For a long time the Wicked One waited in vain, finally in the choir of the *conversi* he found a young novice present only in body and meditating flight. Realising the man was wholly his own he quickly made off with him by means of a three-pronged fork he carried in his hand. The lay-brother later became a common thief and was finally decapitated.

As with other holy men, Robert was on occasions gifted with prophetic vision. Once when celebrating Mass *pro totius mundi salute*, it was revealed to him that the little ship used for freight and fishing by the abbey had sunk and the lives of the crew, two *conversi,* and some servants were lost. Announcing the shipwreck to the assembled community he commended the lost brethren to their prayers and to everyone's surprise, ordered two monks: *go at once to Whitby, and you will find the bodies on the shore under the cliff, give them due ecclesiastical burial.* On their return, they confirmed the truth of the abbot's vision and reported the fulfillment of his command.

Once when visiting a market in Newcastle, Robert encountered a trickster at work cheating the crowd, he scolded him severely and the rogue fled. On another occasion he was visiting conversi in the granges avoiding the highways occupying himself with meditation and psalms as he rode his *sorry beast of burden, no caparisoned palfrey.* He met a nobleman who told his page to ask where he could find the abbot. *When I was at the grange, the abbot was there* was the reply but the great man detected the ruse, proclaimed his own abject state, made Robert mount his own blood-horse, and went on his way with a blessing.

Gossip prospered then as it does now. A noble lady and her husband, who lived in a castle nearby, were so impressed by the life of the monks that in Lent they fasted just as strictly and gave their delicacies to the poor. Delighted at the strength of her faith Robert often visited to encourage her to even greater spirituality. But suspicion arose in the evil minds of some monks, guests and neighbours heard the rumours; at length it reached the abbot. This was Robert's *gravest trial* so he took the long road to Clairvaux to seek the counsel of his Father Immediate. Bernard quickly established the falsity of the rumours and gave Robert his girdle, symbol of chastity, as a token of his belief in his total innocence. Perhaps too he gently reminded Robert that discretion is the mother of all virtues and that *the virtue of discretion without charity is limp and useless while vehement indiscreet fervour leads to ruin.*

The girdle was long preserved among relics at Newminster and was the means of restoring health to many sick folk.

OUTSIDE VISITS

The constitution decreed that the abbot of the mother house make an annual visitation to daughter houses as well as attending the General Chapter in Cîteaux every September: Knowles has calculated that on average a Cistercian abbot spent three to four months a year away from his own community. Bernard voiced the feelings of abbots on the subject of these long absences.

If ye suffer from my absence, think how I must suffer, for ye lack only my single presence but I lack you all ... my longing on my pilgrimage is to see the holy temple of God which ye are: I am not suffered to bring up these babes whom I brought to birth in the Gospel. [11]

In 1157 the General Chapter excused abbots from distant Scotland from attending Cîteaux every year though a later request for a similar dispensation for abbots of English abbeys was refused; however a statute in an amended *Carita Caritatis* allowed the abbot to send a proxy.

It has been argued [12] that Robert had the idea of founding two further daughter houses at Wolsingham and at Finchale in the Wear Valley of County Durham where, apart from the great Cathedral of Black Monks at Durham, there had been very little new monastic activity.

Bishop St Barbe endowed Newminster c.1145 with land at Wolsingham including a forest clearing, the site of the hermitage of Godric and his mentor Ailric; the gift was actually confirmed by Pope Eugenius, a Cistercian, suggesting Robert held some influence in the papal curia. The charter entitled the monks to use the bishop's timber, graze their animals, and build a grange but a clause was inserted forbidding the founding of an abbey, probably by the prior of Durham, Roger, as he feared a new Cistercian abbey in his lands might undermine his authority and draw away his benefactors. In the event no grange was ever established and, ten years later, the lands were relinquished in return for salt works in Blyth and coal mines at Chopwell.

More will be written later of Robert's close friendship with Godric, who established his hermitage at Finchale after moving from Wolsingham. Hermitages were seen as attractive sites for new abbeys: Pipewell occupied a former hermitage, as did Kirkstall abbey founded from Fountains. Robert may have cherished similar ambitions for Finchale, where Godric's zeal and devotion to Mary made him a potential Cistercian recruit. Godric and his fellow eremites may have been searching for a religious order to patronise their settlements; the Cistercians deemed it inappropriate to leave hermits 'to their own whims and intuitions lest they should be deceived'. Finchale was an ideal location: a deep wooded valley with plentiful water from the River Wear, reclaimed forest, cultivated fields, an orchard and fisheries. By 1160 there were two churches there linked by a thatched cloister and a guest house. The policy of incorporation was well established whereby already established local reformers, then communities and properties, were assimilated into the Order.

Again Prior Roger thwarted any such ideas; how much pressure he brought to bear on the ageing Godric we cannot know but Godric chose the Priors of Durham to be his spiritual mentors and became an associate of the Durham community. The hermitage became a dependency of the Cathedral, no visitors were allowed without the prior's permission.

On Godric's death in May 1170 the land reverted to Bishop Hugh Puiset of Durham.

FRIENDSHIP WITH GODRIC

An appealing aspect of the lives of some saints is the close relationship they form with a contemporary who becomes a close friend as well as spiritual director and father confessor, in Celtic monasticism such a person was *anamchara.* In early medieval times the relationship between Herbert, the hermit of Lake Derwentwater, and Cuthbert is a good example. Robert formed such a friendship with Godric, the hermit at Finchale (dale of finches), who finally settled by the banks of the Wear two miles downstream from Durham in a place *wild, overgrown, infested with snakes, liable to floods.*

Godric's biographer, his contemporary Reginald of Durham, gives us a graphic account of the life and appearance of Robert's soul-friend. Born at the time of the conquest, the son of English peasants from the Wash area of Norfolk, Godric had been a peddler, a trader, or a seaman who became a ship's captain (probably Guderic a pirate in the eastern Mediterranean at the time of the Crusades), an inveterate traveller, a steward of a rich household. Weary of the ways of the world, he went barefoot on pilgrimage to Rome and Palestine whereupon he resolved to become a hermit. He tried various locations, first near Carlisle, next at Wolsingham, then in Eskdale before finally establishing his hermitage at Finchale where he was befriended by the monks of Durham Cathedral; here his extreme asceticism marked by severe fasting and long hours of prayer was moderated to some degree as he came under the influence of the Rule of Benedict.

One can readily imagine the eagerness with which Robert would make the short journey to Finchale. Here, as he approached, he may well have seen Godric clad in his hair-shirt praying waist-deep in the cold waters of the Wear. Unusually for a hagiographer, Reginald gives us a detailed description of Godric's striking physical appearance, as remarkable as his career. Robert in his many hours in prayer and meditation and earnest discussion late into the night would see a man short in stature, barrel-chested, with sparkling blue-grey eyes, a long nose and a flowing black beard turning white with the advancing years for he was already well past his three score and ten. As Cuthbert found in Inner Farne, isolation did not bring seclusion as his reputation for heroic sanctity grew. Robert was only one of many visitors: beggars came seeking alms, abbots and even kings came for counselling. When Robert sensed that his days were ending he took his final farewell of Godric conversing more fully of their intimate spiritual experiences. We may conclude that Godric was, like Bernard of Clairvaux, a powerful influence in Robert's spiritual life.

Soon after the observance of Ascension Day 1159, Robert was stricken by a severe fever and received Holy Viaticum. Asked to name a successor he said, *in your obstinacy you will elect Brother Walter to the ruin of your house.* In audible prayer he commended his sons and their common house to the Divine charge and passed from this life to the next. Praying in his cell, Godric saw the darkness of the night dispelled as two bright shining walls of light raised from heaven to earth and angels bearing upwards the soul of the saint in the form of a fiery sphere; he then saw the soul of his beloved friend welcomed by the Blessed at the Gate of Heaven. Godric later protested with tears the truth of his vision. *Would that we were now sharers with him in that glory.* Godric himself lived a further eleven years and died in 1170 at the remarkable age of about a hundred years.[13]

Godric's vision of Robert ascending to Heaven.
Mount St Bernard Archives 1866.

POST-HUMOUS MIRACLES

Robert's body was taken from its original tomb and enshrined more honourably in the choir of the abbey church where it probably still lies. John de Plessey pledged to give five marks sterling to the convent of Newminster and then successors for ever so that two wax lights be kept burning before Robert's tomb. As testimony to his sanctity many miracles were reported: a few examples will illustrate the point.[14]

A young monk suffered from severe attacks of fever alternating between excessive heat and cold; as he grew worse he despaired of human aid and fled in terror to Robert's tomb where he sang the Psalter. Persevering, despite painful mental effort, the fever left him, although exhausted. In time he recovered his strength and forever proclaimed his debt to the virtue of the blessed father.

The same monk was standing on the top rung of a ladder whitening the wall of the dormitory when the ladder slipped and he fell down the hard stone steps descending to the church. Invoking the name of St. Robert as he fell, he landed gently, insensible of any shock. Thanking God and St. Robert he continued his work more carefully.

It was not only monks who benefited from Robert's intercession. John of Netherwitton was cured of insanity at the saint's tomb having first been subdued by Brother Roger, a forester and a man of great strength. John recalled: *As I slept there, there came out of the tomb a monk in a white cowl who loosed my bonds and told me henceforth to lead a better life.* All gave joyful thanks and with devout gratitude John returned home.

A country man stole a beast that was foaled and broken at the abbey; when accused he swore his innocence even on the body of St. Cuthbert in Durham and returned home in high spirits. However his joy was short-lived for he was struck dumb and suffered internal agonies. Coming to the monastery, he so bewailed his sins at Robert's tomb that the merciful saint restored his speech and cured his ailment. Making open confession and full restitution he lived the rest of his life a better man.

Two runaway wagons loaded with wood on a steep descent were about to crush the team of a monk and two youths beneath their wheels. In terror they called on St. Robert and, as an eye witness attested, the wooden splinter bar to which the oxen were harnessed broke, the beasts went free and the wagons stopped; '*twas no natural event.'* They safely resumed their journey to the monastery.

As word of these events spread, Robert's tomb became a place of pilgrimage and his reputation for sanctity grew. It seemed to folks quite natural that God should give miraculous powers to so holy a man. Such incidents also give us revealing glimpses of everyday life in and around the monastery; monks up a ladder, whitening walls, fetching wood felled by foresters by ox-cart, beasts being stolen.

We almost certainly know as much now about Robert as we shall ever know and that is not a great deal; we have no description of his physical appearance such as Reginald gives us of his friend Godric, nor does he bare his soul in any writings as Aelred does in his *Mirror of Charity,* yet the circumstantial evidence is such that we can place him with confidence among the outstanding abbots named above and count him among the forty one early Cistercian abbots who have been recognised as saints. In 1656 the cult of St. Robert was officially approved by the Cistercian Order. His feast day is 7th June.

Yet he remains little known. I know of only four parishes in England and Wales dedicated to St. Robert of Newminster; at Morpeth in which parish the abbey is situated; in Fenham in the west end of Newcastle upon Tyne; at Catforth, Preston in Lancashire, and at Aberkenfig near Bridgend in Glamorgan, South Wales. He has only recently been included in the calendar of saints of Hexham and Newcastle.[15]

Another Robert, monk of Newminster, well taught by the companionship of many brethren ... felt able to fight with God's help against the vices of the flesh and mind, single-handed, with the right arm alone.[16] As son of the mayor of York he had already given up a rich inheritance, now he left the community of Newminster to become an anchorite in a cave above Knaresborough in Niddsdale. As his reputation for sanctity grew his cell became a place of pilgrimage and was visited by King John. After his death in 1235 miracles were attributed to his intercession and he soon became known and venerated as St. Robert of Knaresborough. A Trinitarian monastery was established near his cave ensuring that ensuring that the spirit of monasticism lived on in that place for institutions usually have a longer life than individuals.

LATER ABBOTS

A study of the Cartulary reveals the names of 31 abbots of Newminster[17] from foundation to dissolution; some interesting features emerge which may have applied more generally throughout the Cistercian world.

Naturally abbots were anxious about their successor; on his deathbed Robert warned against the election of Walter as his successor as this would lead to the ruin of the House; the advice was ignored, Walter was duly elected but we hear of no dire consequences. The talent of men entering from other Orders was recognised in the election of the third abbot William, former canon of Guisborough Priory, who received the Cistercian habit from Robert and eventually became Father in Christ to the expanding community of Fountains from 1180 to 1190. Another notable Augustinian convert was Robert Biseth, the second prior of Hexham Abbey, who in 1141 journeyed to Clairvaux to enter the Cistercian novitiate under Bernard; perhaps he had been influenced in his decision by witnessing the life of the White Monks at neighbouring Newminster. William's successor, another Walter, died while at the general chapter of Cîteaux in 1217. John of Thornton brought valuable experience with him for he had been cellarer at Newminster and then served as attorney for Abbot Adam at Cîteaux.

Local men figure prominently; four successive abbots from 1389 to 1478 were all Northumberland men, Robert of Horsley, John of Morpeth, William of Hebescot and John of Birtlee. Promotions were often within the family of Fountains: another Robert, monk of Newminster, was elected abbot of daughter-house Pipewell; Stephen of Eston, who died 1252, moved from the abbacy of Sawley to Newminster, then to Fountains. Times were still troubled, for Robert Butler found it necessary to build Rothley Tower to protect local granges. Robert Charleton was engaged in the appointment of prioress to the Convent of St. Bartholomew's in Newcastle. All abbots right down to the last two, Gerard Duxfield and Edward Tyrry, (Richard Tyrell), were involved in a wide variety of tasks: collecting tithes due to the abbey and to the diocesan bishop, raising funds for the Crusades, receiving and granting lands with attendant rights of passage and pasture, agreeing tenancies, arbitrating in land disputes, negotiating wool prices; all these and other diverse matters had to be dealt with and, once agreed, duly witnessed, signed, sealed and documented as is clear from the wealth of such material in the monastic cartularies. The abbot was required to show business sense and legal acumen, qualities that could never have been foreseen by Benedict composing his Rule or the Cistercian Fathers determining their statutes.

THE BUILDINGS

> *Cistercian art was at the service of monastic life. It was expressed by a harmonious beauty in building which proclaimed the splendour and glory of God.*
>
> ***Pope John Paul II 1998***

We know much more about the layout of the monastic buildings than we know about the life of Robert. The tangle of undergrowth covering the site has already been described yet we can learn not only from the findings of the 1960s dig but also from the knowledge that Cistercian monasteries were built to a pattern that the Black Monks had evolved over the centuries and one that worked best. There were exceptions to the blueprint; at Rievaulx because of the lie of the steep valley sides of the Rye the church did not have the usual west-east orientation; at Fountains Abbey Abbot Huby built a tower on the church, a feature strictly forbidden by the original statutes. It helps too that the site of the daughter abbey of Roche is splendidly preserved, including the range of outbuildings untouched by the archaeologists in the latest dig at Newminster. It is fair to assume that the layout of Roche was very similar to that of Newminster, albeit the church was smaller.

Knowles notes that churches as far apart as Newminster, Whitland (Carmarthen), Quarr (Isle of Wight), Rievaulx (c.1132), Kirkstall (c.1152) and Valle Crucis (c.1201) are similar in all essentials.[18]

The plan reveals the classic Cistercian layout, a four-sided group of buildings around a central cloister and garth. As elsewhere the church dominated the site. Built on the north side facing the Scots and giving shelter from the cold north winds, the church at Newminster was low in elevation, without tower or spire, built of rough stone and unimposing from the outside.

The architectural historian, Honeyman, reckons that *the fragments which remain prove that in beauty and refinement of detail the church at Newminster was the equal of any building in Northumberland.*[19]

PLAN OF PARTLY EXCAVATED SITE OF NEWMINSTER ABBEY

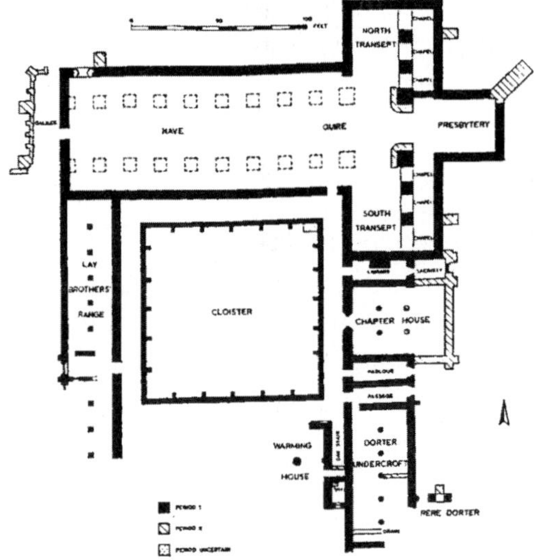

As Cistercian monasteries in the first decades of the 12th century were usually built to the same design and as Roche is a daughter abbey of Newminster it is probable that a full investigation of the site of Newminster would reveal a similar lay-out to that of Roche

DETAILED PLAN OF FULLY EXCAVATED SITE OF ROCHE ABBEY IN SOUTH YORKSHIRE

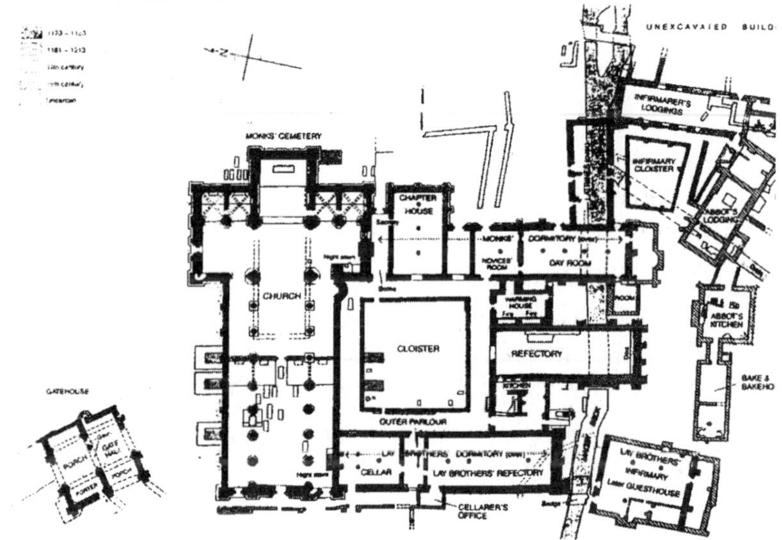

A magnificent ash tree now stands on the site of the high altar.

The plan shows that the church was cruciform in shape, aisleless, with a square-ended presbytery of three bays and a transept each with three chapels. Beneath the floors here were found several stone coffins containing skulls and bones, for this is where abbots and noble beneficiaries were buried, probably one coffin held the bones of St. Robert. The stone walls would be skimmed with white lime and marked with dark red or chocolate coloured lines to simulate coursing. The floor was covered with hexagonal tiles of various colours in geometric patterns described in more detail later; the roof was made of plain red tiles. Notably lacking were any sculptures or paintings, windows were of clear glass, only a large crucifix hung above the entrance to the choir as a constant reminder to the monks that *Our Order is Christ's cross, if you harmonise your way of life with it you can look to share its glory in the degree you have borne its pains*.

A wooden or stone rood screen separated the monks in the choir from the *conversi* in the nave but all worshipped as one community.

There was no *richly polished panelling, no candlesticks as tall as trees, no bronze masses of exquisite workmanship, no monstrous lizards to distract the eyes of the worshipper and hinder his devotion*;[20] all these belonged to the churches of Cluny according to Bernard; here was austerity, simplicity and elegance. Nowhere is this better seen today that in the abbey church of Our Lady and St. Samson on Caldey Island where all is suffused in an exquisite soft green light.

Life was lived on three levels: physical activity was found in the workshops, farms and fields; mental activity in meditation and reading in the cloister: spiritual activity in the cool peaceful interior of the church where the monk sought God in the deepest centre of his being.

The day at Newminster began early, at the eight hour of the night (2 a.m. by our reckoning) as the sleeping monks, wakened by the bell, rose from their straw palliasses on the stone floor of the dorter (dormitory) and descended the night stairs, an example of which is still perfectly preserved at Hexham Abbey, to sing Matins, the first of the seven canonical hours of the daily Divine Office. It remains a mystery how, in an age before clocks, the bell-ringer knew it was time, was it the first cock crow or just intuition? Only flickering light by the altar or ambo lit the shadowy figures of the cowled monks as the church was filled with the rise and fall of the solemn chant of the psalms; the darkness itself symbolised peril. At Lauds, an hour later, the pace quickened until sunrise, symbol of the Risen Christ, was greeted joyfully with the hymn *Iam lucis orto sidere* 'Now dawn has come'. The first rays of light of the day shafted through the rose windows of the eastern walls highlighting the priests celebrating Mass at the high altar and at the side altars in the transepts. The monks within easy reach of the church gathered there to sing the daytime Hours of Prime, Tierce, Sext (about noon) and None and Vespers while those in the fields hearing the abbey bell ringing gathered together for silent prayers and chanting a psalm. The day ended early, about 7 p.m., with Compline, corporate prayer with the apt Psalms 4 and 90, examination of conscience, the singing of the *Salve Regina* in honour of their patroness, and an individual blessing from the abbot before the ascent of the night stairs. The Cistercian day still ends in this way and any guest of the abbey witnessing the service finds it a most moving experience.

The cloisters were the beating heart of the community and, like mortal life, a place of transition where the monks passed from the physical world of workshop or field to the inner peace found in the spiritual world of prayer in church. The cloister garth was a lawn or garden centrally situated and enclosed on four sides by arcaded walls and flagstone walks, as seen in Durham Cathedral today. The lengths of cloister walls visible today, though less so with every passing year as they are covered with ivy, are accurate reconstructions dating from the mid 1920's. The arches are mostly pointed though some are round. The capitals are of the waterleaf variety.[21]

A twelfth century visitor to the cloisters would have witnessed a scene of quiet yet purposeful activity; monks walking the passages meditating on the scripture readings of the day; novices learning the psalms by rote; others busy with daily chores, washing clothes, mending shoes, beating dust out of blankets. Here was where the monks met and lived as a family and grew in fraternal charity, as illustrated by Aelred in his *Mirror*. The other side of the coin was that peculiar menace of the cloister called *acedia*, a weariness of heart, part *ennui*, part *melancholia*. Even the dynamic Bernard suffered: *oftentimes in the early days of my conversion my heart was dried up and withered within me ... more and more it languished, and weariness came upon me, my soul slept in weariness, sad almost to despair, and murmuring to itself: Who shall stand before the face of His cold*? [22]

The chapter house is the most readily identifiable building among the scanty remains and the best place for visiting parties to gather. It was square shaped with four sturdy pillars to divide it into nine rib-vaulted compartments: the base of one pillar can serve as an altar for services of worship. This is where the community gathered each morning at 6 a.m. to hear a chapter from Benedict's Rule, hence the name, to receive orders for the day and hear of punishment for acts of indiscipline by individual monks.

In matters of importance, the whole community met in the chapter house when *the brethren gave their advice with all humble deferenc*e from the most senior monk to the youngest novice for *the Lord often reveals the better course to a young man.* The final arbiter is the abbot acting *in conformity with the Rule knowing that he will have to give an account for all his judgements to God, the most just Judge. He must do nothing without deliberation and 'when you have acted you will not regret* it'. (Ecclus 32).[23] In an age when rank and pedigree were all-important this was a remarkably democratic procedure used in the election of a new abbot.

One can readily appreciate the excitement and emotion generated among the brethren on such occasions. Bede records that the election of Hwaelbert as Abbot of Monkwearmouth and Jarrow as successor to the beloved Ceolfrith was greeted with applause.

The rib-vaulted roof of the chapter house was supported by four sturdy circular pillars whose bases remain. The entrance is marked by a reconstructed stone archway. A lidless stone coffin reminds us that noble benefactors, as well as abbots, were buried beneath the tiled floor of the chapter house.

THE LIBRARY

The small size of the library at Newminster located between the south transept and the chapter house bears no relationship to the importance of its contents, for here were housed the books essential for the *lectio divina* and readers at meal times. Much emphasis was placed on the two to three hours a day set aside for private reading for the former monks of Cluny had found the many hours spent in church there in vocal prayer an insufferable burden. The purpose of the *lectio* was not to fill the mind with information, but to lead the soul to an affective union with God in contemplative prayer.

What kind of books would Cistercian monasteries in England hold? We can only speculate for so much is lost or scattered and catalogues are scarce but from a study of extant manuscripts we can form some idea. There is no reason to suppose that the library at Newminster was very different from the others.[24]

At the heart of the library would be biblical commentaries, the writings of the patristic fathers of Jerome, Augustine and Gregory, meditations, homilies and hagiographies. Two unusual features of Cistercian manuscripts were commentaries with leaves left blank to be filled by the later devotional thoughts, often in verse, of the writer or reader; the *distinctiones* were dictionary type guides on spiritual topics such as the Psalms to assist homilists and confessors. Stephen Langton, one time Archbishop of Canterbury, was a popular exegete sympathetic to the Cistercians who appreciated his moralistic approach to bible studies. Others whose sermons figures at Rievaulx, Byland and Kirkstall were abbot Gilbert of Swineshead near the Wash and abbot Guerric of Igny whose love of nature was evident in the rich agronomic imagery of his writing. At Holm Cultram in Cumbria there was a bestiary without any illustrations, except for one line drawing of an animal; here was austerity even in books.

We may assume that the sermons and letters of Bernard were well represented, especially in view of Newminster's close ties with Clairvaux, similarly too the works of the talented Aelred of Rievaulx, friend and contemporary of Robert. *Speculum Caritatis* (Mirror of Charity) and Spiritual Friendship were, and still are, minor spiritual classics. In the latter Aelred drawns on Cicero's *De Amicitia* which he *seasons with the salt of Holy Scripture.*

The works of the classical authors of Greece and Rome are few in number. Cicero is represented in only four libraries, at Byland and Holm Cultram there was *De Agricultura* by Palladius and also some works by Horace and Ovid; clearly the renaissance of interest in pagan literature in the 12th century passed the Cistercians by, either that or they heeded Bede's advice that it is safer to read the Apostles than the pages of Plato. They would know Alcuin's warning, *What has Ingeld to do with Christ? The gate is narrow, there is not room for both.* Perhaps they had heard of St. Jerome's nightmare in which he was refused entrance to the gates of Heaven: *Thou art not a Christian, thou art a Ciceronian,* accused St. Peter.

Hagiography was popular, more especially in the lives of English saints: Bede's Life of Cuthbert; Aelred on Ninian and Edward the Confessor; Walter Daniel on Aelred, his fellow-monk; Bernard on Malachy and Reginald on Godric of Finchale were all there. In these Lives and in the histories of origins and growth of houses like Fountains, Kirkstall and Sawley, and indeed in the Cartulary of Newminster itself, we detect a strong sense of history and of regional patriotism. It is pertinent to note that the remote Cistercian monasteries of Strata Florida and Valle Crucis in Wales are known as bastions of Welsh nationalism against encroaching Norman influence. [25]

The library at Newminster would be small compared with Rievaulx where a 13th century catalogue records 212 books (about the same size as Bede's library) for Aelred inspired quite a literary tradition there and ruled over as many as 600 monks and *conversi*. Any books brought by the founding group at Newminster would have been lost when the Scots fired the monastery in its first months. The range of books too would be limited with few, if any, pagan authors represented and only a very few books on secular subjects like law, medicine or grammar. No text books were needed for the Cistercians had no boys to educate in schools. Walter Daniel reminded his fellow-monks *that our master Christ did not teach grammar, rhetoric, dialectic in his school; he taught humility, pity and righteousness.*[26] All books were written in Latin with only the odd one in French or English but all revealed a firm and delicate hand and displayed a high standard of calligraphy.

Despite limitations in size and range, as we see it nowadays, one can readily agree that the books present would admirably serve their purpose of providing edifying reading, encouraging and inspiring the monks in their search for closer union with God. Yet Cistercians, then as now, would agree with Bede who, in a commentary on St. Luke's Gospel, wrote: *There is but one theology, which is the contemplation of God, and all other meritorious works and studies of virtue are rightly placed second after this.*

THE ABBOT'S CHAPEL

Adjoining the library was the abbot's chapel, a place of great interest at Newminster and deserving of our close attention for beneath the turf lies the finest undamaged medieval tiled floor in the country rivalling that of Westminster Abbey. The tiles, each 3" x 3", hexagonal in shape and forming geometric patterns, were of many attractive colours: dark brown, golden brown, bottle green, yellow, light red, some decorated with petalled rosettes, patterns of trefoil foliage, heraldic shields commemorating generous benefactors. Detailed descriptions of the floor have been given by H.L. Honeyman;[27] a few examples will suffice to reveal the chief benefactors, all leading Northumbrian families of Norman origin: the Bertrams of Mitford, Umfravilles, lords of Prudhoe, Harbottle and Ridsdale; Percys, not yet connected with Newminster but founders of Fountains Abbey, the mother house, and of Newminster's daughter house of Sawley; Adam of Jesmond, sheriff of Northumberland; Gilbert of Clare, an executor of Magna Carta, William Vesci, lord of Malton and Alnwick; William of Fraglinton (Framlington) and William de Clifton gave lands for the health of their souls; Roger Maudit of Eshott in the parish of Felton bequeathed 20 shillings a year for general absolution and his wife Isabella gave a quarter of wheat annually for making hosts; Sir Robert Taylboys (Taille bois – firewood cutter) of Hepple gave rights of common grazing for the abbey cattle and sheep.

Other Northumberland leading families prominent in public affairs in the north, mainly in the mid 13th century, identified with the abbey include Ros, Bolbec, Greystoke, Somerville, Fitz Roger of Warkworth and Morwick.

Honeyman notes that the tiles adjacent to the altar of the abbot's chapel are well-worn due to regular polishing by generations of novices and *conversi* and the celebrants offering the daily sacrifice. He concludes that the human interest preserved here is *an elegant memorial of the monastic life of Newminster.*

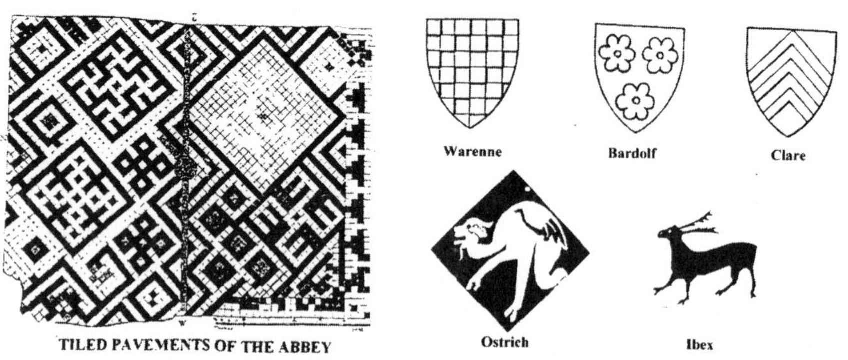

TILED PAVEMENTS OF THE ABBEY

The warming room provided the only fire in cold weather where the monks could gather though they were not allowed to speak or read there and could only stay a short while.

Above these ground floor buildings in the east range was the dorter (dormitory) with a rere-dorter at the end above the fast-flowing stream to carry human waste quickly away.

LAY BROTHERS

The entire western side of the square of monastic buildings was taken up by the lay-brothers' range refectory at ground level, undercroft for storage beneath and dorter above. The size of the building indicates that there was a good number of *conversi,* though we cannot be precise; at Rievaulx some two-thirds of the 600 strong community were *conversi,* although at Newminster the numbers would be much smaller, the proportion of lay to choir monks would probably be similar.

The rapid expansion of the Order in the first decades required new buildings to accommodate the growing numbers of novices, the expense was largely met by borrowing, so that the monks soon ran into debt. When Aaron, the Jewish moneylender of Lincoln, died in 1186, Newminster was one of nine Cistercian abbeys that together owed him the large sum of 6,400 marks.

The Cistercians were the first Order to use lay-brothers on a great scale and in an organised way to do the work in the fields, thus freeing choir monks for spiritual duties. They took simple vows, observed the rule and were taught the *Pater noster, Credo and Gloria* by rote, though not, it is thought, taught to read or write; however not all were *illiterati* for one old soldier staying at a guest-house at a French monastery recognised the lay-brother waiting on him at table as his former general.

The call to the vocation of Cistercian lay-brother held a wide appeal and met a real need, for it offered a secure life with a regular meal and a roof overhead, all the more attractive in an age ravaged by famine and civil war. The prospect of healthy outdoor work in the fields and on the farms, the companionship of like-minded brothers and the solace of a life of spiritual exercises found a ready response. The numbers at Newminster were sufficient to staff the daughter abbeys of Pipewell, Sawley and Roche with a complement of lay-brothers about equal to that of the twelve choir monks and the founding abbot. Abbot Huby of Fountains called the *conversi* '*pious draught-oxen of Christ'*.

The numbers of lay-brothers declined as rapidly as they had risen. As the reasons were universal throughout the land rather than local, it is fair to assume that Newminster fared no differently from other abbeys where we do know numbers. At Meaux in Holderness there were 60 choir monks and 90 lay-brothers at the start of the 14th century but by 1393 there were only 28 monks and no lay-brothers; similarly, at Rievaulx by 1381 the community was down to 15 monks and only 3 lay-brothers.

The plagues that struck thrice in the mid 14th century, in 1348-49, 1361 and 1368-69 wiped out one third to half of the population of England and were most devastating in closed communities.

The consequence of shortage of labour drove up wages so that monasteries found it more economical to lease their lands rather than exploit them directly themselves. The recruitment of *conversi* was then actively discouraged so that by the dawn of the 15th century it had all but disappeared. An immediate problem for abbots was all the surplus accommodation, a problem familiar to some seminaries today. At Sawley a wall was built across the church to seal off the nave where formerly the *conversi* gathered from the presbytery; elsewhere the empty ranges were adopted as abbot's lodgings, guest-houses or simply allowed to fall into ruins.

An interesting group of buildings formed the southern boundary of the monastic site across the stream. Archaeologists have not explored here but, if the lay-out of daughter abbey Roche is anything to go by, these would include a lay-brother's firmary, lodge, a bake-house adjoining the kitchen, an abbot's lodge and little cloister. Around the central complex would be a variety of ancillary structures such as granaries, barns, stable, workshops, malt-house, dove and pigeon-cotes.

The monastic garden, like the library, was a place of great significance in the life of the community for it served both the body and the soul of the monks. Archaeologists focus mainly on buildings but from records from Rievaulx and St. Gall in Switzerland we can gain some ideas on what a visitor to a 12th century monastic garden like that at Newminster might have seen. [28]

In charge was the *hortulanus,* the monk-gardener, who also played a key role in the liturgy bringing the first fruits of a new season to the altar for blessings and chanting the antiphon *O Radix Jesse* (O Root of Jesse) during Advent. For the *hortulanus* and his helpers work in the garden was healthy, fulfilling and an excellent remedy for acedia.

To save time and energy the vegetable garden was located near the kitchen and the refectory and near the hen and goose-houses, the barn and the monks' latrine so that there was a ready supply of nitrogenous fertiliser to enrich the soil. Thus, in model recycling, the community fed the soil and the soil fed the community with a variety of fresh vegetables, peas, beans, lentils, cabbages, onions, leeks, borage for salad, perhaps alexanders too for they still flourish in the ground outside Tynemouth Priory.

In an age when most medicines were herbal and when the most knowledgeable practitioners were monks and nuns the herb garden took on a special importance, growing a wide range of plants used for treating diverse ailments. At Newminster, as elsewhere, we would almost certainly have seen rosemary, sage, rue, mint and parsley as well as comfrey (knit bone) used for poultices, henbane for sedatives, St. John's Wort as a salve and anti-depressant, tansy, marigolds and santolina (holy oil). Herb-robert (geranium robertianum) was used in a compress to arrest bleeding and is probably named after Robert of Molesme, first abbot of Cîteaux, whose knowledge of the medicinal properties of plants was well known. The laxative qualities of certain plants were widely recognised; when the contents of the latrines of the monks at St. Alban's were excavated recently they revealed many berries of the buckthorn bush.

Apples would be the main fruit gathered from the Newminster orchard. Although the climate was warmer in the Middle Ages, it was still too cold for vines though there is evidence of vineyards as far north as Yorkshire and Lincolnshire.

The masses of snowdrops flowering on monastic sites like Brinkburn and Roche in early February almost certainly have medieval origins for their pure white flowers were collected to adorn monastic and parish churches on the Feast of the Purification of the Blessed Virgin Mary, Candlemas, on 2nd February. A search of the abbey site and its banks at Newminster by a local botanist revealed no plants of obvious medieval origin as can, on occasions, happen elsewhere on old sites.

In summer the monastic gardens would be full of fragrances and alive with birds, bees and butterflies, an earthly paradise where the monk could find space for meditative prayer and enjoy his period of *otium,* sanctified leisure. In his scriptural readings he would find ample sources of inspiration in the Song of Solomon, in the New Jerusalem in Revelations and in the book of Sirach where the Gardener speaks to those in the garden: *Burgeon like a rose-bush, blossom like the lily, and smell sweet and put forth leaves for your adornment.*

In his reading too of the earlier Christian monks he would learn that the father of monasticism, Antony of Egypt, cultivated a garden in the desert to supply crops for his own needs and where visitors could *find relief from the hard trip*; in the 6th century the delightful watered gardens of Cassiodorus in his monastery at Vivarium near Naples helped to restore pilgrims and those in need. The sermons of the contemporary abbot Guerric of Igny were rich in gardening imagery; Mary, a fruitful vine, John, a cedar, Peter and Paul, olive trees, but *you are the true gardener, the same Creator who cultivates and protects your garden. You plant by your word, water with your spirit, give growth by your power.*

Perhaps the finest expression of the power of gardens to inspire praise was found above the entrance to the Benedictine abbey of Liesse in Northern France: *May the beauty of flowers and other creatures draw the heart to love and admire God, their Creator. May the garden's beauty bring to mind the splendour of paradise.*

BENEFACTORS

The abbey charters set out meticulously the stages by which the monks of Newminster acquired lands, properties and rights throughout Northumberland. Some fifty eight families are listed in the Cartulary as benefactors in return for the promise of prayers and Masses by the monks, offered for the health of their souls and for those of their antecedents and successors.

After the de Merlays, the most generous patrons were the Umfravilles, lords of Prudhoe and Harbottle Castles, and of the Liberty of Redesdale. the most powerful baronial family in the county in the 12th and 13th centuries. In 1181 Odinel II Umfraville granted Newminster the grazing in the forest of Alwent (Alwinton) and Kidland for 29 years, for which the monks paid 220 marks to Odinel, 3 marks to his wife Alice and 5 to his eldest son Robert. In 1184, on the death of his father, the rent was increased by 40 marks. Throughout the next century further grants were made of lands at Scorthorpe, Fastside, Hepden (formerly owned by Henry the crossbowman) and Shillhope Law. In 1226 Gilbert de Umfraville gave the monks a licence to build a fulling mill and mill pond at Hepden (Barrowburn) and a grange at Rowhope 'for the salvation of my soul and the souls of my ancestors and heirs'. It seems likely that fleeces from sheep shorn at Rowhope were processed a mile downstream at Hepden. Local historian David Dixon claimed[29] that in his time many of the freestones used in local farm buildings came from the old fulling mill whose foundations could still be seen at low water in the Coquet.

Dixon describes Kidland as a wild and sparsely populated waste of steep and lofty hills divided by narrow winding glens[30]. It is a remote and beautiful corner of Northumberland beloved of hill walkers, now quite extensively forested; in medieval times, though much given to brigandage and livestock raiding, it was successfully grazed by the flocks of Newminster Abbey for the sweet bent grasses of the hillsides provided ideal pasture.

A charming story is told of a monk looking after the flocks which grazed in the hills of Kidland from April to August for their summering or shealing. He spent the time making straw skeps for bees, one a day, as he knew when he had made six the next would be Sunday. Once he mislaid a skep so when the local country folk arrived for Sunday Mass they found him still busily at work.

A building called Memmerkirk at the confluence of the Sting and Yoke burns originally believed to be a chapel is now recognised as a former shepherd's dwelling.

The monks continued the centuries old practice of transhumance, moving livestock from lowland granges in winter to upland pasture in summer shielings. Various wayleaves are recorded: Thomas de Clennel, John de Clavering, Robert de Heppel and the Umfravilles, gave free right of way to all monastic servants, carts, carriages and animals to facilitate the passage of flocks and herds to and from the hills.

The Charters carefully record how the boundaries of lands granted by patrons were to be marked. Wherever possible, natural features were used: the river Koket (Coquet), the Osweiburne (Uswayburn) or the hanging willows; elsewhere ditches were dug or pre-existing drove roads like Ernespeth (Clennel Street) used.

The agreements included some interesting clauses: the monks could take what they wanted from the forest by order of the lord's forester but their hunting dogs were to have one foot cut off to prevent them chasing the lord's game. In 1226 Gilbert quitclaimed hunting rights on Cheviot and Coquetdale moors 'for the sake of his father's and ancestor's souls' to give the monks the sole rights to hunt wolves and foxes on his land, it was agreed that the monks would return all straying horses to the local lords.

As Kidland was formerly part of Alwinton parish an agreement was made between Thomas de Rule, the vicar, with the abbey of Newminster that the abbot should pay to Thomas half a mark of silver, 1 lb. of pepper and 1 lb. of incense yearly at Michaelmas in lieu of tithes.

The Umfravilles stood to gain spiritually, financially and economically from their dealings with Newminster abbey: the charters promised prayers from the monks for the sake of the lord's soul, his family and ancestors; the sum of 268 marks paid as annual rent by the abbot of Newminster represented a considerable and steady income for the lord; the uplands of their liberty were developed and managed by the diligent and enterprising Cistercian monks and *conversi*. Monastic investment was encouraged by the security afforded by the dominant presence of Harbottle Castle, in contrast with the more lawless neighbouring valley of Redesdale where there was little monastic interest.

Other beneficiaries of the abbey in Upper Coquetdale were Patrick de Kestern, and later his son John, who granted 113 acres of land for grazing on the Caistron area and also permission to build a corn and fulling mill. They also gave a pittance of bread, good ale, salmon and other fish to the monastic community to celebrate the feast of the Blessed Virgin Mary. At nearby Flotterton William, son of David, gave around 100 acres for grazing rights of passage, and licences to build a mill and dig marl. At Bickerton Thomas allowed the monks to cultivate osiers (willows) on the banks of the river Coquet for basket making.

The charters also refer to two local hermits, John of Maydenle and Hugh of Hepal who settled on a site near Caistron and cultivated seven acres of land granted by John de Kirsten.

The monks were also active on the Northumbrian coast. At Warkworth at the mouth of the Coquet grants of saltworks were made by Roger, son of Richard and Simon, Earl of Northumberland. In one of the earliest references to the river Blyth in 1140 Robert of Winchester gave a grant of two salt pans at the mouth of the river and fishing rights from Sleekburn to the sea. Salt was exported to London, Yarmouth and Hull along with grain transported by mule and pack horse to the granary owned by the monks on Cambois Links. In return for salt, George Matheson of Hull sent two tonnes of Gascon wine, wax, pitch and tar in a ship to Blyth for the abbey. The pans were later let to the yeoman, Roger Pye, for seven years, at £24 rent who would *delyver from tyme to tyme free as moche salt as shall be spent in the kychying of Newmynster paying nothing but carriage of same.* The road between the abbey and Blyth was well used.

Two benefactors resided in Kambus (Cambois): Adam quitclaimed all rights to grazing on the Snook and to his saltworks in favour of the monks, and allowed them to collect sea-coal and sea-weed to use as fertiliser; Walter made maintenance of food and clothing for a bedesman to reside in the gatehouse of the monastery whose duty was to serve as porter and pray for the souls of the deceased. Eustace of Balliol gave lands at Newbiggin and Seaton and a fishing boat.

A few examples from elsewhere in the county will suffice to show the wide range of activities of the White Monks and the variety of benefactions they received, at times with conditions attached.

Mining was important. Coal was extracted from the steep banks of the river Blyth at Plessey, one of the earliest references to coal mining in the area, and was also mined at Chopwell in the Derwent Valley. Stone was quarried at nearby Mitford, the most likely source of the stone used for building the abbey, and peat dug from the moors around Edlingham. Grazing rights granted by John around Stobswood, excepted goats.

The fisheries at Benton on Tyne were next to be sub-let; Roger Maudit provided for dole for poor at the monastery gate on the feast of the Blessed Virgin Mary; two oatcakes and two herrings were given to 100 poor people on the feast of St. Catherine thanks to

Roger Bertram of Mitford: grants of land were made by William Frebern as far north as Berwick; Henry of Pandon provided stalls or booths in Newcastle Bigg Market where the monks could sell their goods, Robert Baynard, Gilbert de Langwitton and others paid for pittances of salmon and good ale to the monks to celebrate the feasts of their favourite saints, St. Lawrence, St. Catherine and St. Mary Magdalene.

The monks paid Merton College, Oxford, 8 marks in lieu of tithes for Horton Grange and undertook to build and repair the bridge over the nearby river Pont. Some benefactions provided for the elements used in the Mass: German Tyson of Schipibartil for wine on the feast of St. Valery; Roger Maudit ¼ wheat for making hosts. Robert Meriwyn de Meldin, William Faber, Christiana de Mitford and Reginald, Abbot of Fountains, were among the benefactors ensuring that lights were kept burning before the shrine of St. Robert, a sign of the esteem in which he was held.

Not all beneficiaries were nobles or rich landowners: Almer, the *carnifex* (butcher) of Morpeth gave a pittance on St. Francis Day; Richard and Alvery, both masons, gave land for grazing; Ralph, the smith, donated one acre and his wife, Lucy, a pittance on St. Barnabas Day.

The White Monks devised their own solution to the problem of supplying *conversi* on farms more than a day's journey distance from the abbey. Granges consisted of a chapel, a refectory and dormitory with associated farm buildings such as barns and granaries. A monk who was a priest supervised the *conversi.*

With the probable exception of Rowhope in Upper Coquetdate, the granges of Newminster, at Horton (where there is still a farm), Nunnykirk, Rittons, Highley and elsewhere (see map) lay no more than ten miles from the abbey and therefore well within a comfortable day to journey on foot or on horseback. It is doubtful that on major feast days even with the whole community present the church was ever so full as to resemble 'a hive of swarming bees' as at Rievaulx.

The impact of all these activities over four centuries on the landscape of medieval Northumberland would be considerable.

Grazing was extended into the uplands, new arable land brought into cultivation, roads and bridges built, ditches dug, land drained, granges established, mills erected and mill ponds formed. In an open landscape very different to the present patchwork of woodlands, moors and fields bounded by hedges or fences the difficulties of marking boundaries between adjoining lands have already been noted.

It is difficult to assess accurately the effect of the monks of Newminster on agriculture, industry, trade and commerce in the county but all would certainly be stimulated by the hard work, practical skills and business acumen of the pioneering White Monks who, for the first time, developed commercial farming on a large scale. More especially too in the 14th and 15th centuries Newminster Abbey would be the biggest employer in the county either directly with hired labour or indirectly, after the decline in numbers of the *conversi*, through their tenants; in their service generations of country folk would find gainful employment in honest toil as shepherds, cowmen, ploughmen, dairymaids, millers, fullers, tanners, dyers, quarrymen, foresters and fishermen and in general labouring building and repairing ditches, roads and bridges. The evidence is plain to see in the immense detail of the Cartulary.

As the most enlightened farmers of the age the White Monks would contribute much to agricultural science in Northumberland and throughout the land; they cross-bred the best animals from different flocks; the sheep might graze on the open moors and hills by day and fold at night on ploughland; they fully appreciated the value of droppings as fertiliser. Trade was stimulated too for raw wool was sold in local markets and sent abroad from developing ports like Newcastle. Newminster owned several buildings along the Tyne for storing wool prior to export, perhaps in the abbey's own ships.

The expanding textile industries of Flanders and Italy provided an eager market; around the year 1300 their merchants bought 76 sacks of quality wool from Fountains and 60 each from Rievaulx and Jervaulx. We have no such figure for Newminster but in the Cartulary we read of Abbot Adam writing to Edward I giving details of negotiations with Florentine merchants over the sale of wool in 1274 and the next six years, in breach of the Cistercian Statutes.

'The Monks of our Order should obtain their livelihood chiefly by manual labour, agriculture and the rearing of cattle'.
Cistercian Constitutions.

HOW IS THE GOLD BECOME DIM AND THE FINE COLOUR CHANGED?[31]

The story of Newminster is the story, in miniature, of the Cistercian Order throughout the four centuries of the Middle Ages. In the twelfth century strict adherence to the rule of Benedict and observance of the Statutes together with discipline and effective administration ensured by the system of annual general chapters and visitations resulted in the very highest standards of spiritual excellence, exemplified in our own case by the holy life of the saintly Robert, first abbot. The system was so manifestly successful that Pope Innocent III at the fourth Lateran Council, 1215, decreed that all monks and regular canons adopt similar procedures but already by that date the early brilliance was fading. The annual visitation by the abbot of the mother abbey had been replaced by commissioners with plenary powers and the right of deposition; a change not universally welcomed for as late as 1500 the Abbot of Newminster warned the commissioners away from his abbey and from daughters Pipewell and Roche for he still claimed his old rights.

Clearly external factors did not help: the ravaging effects of the Hundred Years War and the Black Death; the rising popularity of the new Orders of mendicant friars; but the rot began within the Cistercian Order itself. The prohibition by the original Statutes on accepting parishes and tithes and other revenue from beneficiaries was ignored. By exploiting lands, often marginal, with a skilled, diligent and well directed labour force of many *conversi* operating from far-flung granges, monks who had set out eating roots and grass in the forest of Cîteaux and Fountains found their Order becoming rich land-owners generating much wealth from grain, oil, wine and, most especially in this country, wool from the flocks of sheep grazing freely on moors, downs and wolds. Wool became to the White Monks, and indeed to the economy of medieval England, as important as coal in the 19th century or the export of wool to the growth of modern Australia.

It was not the individual monks who were corrupted by the material success of their enterprises but rather the purity of the original spirit of a life of prayerful contemplation in poverty and austerity.

The location of the Newminster Abbey was the cause of two distinctive features of life there over the centuries; proximity to Scotland meant fear was ever present of raids, which might repeat the events of 1138 when the abbey was burned down by a Scottish army. Far from being in an isolated place removed from the comings and goings of men, the community quickly realised they were on the main north-south road to and from England and

Scotland and were called upon to host visiting kings and armies far more frequently and at much greater expense than ever imagined.

Between 1310 and 1314, Edward II visited the abbey with his extensive royal entourage three times and dated statutes there. Edward III was there again with his army in 1334. As late as 1502 Margaret, eldest daughter of Henry VII, went to the abbey where *she was recyved by the abbot and religious at the gait of the church with a crosse.* In early January 1515 Margaret, Queen of Scotland, who had only just given birth to a daughter in Harbottle Castle, visited Morpeth where she was met by Lord Ogle and the Abbot of Newminster.

DISSOLUTION

In his book *Stripping the Altars*[32] Eamon Duffy produces a wealth of evidence to show that parish life in medieval England was far from being decadent or decayed but was strong and vigorous. Margaret Harvey reached a similar conclusion locally where she found religious institutions were flourishing in Durham on the eve of the Reformation[33]

The liturgy of the Church was an integral part of the lives of the people and found expression in many ways: Sundays and major feast days were marked by worship in church at matins, Mass and Evensong. The number of parish churches of Saxon or Norman origin within a radius of a few miles of Newminster – thirteen are listed in the Anglican Deanery of Morpeth – indicates that there was a real need for accessible centres for worship and for lively and widespread parish and guild participation in the life of the church. It is realistic to visualise St. Andrew's, Bolam, with its tall unbuttressed Saxon tower and St. Mary the Virgin at Woodhorn, reputedly a gift to the Community of St. Cuthbert by King Ceolwulf when he entered Lindisfarne as a monk in 737, packed with worshippers on Sundays and Feast Days.

If that itinerant Tudor traveller, John Leland, had visited Newcastle on the Feast of Corpus Christi in 1536, he would have been struck by the vibrancy of the social and religious life of the city, for the old faith was still very much alive.

In medieval cities like Newcastle, York and Chester colourful and popular mystery plays on feasts such as Corpus Christi *gave worship to God and honour to the citie*; in so doing civic pride was promoted, social structures reinforced, church and secular authorities brought together and *religious truths were taught to those who could not read.*

All these celebrations were in stark contrast to the state of the smaller monasteries already falling silent and into disrepair as the monks dispersed with their pensions and the stone-robbers moved in. Sadly, the mystery plays soon went into decline for in 1548 the feast of Corpus Christi suffered the same fate as the monasteries when it was suppressed by Cranmer, later the plays were banned. The last recorded play in Newcastle was Noah's Ark, appropriately by the Shipwright's Guild, and featuring the time-honoured struggle between good and evil with such characters as Deus, Diabolus, Noah, Uxor Noah and Beelzebub.[34]

The speed with which the storm broke in 1535 took everyone by surprise.

The Act of Supremacy of 1534 was unequivocal, The King and his successors were to be 'the only supreme head of the Church of England called Ecclesia Anglicana'. Once this Act and the Treason Act became law it was an offence punishable by death to deny the royal succession. King Henry VIII was now the supreme head of the church in England.

Already by the summer of 1534 seven Carthusian monks had been executed for refusing the Oath of Supremacy followed by John Fisher, Bishop of Rochester, just promoted Cardinal, and Thomas More, recently Chancellor, for refusing the Oath of Succession.

Immediately after these executions Thomas Cromwell's Commissioners began their mammoth task of visiting, and reporting on, and assessing the value of some 318 houses, including 103 convents of nuns, where the annual income was less than £200 and where there were fewer than 12 residents. The economy was in a parlous state after constant expensive wars with France and impending wars with Catholic Europe were looming. Covetous royal eyes were cast on the monasteries whose annual income estimated at some £300,000 exceeded that of the Treasury: thus the Act for the Dissolution of the Lesser Monasteries was passed and the Commissioners working in pairs completed their task in seven months.

Cromwell's wish was that the reports of the Commissioners would provide him with sufficient ammunition to abolish the monasteries, not reform them. Predictably they found that manifest sin, vicious carnal and abominable living is daily used and committed among the little and small abbeys. This was in sharp contrast to the divers great and solemn monasteries of this realm wherein (thanks be to God) religion is right well kept and observed – monasteries such as Westminster and Christchurch, Canterbury, with annual revenues approaching £2,500. Yet by 10th April 1540 all monasteries and convents, little and great, had been dissolved and were the property of the King. Their money went to the Court of Augmentation, the royal treasury.

Even as late as January 1535 abbot Edward of Newminster was leasing to *Sir Philip Dacres, knight, and Roger Pye, yeoman, seven saltpans at Blythe snoke with the wider granary there for the keeping of salt for seven years for a rent of 24 l.* In the same years the lease of *a water mill at Stannington to Thomas Ray, his wife Marion and lawfully begotten children* was for thirty years. Was the abbot being naive, unduly optimistic or simply building up credit? When notice was given that the King's commissioners were coming it is not difficult to imagine the sense of impending doom that would prevail, nor the air of courteous resignation with which they would be received.

Newminster was at least spared the fate of Roche. An eye-witness account survives of events following the surrender of daughter abbey Roche on 23 June 1538. One wonders how often events elsewhere followed a similar pattern. There was a brief ceremony in the chapter house when fourteen monks and four novices signed the deed of surrender and received their pensions and 20 shillings each towards new clothing. The plan was for an orderly dismantling to take place, followed by an auction, but before this could take place the mob moved in quarrying the walls for stones, setting fire to the choir stalls to melt the lead from the roof, prising up paving and tiles; *all things of price were either spoiled, carped away, or defaced to the uttermost ... every person bent himself to filch and spoil what he could ... nothing was spared but the oxhouses and the swinecoates.*[35]

By 1540 not only were the 800 or so monasteries and convents gone, but the very fabric of the social and religious lives of the common people had been violently ruptured. The new laws aimed unerringly at the centuries old devotional practices underlying their faith; devotion to the Virgin Mary, veneration of holy relics, pilgrimages to shrines like Walsingham, celebration of saints' days, prayers for the dead. Sacred objects like crucifixes and statues were idolatrous and were to be destroyed. Priests were soon to be branded wicked imps of the anti-Christ. Well might Simon Schama in his *History of Britain* pose what he calls *one of the most poignant questions in the nation's history: 'Whatever happened to Catholic England?'*[36]

Henry's Commissioners found no fault in the community of 17 choir monks, 3 novices and 4 choir boys resident at Newminster. This was a small community but except in first halcyon days it had probably never been much greater, especially after the ravages of the Black Death. Around 1530 comparable numbers were found elsewhere, 17 at Alnwick, 15 at Tynemouth, 20 at Hexham, 10 at Brinkburn and 9 at Blanchland, only Durham with 66 was well in excess. The intended figure for Hexham was only 26 and Brinkburn's figure was only two less than at its foundation. The conclusion is that though numbers were down the communities were not seriously under strength.

In their *Valor Ecclesiasticus* the Commissioners valued the annual revenues of Newminster at only £100 8s.10d. yet the King's Surveyors in 1536 gave the figure as £265 10s. 0¼ d., even the last farthing is recorded. The big discrepancy is suspicious; crown policy was to close first all houses with an annual income of £200 or less. Were the figures deliberately falsified to drag not only Newminster but also Hexham (£267), Alnwick (£256) and Finchale (£206) into the net? Was it a case of payment by results for the commissioners? Ten other houses in the county from Lindisfarne (£110) to Lambley Nunnery (£5) stood no chance.[37]

In effect, Newminster Abbey was among the first to be dissolved; Hodgson records: *this House fell on 27 Hen 8 1535.*

NEWMINSTER PROPERTIES AT THE DISSOLUTION 1535

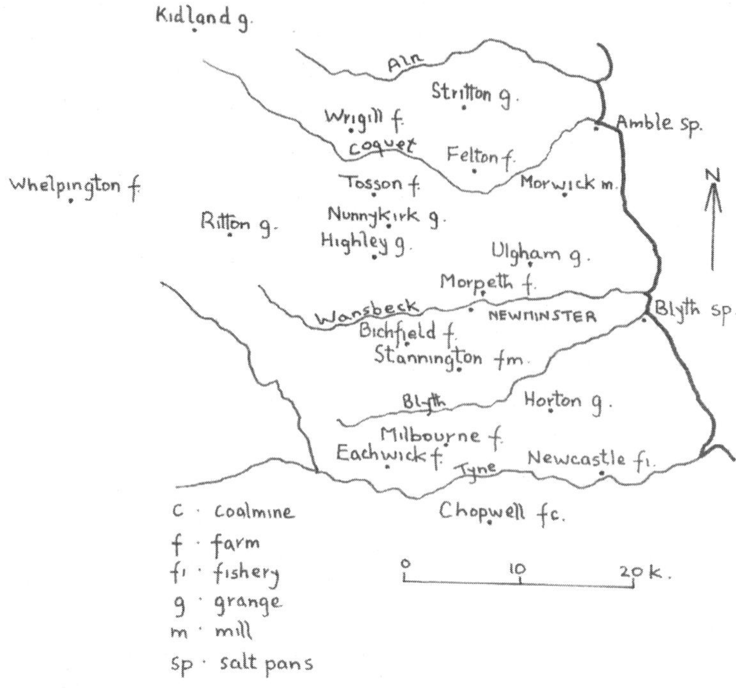

The Commissioners' report has much historical interest as it lists the many scattered holdings of the abbey and their worth; here are a few examples:

Ulgham £13 6s. 8d.	farm and grange
Blithesnok £14 0s. 0d.	farm, barn, coal mine, 7 salt pans
Stannyngton £ 4 0s. 0d.	farm, 2 windmills
Whelpyngton £12 0s. 0d.	farm, rectory
Novum Castrum super Tinam £ 4 0s. 8d.	farm of 8 tenements
Morwyke £ 3 6s. 8d.	farm, fulling mill

The two parishes with which Newminster had been endowed generated £26, only about 10% of the income but then the Order originally forbade the owning of any churches.

There is no evidence to suggest that the monks of Newminster played any part in the popular northern uprising called the Pilgrimage of Grace; like the clergy of most religious houses it seems likely they remained inactive believing vainly, as it turned out, that this was the best way to safeguard their own future. The rebels had social and economic grievances, as in the Rising of the North in 1569, but a foremost demand regularly made by Robert Aske and other leaders was the restoration of the monasteries.

Some Cistercian monasteries in the north did show active support. At Kirkstead the community, under threat, joined the rebels for four days unadventurous campaigning before rejoining the abbot who had pleaded sickess; at Furness the abbot and the monks were most outspoken in their condemnation of royal supremacy; at Holm Cultram the abbot acted as envoy for the rebels to the authorities in Carlisle; at Sawley the commoners restored the community, as happened in houses in York, and the abbey became a centre of resistance and source of the marching song of the rebels. At Jervaulx upon pressure from the insurgents to join them, Abbot Adam *conveyed himself by a back door to Witton Fell where he tarried on a great crag for four days* returning only when the commoners threatened to burn the house down.[38]

The only evidence of resistance was at the Augustinian House of Hexham where the sub-prior closed the gates of the monastery and paraded the whole community of canons with the sixty armed men on the Green at the approach of the Commissioners. The prior was away seeing Cromwell at the time, without any success. This show gained the priory a few months' grace before surrender. Much alarmed by these reports the King ordered Norfolk *to repair to Sally, Hexham and Newminster without pity or circumstance and cause all the monks and canons that be in anywise faults to be tyed uppe without delay and ceremony to the terrible example of others.* An order to the Earl of Derby singled out the abbot of Sawley for special treatment for *the said abbot and certain of the chief of the monks were to be hanged upon long pieces of timber, or otherwise, out of the steeple.*

In the event, the Abbot of Sawley, William of Trafford, along with fellow abbots John Paslew of nearby Whalley, William Thirsk, retired abbot of Fountains and Abbot Adam Sedbergh of Jervaulx did suffer for, with two White Monks of Whalley, they were executed at Lancaster on 10 March 1537.[39]

Local tradition has it that the last Augustinian prior of Hexham Abbey, Edward Jay, was hanged at the gates of his own monastery.

The fate of the last of the thirty-one abbots of Newminster, Richard Tyrell, who ruled in the last decade of the abbey's four centuries of life, was typical of the majority; he was given a pension of £30 p.a. and died at Pontefract in 1541. An extant record dated 1553 states that the only sum in charge to the Crown 18 years after the surrender was £6. 13s. 4d., for the abbots and all monks except one were provided for or dead.

The Crown sold the site of the abbey and its lands into private hands;[40] among the more notable future owners were Sir Ralph Grey of Chillingham, William Lord Eure and Robert Brandling of Felling. The site remains in private hands. Future archeological or restorative work seems most unlikely: a return of the site to nature is the probable fate.

EPILOGUE

While one marvels at the grace and elegance of the architecture of the substantial remains of Rievaulx, Fountains, Bylands, Sweetheart and elsewhere for here surely is Cistercian spirituality wrought in stone in all its austere beauty, yet it is among the tumbled and fragmentary ruins of monasteries like Newminster that the eloquent words of David Knowles resonate most deeply:

'The ghost of medieval monasticism remains to haunt this island. The grey walls and broken cloisters, the bare ruin'd choirs where late the sweet birds sang speak more eloquently for the past than any historian dare and pose for every beholder questions words cannot answer.'[41]

One has a keen sense of the presence of a greater company when visiting 'the bare ruin'd choirs' of Newminster Abbey whether alone, standing beneath the majestic ash now growing on the sanctuary floor of the abbey church, or as a member of a party of pilgrims gathered on the flower-decked turf of the chapter-house to celebrate with joy the Eucharist, using the base of a fallen column as an altar. There is a growing awareness that this is indeed holy ground sanctified over four centuries by the work and worship of good men striving to lead selfless lives in a spirit of fraternal charity: the communion of saints becomes a reality as history and faith embrace.

NOTES AND REFERENCES

1. REV. JOHN HODGSON. (1779 – 1845). A History of Morpeth 1832, reprinted 1973, Newminster Abbey, p.41.

2. Ibid p.42.

3. Archaelogia Aeliana (AA). Vol. XLII 1964. p.85 – 171. Excavations at Newminster Abbey. B. Harbottle. P. Salway.

4. Memorials of Fountains Abbey. Surtees Society (SS) 1876. Vol. 1, p.58.

5. Chartularium Abbathiae de Nova Monasteria. The Newminster Cartulary. SS Vol. 66. 1876.

6. Two 14th century lives of St. Robert are extant, both probably versions of older documents now lost; one, unpublished is in the British Museum. Lansdown MS 436. The other is in John of Tynemouth's Santilogium Anglic printed in 1516 in *Nova Legenda Anglie* re-edited Horstman, Clarendon Press 1901. Part of this second life is in Nova Legenda Acta Sanctorum, edited by the Jesuit Bollandists, Jun 11, tom II p.47, W. Williams, St. Robert of Newminster, Downside review VII 1939 is taken from the Acta Sanctorum. Source of stories of everyday life.

7. Memorials op cit. Vol.II Appendix p.117.

8. John, Augustinian prior of Hexham Abbey c.1150 'distinguished in learning and eloquence' wrote continuation of History of Simeon of Durham, cited by W. Percy Hedley in Northumberland Families. Vol. 1 1968, p. 196.

9. JOHN LELAND. (d.1552) Tudor chronicler and Traveller, visited Northumberland c.1539 searching for antiquities.

10. JANET BURTON, The Monastic Order in Yorkshire 1069 – 1215. 1999. p.120.

11. Cited by G. Coulton Two Saints St. Bernard and St. Francis 1932. p.47.

12. TOM LICENCE. The Benedictines, the Cistercians and the Acquisition of a Hermitage in Twelfth Century Durham. Journal of Medieval History, Vol. 29. Dec. 2003.

13. Benedict's Disciples ed. D.H. Farmer 1980. V.M. Tudor St. Godric of Finchale, p.195-211.

14. Stories recorded by W. Williams op. cit.

15. I know of two parishes in the U.S.A. dedicated to St. Robert of Newminster, at Milwaukee and at Shorewood, Wisconsin.

16. The Rule of Benedict for Monasteries. Ealing Abbey, edition 1939. Chapter 3.

17. A.A. vol. XII. 1915. A.H. Oliver. List of the Abbots of Newminster p.206 – 225.

18. DAVID KNOWLES. The Monastic Order in England, 1963 edition p. 647 in Volume 4.

19. H.L. HONEYMAN, Northumberland 1951. P.172.

20. BERNARD APOLOGIA AD Willelmum CXII cited in D. Knowles Christian Monasticism. 1969 P.82

21. N. PEVSNER. The Buildings of England. Northumberland. 1992 p.518.

22. From G. Coulton op.cit. p.55.

23. The Rule of Benedict op.cit. chap.3.

24. C.R. CHENEY. Medieval Texts and Studies. 1973. CHAP. 17. English Cistercian Libraries. The First Century.

25. OLIVER DAVIES. Celtic Spirituality 1999. Introduction.

26. WALTER DANIEL op.cit.

27. H.L. HONEYMAN. The Tile Pavements of Newminster. A.A. VOL. VI 1929. P. 95 – 104.

28. G.K. ANDERSON, Cistercian Studies vol. 36.4 p.457 – 471. Designed for prayer: An Essay on Medieval Monasticism for Contemporary Designers and Gardeners.

29. David Dixon. Upper Coquetdale. 1903. p.21. See also Historic Village Atlas.Northumberland National Park Authority. 2004, especially 9. Harbottle p.303 – 342 and 11 Holystone p.363 – 387.

30. Ibid p.39.

31. Lamentations 41 quoted by Knowles in Christian Monasticism op.cit. p.89.

32. EAMON DUFFY, Stripping the Altars. 1992.

33. MARGARET HARVEY. Lay Religious Life in Late Medieval Durham. 2006.

34. HELEN TURNBULL. The Corpus Christi Plays of Newcastle, Tyne and Tweed 2002, pp. 53 – 56.

35. Roche Abbey, English Heritage handbook 1994. P. 24.

36. SIMON SCHAMA. A History of England 3000 BC – AD 1603. P.274.

37. RICHARD LOMAS. North-East England in the Middle Ages 1992. Chapter 8. The Church: The Religious Corporations.

38. D. KNOWLES. Bare Ruined Choirs. 1976 ed. Chap.17. The Northern Rising, pp. 205 – 220.

39. Ibid.

40. See John Hodgson op.cit. pp. 49 & 50.

41. D. KNOWLES, Ibid p.320. Title taken from Shakespeare Sonnet No. 73.

APPENDIX A

SEALS OF NEWMINSTER ABBEY

1. Seal of Robert of Newminster: oval 1.5 in. x 0.75 in.: the abbot's hand holds a crozier
   SIGNUM ABBIS DE NOVO MONASTE.
   Attached to testimonium of Bp. William de St. Barbara settling dispute between Roger, Prior of Durham, and Wazo, Archdeacon of Durham, 1147.
   The simple design reflects the spirit of the early Cistercians.

2. 14th Century seal of Abbot John appended to receipt of tenths showing head of John the Baptist.

3. Seal attached to obligation of Convent of Newminster to found a chantry in Morpeth Church, dated A.D. 1334, 2.5 in. x 1.5 in.
   Our Lady, robed and crowned, seated in a canopied niche, holding an apple to the Christ Child, an allusion to the fall of man. On each side, a crescent enclosing a star, with a fleur de lys above, symbols of Our Lady. Below the pediment a tonsured demi-figure of an abbot praying and holding his crozier: above the abbot AVE MARIA.
   S'COE: ABBIS ET COUETUS
   SCE MARIE: DE NOVO MONASTERIO

4. Attached to document printed in Priory of Finchdale: 1220.

5. Seal of Abbot John, 1311, attached to receipt for tenths; symbols of a crescent, a star and fleur de lys illustrate the deep devotion to Our Lady of the Cistercian Order.

Illustrations published by Surtees Society, 1876.

APPENDIX B

Excerpts from

THE MORPETH HERALD AND REPORTER

FRIDAY, JUNE 10, 1927.

NEWMINSTER ABBEY PILGRIMAGE.

20, 000 Catholics Take Part in Procession.

IMPROVISED ALTAR ERECTED AMIDST RUINS.

High Mass Performed by Bishop Thorman.

INSPIRING AND IMPRESSIVE SIGHT.

There was a great invasion of Catholics from the Diocese of Hexham and Newcastle into Morpeth on Tuesday morning to take part in the pilgrimage to Newminster Abbey on the occasion of the 800th anniversary of St. Robert, the first Abbot of the Abbey, which was founded in 1138 by a band of Cistercians from Fountains Abbey, Yorkshire. Amidst the ruins, the huge congregation numbering 20,000 made public demonstration of their loyalty to the Catholic faith.
St. Robert of Newminster is famed as being one of a colony of monks who were brought from Fountains Abbey in Yorkshire in the year 1138 by Ranulph de Merley, Baron of Morpeth, who founded a Cistercian monastery for the community which he himself built that year.

WIDESPREAD INTEREST

Shortly after nine o'clock in the morning, all roads seemed to lead to Morpeth. Several hundreds of special 'buses, one hundred being from Durham alone, ,brought thousands of pilgrims into the town, but so complete were the arrangements that there was at no time any serious congestion in the streets. There were also four guaranteed excursion trains from Stockton, Wallsend, South Shields and Newcastle. It was a wonderful sight to see the pilgrims forming up in the New Market extension to take their places in the procession. Even outside the Catholic community widespread interest was created in the great pilgrimage, which has never before taken place in Morpeth. It was a magnificent spectacle to watch the procession moving slowly on its way to the Abbey ruins.

CIVIC WELCOME

Father Kershaw, of St. Robert's, Morpeth, introduced Bishop Thorman to the Mayor, who then introduced the alderman, councillors and officials individually to the Bishop.

The formal introduction over the Mayor then addressed words of welcome to the Bishop and forty clergy assembled in the following terms:-

My Lord, Right Reverend and Reverend Fathers, ladies and gentlemen, - On behalf of the inhabitants of the borough, I have the honour of welcoming you to this town. We have not had on any previous occasion the privilege of a visit of a similar kind from the Roman Catholic Church. It is therefore with distinct pleasure that I extend to you a cordial welcome. Your pilgrimage to Newminster Abbey is a sacred one. We regard it with feelings of respect and reverence. It was in the year 1138 on Christmas Day that a party of monks made a pilgrimage from Fountains Abbey in Yorkshire and were received into Morpeth Castle by Ranulph de Merley, who was "powerful in Northumberland."

It is said that from that pilgrimage in 1148 the foundation of Newminster Abbey was established under Ranulph de Merley's patronage and protection. But for centuries the Abbey has lain in desolate stillness, " The keepers of the Tombs and the Servants of God have long been driven from the sanctuary, and the destroying hands of time and man have levelled its altars and towers with the earth."…..

PRAYERS AND INTERCESSIONS

Today for the first time in many generations prayers and intercessions will be restored. Solemn music will again be heard within its sacred precincts.

It has been a matter of regret to many Morpethians that the Abbey lay so long desolate and destroyed. Graves of past grandeur lay beneath rugged grounds……

We earnestly hope, My Lord, that your pilgrimage today will be a solace and inspiration to your people and I desire to extend to you on behalf of the inhabitants a cordial welcome. I ask you to accept it as a sincere expression of the honour that we feel in your presence here today. (Applause)

THE BISHOP'S RESPONSE

Rising to respond to the civic welcome Bishop Thorman said: I wish to give in simplicity and in a few words an expression of the feelings of kindness and friendliness which we , Catholics, feel in the cordial reception you have accorded to us this morning..

In coming here today there is emphasised the fact that in so far as we are Catholics we have another connection with this ancient borough, and one more deeper and more solemn than the obvious things of the earth – that is the link that binds us is most true, and to us most sacred union with the ages that are past. I must speak, of course, with consideration for varied opinions, but in this our own sentiments are extremely deep and real to us. We feel a kinship with those who in the ages past travelled far into what was then a wild and rugged country, and built for themselves a home where they could dwell in peace where they might worship God and exercise works of charity. Building for themselves, and a beautiful home it was, and cultivating the country.

It is a fine inspiration when visiting and revisiting these scenes of times long past, feeling they are indeed our forefathers. We come with a certain feeling that we have a right to come in this day of wider opportunities to renew as much as we can the old splendour, the ceremonial of those past ages, to most people partly not more than a memory. I thank you for your kind reception and support. I thank you also in the name of the clergy of the diocese of Hexham and the Catholic people of Northumberland and Durham for having received us so kindly and made our coming here so pleasant. I hope that the memory will long remain with them. After all these sad ruins of Newminster do speak as to the works of God and the permanence of a principle. While men just go the ruins remain. It may be in God's good time that our desire will be fulfilled. (Applause.)

THE PROCESSION

The Market Place and Newgate Street on both sides were crowded with respectful onlookers as the procession slowly wend its way to Newminster. Each pilgrim was wearing a Maltese Cross with the ancient seal of the Abbey affixed to the cross and with the Papal colours, yellow and white ribbon, attached, a suitable memento of the occasion. Banners of different fraternities, several having the papal coat of arms emblazoned on them, were carried. The procession was led by the Cross Bearer and two Acolytes, candle bearers, in purple cassocks. Then came a body of boy scouts followed by the Morpeth people with the statue of the Sacred Heart carried by four men, and the banners of Our Blessed Lady and St. Joseph. On the way the pilgrims recited the Rosary and sang the hymn "Hail Queen of Heaven." About 10.30 the head of the procession had reached the ruins, but it was 12, noon before everybody had arrived at the sacred spot and taken up their places for the Mass to commence.

ALTAR RAISED ON SACRED SPOT

Within the enclosure of what remains of the Abbey an improvised altar had been erected with frontal and canopy of crimson and gold. There was a crucifix and six tall candles. The altar, it was believed, was raised over the grave of St. Robert..

The impressive service was pontifical High Mass, Bishop Thorman being the celebrant, Father E. Wilkinson deacon and Father J. Farrow sub-deacon. The Canons of the Throne were Canon Harris and Canon Rodgers, and Canon Newsham acted as assistant priest.. The Masters of Ceremonies were father F. Dunn and Father C. Conway. Father J.H. Whitaker of St. Mary's Cathedral was in charge of the music.

There was about 200 priests present comprising Dominicans, Benedictines and Redemptorists. A notable figure was a Franciscan Friar in his brown habit.

The huge congregation sang the hymns "Sweet Sacrament Divine" and "Hail Queen of Heaven" whilst the pilgrims were assembling.

The Bishop wearing the Cappa Magna with his Canons and the choir of priests approached the altar singing "Faith of Our Fathers" and this inspiring hymn accompanied by a Brass Band was taken up by all the thousands present.

During the service the sky became overcast and there was a heavy shower, but now and again the Abbey ruins and the congregation were bathed in brilliant sunshine.. It was not the good fortune of many to see what was happening at the altar but all followed the service with zeal and devotion. The music was impressive throughout all those who participated in the memorable service will not soon forget it.

THE SERMON

In the incense-laden air the pilgrims disposed themselves to listen to the sermon by Father Geo. McBrearty of St. Lawrence's Church, Byker. Speaking from a temporary pulpit erected not far from the altar, Father McBrearty, who is a powerful preacher, said: Here we are assembled in pilgrimage this morning. Here we are the successor of St. Robert offering up on an improvised altar solemn sacrifice of the Mass in this waste where scarce a stone now stands upon a stone and here in the days when all England was Catholic stood the Abbey of Our Lady of Newminster. Beautiful they say it was, and as fair if not fairer than its mother of Fountains. For from Fountains it sprang. Ranuloh de Merley, of Morpeth, had seen the men living so wonderfully with God, reflecting much of Heaven living so near to God, that he desired to have them on his own demesne here to pray for his soul and also for his wife and children, and for the souls of his parents and of all the faithful departed, and so there came North a small band of monks to make themselves a new Fountains, and there came St. Robert. But our St. Robert was not a French monk. He was a Yorkshireman, born at Craven, and had been a parish priest before he came…..

A HALLOWED SPOT

Newminster was a thoroughly English monastery English in its birth and English in its rule and the only un-English thing about it was its death or destruction, After it had stood in all its grandeur for well nigh four centuries it was reduced to a heap of ruins as they saw it that day. Yes, a heap of ruins, but forever a hallowed spot. For four centuries Newminster was as heaven brought down to earth, or life lived in heaven. Its inmates spent their lives there as the higher congregation of the angels spent their immortality in heaven, worshipping, praising and glorifying God. That was, after all, the greatest and noblest activity of man. Then the blow fell, and at the word of the greatest tyrant that ever sat on a throne Newminster and other monasteries in England were condemned to extinction, and in a few years all that remained of them was here and there a few crumbling walls or a name or a memory that refused to die. There was no real or right reason for the suppression of the monasteries. Henry VIII fabricated a case against the monks. It was to vindicate the memory of thousands of their fellow countrymen; to give the lie to all the misstatements and misrepresentations against their faith and religion that had been uttered against them, that they were assembled at Newminster that day.

SACRED RUINS

" We proclaim a veneration for this spot " declared the preacher, " and we profess that it is sacred in our eyes. There is nothing on earth so noble as a life consecrated to God. We thank God for the gift of the true faith in which we rejoice. It is not for ourselves that we grieve as we stand within these silent ruins, but for this realm of England so long of this faith and its blessing; this England so materially great yet so spiritually poor and in need. We are asking Our Lady of Newminster to intercede for this land. Let us all pray for this land so violently deprived of the true faith, that this faith may be restored to it. "

At the end of the Mass the solemn Te Deum was sung by the choir priests and pilgrims.
At the close of the celebrations the Bishop and thirty of the clergy, together with the Mayor (Councillor J. Wilson) , and the Town Clerk (Mr E.C. Jackson) were entertained to lunch by Sir George Renwick. It was by the kind permission of Sir George that the pilgrimage was held, the ruins of the Abbey being on his estate.

BENEDICTION AT ST. ROBERT'S CHURCH

At 5 p.m. His Lordship gave benediction at St. Robert's Church. There was a large congregation, too large for the seating accommodation of the church. Those unable to obtain entrance were accommodated in the grounds, and the Bishop bearing the Monstrance under the canopy carried by bearers gave the blessing to the waiting crowds outside.
The whole of the day's proceedings were carried through with great success.

I have been unable to find any photographs* of this great occasion but the picture above shows how the abbey site would have looked at the time of the pilgrimage. The extent of the reconstruction work of the 1920s is clearly evident: contrast this with the present overgrown state of the ruins.

*See Addendum

Newminster: sketch of 18th Century scene.

Sir George Renwick, landowner, and labourer. c. 1920.

PARISH PILGRIMAGES
1995

2005

The Lady's Walk 'On the hitherie bank of Wanspeke' from Morpeth Town Centre to Newminster Abbey, about 1 mile.

A brief history in the old chapter house.

Reading from the Rule of Benedict.

The Offertory.

The Communion.

The picnic.

From Colombia and Ecuador to Newminster.

APPENDIX D

Summary of letter from English Heritage

Dear Mr. Thornton

NEWMINSTER ABBEY, MORPETH, CASTLE MORPETH, NORTHUMBERLAND
COUNTY MONUMENT NUMBER ND 165

Thank you for your letter of the 3 June 2008 enquiring about the above scheduled monument. We spoke on the phone today and I said I would write to you confirming the main points of our conversation

Your recent research into Newminster Abbey has prompted you to establish English Heritage's interest in the monument. Newminster Abbey is a scheduled monument and as such legally protected as a nationally important archaeological site. Scheduled monuments are designated and added to a 'schedule' by the Secretary of State for Culture, Media and Sport (DCMS) under powers contained in the Ancient Monuments and Archaeological Areas Act 1979. Once a site is scheduled written consent must be obtained for any works that affect it. English Heritage provides advice to the DCMS on all applications for consent.

English Heritage is the Government's statutory advisor on all aspects of the cultural heritage – including historic buildings and areas, archaeology, historic parks and gardens, and the wider historic landscape – with a duty to promote public understanding and enjoyment of the heritage. We provide the DCMS with advice on scheduled monument consent applications and the Local Planning Authority (Castle Morpeth) with advice on planning applications that affect the monument. We are also able to provide the owners with advice, including preparing applications for scheduled monument consent, planning applications or practical advice from our specialist teams on methods of survey, repair and interpretation. Newminster Abbey is privately owned and not managed by English Heritage. If you wish to gain access to the site you must contact the owners for permission to do so.

You may also have noticed that Newminster Abbey is on our *Buildings at Risk* register. This is because we believe it is at risk and in slow decline. We put buildings like this on the register to highlight the problems faced by their owners and managers. We understand that monuments like Newminster Abbey require the skills of many different kinds of specialist to arrest their decline and these are not necessarily skills that owners have, or ones they can easily obtain without assistance. English Heritage and the Local Planning Authority can help with this work and we encourage owners and occupiers to approach us for advice and assistance.

I hope this has answered all your questions. Should you require any further information please contact me again at our Newcastle Office.

Yours sincerely

Kate Wilson
Inspector of Ancient Monuments
kate.Wilson@english-heritage.org.uk

INDEX

Front Cover

Postage stamp issued in March 1997 to commemorate the 1400th anniversary of St. Columba.

Courtesy of the Post Office

Back Cover

King Egfrid landing on Inner Farne to summon Cuthbert to become bishop.
William Bell Scott (1811-1890), Wallington, The Trevelyan Collection.

Courtesy of the National Trust

All profits from the sale of this book will be sent to Father Bernard Phelan (see page 28) to help finance the sinking of 30 new deep boreholes to provide clean fresh water for 21,142 people in his parish of St. Joseph's, Kotido, Karamoja, Uganda, a semi-desert region where diseases are rife. Any donations sent to me at the address below will be most gratefully received and immediately forwarded. My wife and I spent the first five years of our married life in Uganda: half a century later that country remains close to our hearts.

Gods, Saints, and a Scholar, is available from St. Mary's Cathedral Bookshop, Clayton Road West, Newcastle upon Tyne NE1 5HH (Tel. 0191 2316040) or from G.B. Thornton, c/o St. Robert's R.C. Church, Cedar Road, Fenham, Newcastle upon Tyne NE4 9PH: Price £10 + £3.00 postage and packing.

ADDENDUM

These photographs of the Diocesan Pilgrimage of 1927 to Newminster Abbey were received on the day of going to press. As they are part of a private collection we believe this is the first time they have been published.

Courtesy of Helen Feeney.

J.W. HA

GARAGE.

NOTES

NOTES

NOTES

NOTES

NOTES

NOTES

NOTES

NOTES